The Kentucky Derby

MUSEUM

Cook Book

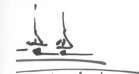

Library of Congress Catalog Card Number 86-82577
International Standard Book Number 0-9617103-0-6

Proceeds from the sale of this book will be used to support
The Kentucky Derby Museum, a non-profit organization,
dedicated to the preservation of the history and traditions
of the Kentucky Derby and Thoroughbred Racing.

First Printing December 1986
Second Printing June 1987
Third Printing March 1988
Fourth Printing December 1989
Fifth Printing July 1992

Printed by Commercial Lithographing Company
Louisville, Kentucky

Graphic Design by Unigraphics, Inc.
Louisville, Kentucky

Acknowledgements

The Kentucky Derby Museum Cookbook Committee wishes to express its appreciation to the many talented friends and professionals in our community who have helped us pull our volunteer efforts together to produce this cookbook.

The Courier-Journal and Louisville Times, C. Thomas Hardin, Director of Photography, Gary Chapman, Staff Photographer, Pam Spaulding, Staff Photographer for Courier-Journal Magazine, Elaine Corn, Past Food Editor, Sarah Fritschner, Food Editor, Alice Columbo, Assistant Food Editor; Diana Williams Hansen, Syndicated Food Columnist and Cookbook Editor; Jim Bolus, Louisville Sports Writer; Kinetic Corporation, Richard Duncan; Warren Lynch; Grisanti, Inc.; Maria K. Beckman, Louisville Photographer; Kentucky Derby Festival, Inc., Photographers Richard Bram, John Nation and Dick Wilson; Historic Homes Foundation, Mr. Charles Hill; Donna Lawrence Productions; General Electric Company and their "Microwave Guide and Cookbook;" The Kentucky Derby Museum Staff, Tim Powell, Staff Photographer; The Finish Line Gift Shop; Betty Fawcett, Meredith Grider, Susan Grubbs, Cathy Henry, Joanne Heumann, Anne Joseph, Genie Potter, Sally Schneider, Shirley Sotsky, Priscilla Veatch, and Bill West.

The Kentucky Derby Museum
Cookbook Committee

The Kentucky Derby Museum Cookbook is respectfully dedicated in memory of Laurie Lussky whose creativity and dedication helped ensure its success and popularity.

4

Introduction

The Kentucky Derby and Churchill Downs are synonymous with the biggest and best in the world of Thoroughbred racing. The Kentucky Derby Museum, by its very design, has embodied the heritage and pageantry associated with the Derby and the Downs. Through the exhibits and programs of the Museum, we are able to share that same excitement with visitors from all over the world.

It is seldom that any museum has the opportunity to capture the essence of its purpose and package it for the enjoyment and enlightenment of all.The Kentucky Derby Museum Cookbook has accomplished just such a feat and, with the advent of this fifth printing, has truly become an entertainment phenomenon.

This cookbook faithfully reproduces many unique Derby Party recipes and happily takes note of traditions and anecdotes that also lend "flavor" to special occasions. The recipes were lovingly gathered and tested by volunteers who were thoroughly professional in their attention to quality, creativity, detail and having a wonderful time. We cannot thank them enough for their hundred of hours of dedicated effort on this project. In the selection of recipes they handicapped a winner every time!

We sincerely hope The Kentucky Derby Museum Cookbook will enliven and enrich your everyday entertaining and dining pleasure, and most importantly, make your Derby celebration a grand and glorious occasion.

Bon Appétit!

RANDY W. RAY
Executive Director
Kentucky Derby Museum

Churchill Downs

The Louisville Jockey Club and Driving Park Association, as it was called in 1874, was founded by Col. M. Lewis Clark. The twenty-nine year old grandson of William Clark (of the Lewis and Clark expedition), spent two years in England and France studying racing, European fashion, before returning to America to establish a new race track in Louisville, Kentucky.

Churchill Downs was named, in 1929, for John and Henry Churchill, uncles of Clark, who had agreed to lease him the land for the track back in 1874.

Work on the grandstand was completed just in time for the opening of the track and the first Kentucky Derby, on May 17, 1875. Won by Aristides, the Kentucky Derby, fashioned after the Epsom Derby in England, has become the premiere racing event in the country. The original grandstand was dismantled in 1895 and was replaced with new stands topped by the world famous twin spires, symbol of thoroughbred racing at its finest.

Kentucky Derby Museum

The Kentucky Derby Museum, dedicated to the entire Thoroughbred industry and the Kentucky Derby in particular, stands proudly next to American racing's most famous arena, Churchill Downs.

A separate nonprofit corporation, the Museum was built to provide visitors with a comprehensive overview of Thoroughbred racing in an entertaining atmosphere, and to preserve and promote the heritage and traditions of the "Sport of Kings."

Opened in April, 1985, exhibits in the $7.5 million facility feature the Kentucky Derby as America's greatest race, show the visitor a backside and inside view of the racing industry, and allow for "hands on" experiences with computerized handicapping, horsepower machine, authentic starting gate, and much more. Film highlights of past Derbys and other great races from around the world are featured. And, the award-winning multi-image show "The Greatest Race — A Kentucky Derby Panorama" surrounds the visitor with one of the world's largest 360 degree sensory adventures, capturing all the color, excitement, beauty and action of Derby Day in Louisville.

Entertaining and educating over 150,000 visitors a year, the Museum is one of the leading attractions in the Commonwealth of Kentucky. There are exceptional exhibits to browse, a live Thoroughbred to pet, a tour of Churchill Downs to enjoy and a relaxing mint julep just waiting on the restaurant terrace.

The Museum maintains the traditions of Kentucky hospitality and Thoroughbred racing and invites the world to share them.

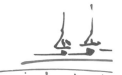

The Kentucky Derby

"The greatest two minutes in sports", first run in 1875, has become racing's most important victory for horsemen, the show to watch for a vast international television audience and the place to be, if you are in Kentucky on the first Saturday in May.

Of the thousands of thoroughbred horses who celebrate their third birthday in January, no more than twenty will reach the starting gate in the most famous of races. Each will have been bred, trained and nurtured in hopes of outrunning the competition to win a place in history, the gold trophy and hundreds of dollars in prize money. The first Kentucky Derby, won by Aristides in 1875, netted the winner $2,850. The highest earnings, won by Ferdinand in 1986, were $609,400.

Nominations for the Kentucky Derby are made by paying $600 to Triple Crown Productions, Inc. as agent for Churchill Downs® Incorporated. This also nominates the entry to the Preakness and Belmont Stakes, the other jewels of the Triple Crown®. An additional fee of $10,000 and a starting fee of $10,000 are required to run in the Kentucky Derby®. On Thursday before Derby the positions in the starting gate are determined by a random drawing held in the Winner's Circle of the Kentucky Derby Museum. This is an event widely covered by the world's turf writers and media and is attended by the owners, trainers and breeders.

On Derby Day, racing fans begin to pour into Churchill Downs® during the early morning hours and continue to arrive right up to post time for the Kentucky Derby®, which is run at 5:30 p.m. Seven races preceed the Derby with an hour between each race. This spacing allows the crowds of people to make their way to the mutual windows, or to enjoy the other Derby traditions, including promenading in the latest Spring fashions and hats, socializing with friends, strolling the flower gardens or viewing the horses in the paddock.

A few minutes before the Derby the pace picks up. Fans seem to feel the need to be in their seats and with their friends for the running of the Derby. Feet start to shuffle in the betting lines as impatient patrons, eager to place their bets and get back to their seats, become anxious. Old friends tear away to get themselves situated for the race, young people in the infield vie for a spot next to the fence so that maybe, just maybe, they will be able to say they saw a horse race on Derby day. Mint julep vendors sell one last julep to toast the winner, the loser will at least have the souvenir julep glass to take home.

In the jockey's lounge, tension builds as the athletes slip into the colorful silks representing the owner for whom they ride. Each race is run for the purpose of winning, but the Derby will insure a place in history for the jockey, owner, trainer, and breeder. Other races may be richer in winnings, but none is more coveted by those in the thoroughbred industry.

After the weigh in, the jockey and his mount enter the parade to the post, where they strut past 125,000 spectators on the way to the starting gate. Those fans who have not already chosen their favorite will pick one now, even if there is not time to run to the betting window.

A hush falls over the crowd and the rustle of the program can be distinguished as those who may not know every verse turn to the page where "My Old Kentucky Home" is printed. This is what they came for. To be part of the tradition. To take part in an event that has been taking place every Spring for over a hundred years. The band begins the familiar song and the thousands of spectators softly join in. "Weep no more my lady" brings out the best in everyone and for that moment each becomes a Kentuckian, swelling with pride. For at this moment memories fly; Derbys past, old friends, old times, old memories. . ."Old Kentucky Home far away." A catch in the throat comes as a surprise, but it is difficult not to get caught up in the moment. Then the loudspeaker breaks the spell with the booming declaration "aaaand They're Off." The starting gates fly open and the field of horses bursts onto the track.

The sound of the crowd builds like an enormous wave, first random screams and shouts as one after another the horses take their places for the trip around the backside. Then as they round the turn, everyone who has a favorite is urging him on. One leader is replaced by another and is challenged by a third. The positions on the giant tote board in the infield change and bring on even more screams, and fans are beginning to stand up on their chairs for a chance to see the winner cross the finish line.

A leader emerges and crosses the finish line to the hysterical rejoicing of thousands of people waving their programs, toasting with juleps and hugging each other in delight. Another Kentucky Derby® has come and gone. Another page has been added to racing's history book.

"I am fulfilled and weary. This Kentucky Derby, whatever it is — a race, an emotion, a turbulence, an explosion — is one of the most beautiful and violent and satisfying things I have ever experienced. And I suspect that, as with other wonders, the people one by one have taken from it exactly as much good or evil as they brought to it.

What an experience. I am glad I have seen and felt it at last." —John Steinbeck, May 6, 1957, in the Courier Journal.

The Great Balloon Race

One of the most popular events of the Kentucky Derby Festival is the Great Balloon Race.

The first balloon race was held in 1973 and has become one of the most prestigious among the nation's aeronauts, creating a waiting list for competition.

Spectators gather at daybreak at the launch site in anticipation of the balloon race lift-off. There is excitement as a maximum of fifty-one multicolored balloons become filled with hot air from the gas burners, inflate, and rise into an upright position. After lift-off, from the spectators viewpoint, the sky becomes a panorama of spectacular colors and shapes floating through the morning air. While the aeronauts view the metropolitan area, they experience the roar of the gas burners, yet can hear the voices of conversations below, the barking of dogs, or the crowing of roosters.

The race is a hare and hound race with the previous year's winner having the distinction of acting as the hare. The race is held the Saturday before Derby in the early morning at the Kentucky Fair and Exposition Center and usually ends in the wide open spaces of a friendly farmer. For those who cannot actually be there, the local radio station personalities are on board several of the balloons to give an account of the event to the listening audience.

The Great Steamboat Race

Pride and perseverance paved the way to establishing both the Belle of Louisville and The Great Steamboat Race. In 1962, despite intensive political criticism, Jefferson County Judge Marlow Cook purchased an old, delapidated stern-wheeled riverboat named the Avalon, for $36,000, renamed her and challenged Cincinnati and the Delta Queen to a steamboat race.

There was frantic struggle to get her under steam. In her maiden race, she was a disappointing and humiliating twenty minutes behind the Delta Queen at the finish. Race II provided an exciting photo finish victory and the race captured the imagination, loyalty, and warm hearts of her admirers.

Every Wednesday before Derby Day thousands of spectators line the banks of the Ohio and fill highrise apartments and office buildings to view the riverboat rivalry. High-spirited passengers wave to the crowds and the hundreds of pleasure boats converging in order to witness, first hand, the traditional presentation of the Golden Antlers to the winner of the race.

The Kentucky Derby Festival Pegasus Parade

The Kentucky Derby Festival Pegasus Parade has grown tremendously in local stature, overcoming its humble beginning in 1956 when it was produced for a grand total of $640. The Parade now enjoys the status as the most popular of all the Festival events as 250,000 enthusiastic spectators line the Parade route, Broadway in downtown Louisville, from Campbell to Ninth Streets. Tickets for every available seat for the Parade are now sold out well in advance and as many as 250,000 viewers can enjoy the Parade at home by virtue of the live, local television broadcast.

Thanks to the dedication and hard work of many Festival volunteers and the foresight of the Festival administrators, the Pegasus Parade has become such a successful event. Celebrities such as John Wayne, George Peppard, Jack Klugman, Rosemary Clooney, Dolly Parton, Roberta Flack, Kenny Rogers, Esther Williams, Gary Collins and Mary Ann Mobley have added luster to the Parade. The cheering throngs along the Parade route also look forward to seeing the 20-25 marching bands, clowns, specialty units and twenty or more elaborately designed and constructed floats. The Pegasus Parade averages 100 units and lasts for about 1½ to 2 hours.

Kentucky Derby Festival

The Kentucky Derby Festival began in 1956 with one event, the Pegasus Parade, and a budget of $640. It was estimated that 125,000 people lined the parade route, which began at 12th Street, ran east down Broadway and then up Fourth. Then Mayor of Louisville, Andrew Broaddus presented trophies to winning floats and specialty units and declared the whole affair a huge success. From this single event evolved the 10-day civic celebration known as the Kentucky Derby Festival.

Today, the Kentucky Derby Festival boasts a $1.8 million budget and a 10-day extravaganza of over 70 events. The Pegasus Parade remains the most popular event for the Festival with over a quarter of a million spectators along the Parade route on Broadway and another 250,000 people viewing the Pegasus Parade live on TV. There is the Great Balloon Race, the Great Steamboat Race, the Mini Marathon, plus a barrage of sporting events and concerts. In addition, the famous Chow Wagons offer Louisvillians, as well as visitors to the city, a chance to participate in the festivities.

Entertaining over 800,000 people each year, the Kentucky Derby Festival maintains an important position in the community. By constantly searching for new and innovative ideas for events, and maintaining the standard of quality in the events currently offered, the Kentucky Derby Festival will always strive to accomplish its mission to provide "creative and unique entertainment and community service for the people of the Greater Louisville area."

"Derby Fever"

The Kentucky Derby is more than just a race among three year old thorough-breds; it is a season of the year. In his book "Run for the Roses", Jim Bolus quotes General Basil W. Duke, prominent Kentuckian on the subject of the first Kentucky Derby. "Today will be historic in Kentucky annals as the first "Derby Day" of what promises to be a long series of annual turf festivities which we confidently expect our grandchildren, a hundred years hence, to celebrate in glorious centennial rejoicings."

The expectations of General Duke were more than justified. What has become known as "the greatest two minutes in sports" is now one of the major sporting events of the year. Millions watch on television while over a hundred and twenty-five thousand watch in the shadows of the Twin Spires atop the famous symbol of thoroughbred racing, Churchill Downs.

For well over a hundred years, the Kentucky Derby has been the opening event to herald Spring. The parties given in Kentucky prior to Derby are legend. During the ten days before the Derby, events become reasons for various kinds of enter-tainment. From Balloon Race baskets for early morning breakfasts to riverbank picnics enjoyed while the steamboats are racing down the Ohio River, the people of Kentucky begin to enjoy entertaining long before the actual day of the Derby.

Parties abound after the Friday races preceding the Derby, featuring "The Ken-tucky Oaks". "The Oaks" is the race to determine the fastest three year old filly. Many attend "The Oaks" every year to enjoy the pleasure of walking through the tulip gardens and people-watching without the added excitement that accom-panies the Derby Day festivities. For the party enthusiasts, it is another event for showcasing delicious regional specialties and Kentucky hospitality.

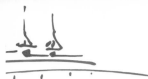

Springtime in Kentucky is a wonder to behold, even without the additional excitement Derby brings. The azaelas, tulip trees, and pink and white dogwood trees seem to know something special is happening. They burst with color just days before Derby and cling to their beauty as though by decree, until the middle of May. At that point, other flowering plants take their places. Mint, of course, is one of the most important items in the yards and windowboxes of Kentuckians and serves an important function in the preparation and decoration of the legendary Mint Julep. Brightly colored geraniums, petunias and other Spring flowers bursting over the tops of their containers (recycled whiskey barrels are popular) appear, as if by magic, on Thursday and Friday to decorate yards, porches and patios. Kentucky does dress up for Derby.

For those not attending the races, it is no less festive. Few people ever watch the Derby alone. House parties are a favorite way to entertain and watch the race with friends. Many who have enjoyed a Derby party while in Kentucky have taken the tradition to other parts of the country and now Derby Parties are enjoyed the world over. Contingents of former Kentuckians often gather in cities and towns everywhere to watch the Derby together, reminisce, and enjoy some of the regional foods that have become such a part of Derby entertaining.

Others will journey back to Kentucky, often bringing groups of friends to share in the fun of the most festive weekend of all. This is a popular time for the college student to introduce his friends to Louisville and "the infield".

Many who have witnessed a Derby have had interesting things to say about Louisville and the Derby. Irvin S. Cobb, noted humorist, put it this way. "You ain't never been nowhere and you ain't never seen nothin' until you go to Kentucky in the springtime and with your own eyes behold a Kentucky Derby."

Suggestions for Derby Entertaining

Centerpieces or table decorations set the mood and excitement of special occasions. This is especially true for Derby entertaining. Plan your menus and preparation of your food well in advance so you will be able to enjoy all of the Derby festivities and still be a refreshed and gracious hostess.

Greet your guests with traditional mint juleps served in silver julep cups or tall frosted glasses.

Center pieces of red roses or colorful spring flowers will capture the Derby spirit.

This is a perfect occasion for displaying sterling silver for an elegant dinner or buffet.

Place a red rose at each ladies' place-setting and use red or silver bordered placecards for a sit-down dinner.

Fill a silver wine cooler with long stemmed red roses as a centerpiece encircled by silver julep cups filled with fresh mint.

Fill large vases or unusual containers with azaleas, dogwood or any flowering greenery from your yard. The aroma and color will enhance your home and add a touch of "Derby Fever".

Garnish silver serving trays with rosettes of tomatoes and radishes. Watercress, Bibb lettuce and mint are also traditional and attractive to use with molded salads, terrines and appetizers.

Carved ice or tallow-sculptured horseheads are conversational selections as well as unusual decorations. These are especially adaptable to areas which are spacious.

Add a whim or fancy to a punch bowl for Mock Champagne Punch by adding a ringed water mold of roses and mint.

Buffet tables can be accented by wrapping red napkins around silver flatwear and tying with narrow white satin ribbon. Red or jockey silk colors make colorful runners for tables.

If you are using a lace table cloth, have a red taffeta cloth made as an undercloth. The expense is well justified because the cloth will also make an attractive addition for your table during the Christmas holidays. Quilts also serve as unusual and traditional table coverings.

Baskets filled with·red geraniums or tulips create an informal atmosphere. They can be used for tables, patios and outdoor barbecues.

For a Derby breakfast or brunch, racing enthusiasts are always thrilled to receive the Racing Form and "tout" sheets. These are available early Derby morning at stores and shops throughout the city. The Official Derby programs, listing all the races including the Kentucky Derby, are now available at stores in Louisville early Saturday morning. These programs may be obtained for Derby parties given throughout the country.

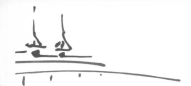

Depending on the extent of your "Derby Fever," the following is a plan for a Derby Day party:

"Setting the Pace," Invitations

Once you've decided to have a Derby party you automatically get "Derby Fever" and are "Off and Running" with party plans and ideas galore for a "Winning" Derby day. After planning the guest list, the decision is to either phone your guests or send invitations. Whichever is more convenient is proper. Try not to include so many that you cannot comfortably entertain. Many pre-printed cards are available, and invitations can be purchased through the "Finish Line" shop at the museum. You may choose to personalize your own invitation by using blank cards and following a simple race track theme:

POST TIME: time party will start.
PROGRAM INCLUDES: buffet, cocktails and barbecue.
TRACK LOCATION: your address.
SILKS: dress code—casual, formal; costume (Stephen Foster or Riverboat
       gambling days).
TRAINERS: your name

T shirts could be printed with your invitation and mailed to guests. The whole concept of your invitations should set the pace of your party, whether formal, informal or casual.

"Parade to the Post" No matter how elaborate or how creative you want to be, the theme is set by your own imagination, time and budget.

Buffet serving seems most popular during Derby week as it is an easy way to entertain a maximum of friends with a minumum of space and help. There is the traditional buffet supper, where guests serve themselves and dine throughout the home, and the "seated" buffet supper, at which guests serve themselves and eat at set tables.

The menu is the most creative part of party planning. In order to ease the last minute work load, plan ahead and choose food items that can be frozen or re-frigerated a day or more ahead.

Party checklist: Explore rental facilities.

Cocktail equipment	Favors	Silver/Flatwear
Bartenders	Flowers	Caterers
Waiters/Waitresses	Food	Trays/Platters
Candles	Music	Hot trays
Chairs/Tables	Place cards	Tea/Coffee service
Decorations	Table linens	Tents

Make your food table festive by using horseshoe-shaped molds for aspics and patés. Garnish trays with tomato roses or piped cream cheese roses. Garnish plates with rinsed and dried flower petals, or scatter them on the table around the centerpiece. Roses, tulips, violets, mums and nasturiums are edible flower petals. Cake molds of horseshoe and hot air balloon shapes are available. There are also candy molds of roses, horses and other decorative molds. Kentucky candies, such as the famous Bourbon Balls, are impressive to pass at the end of dinner or to give as gifts.

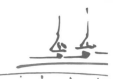

A fifth of Kentucky Bourbon frozen in a block of ice is a conversation piece. The Bourbon is set in an empty half gallon milk carton, filled with water, sprigs of greenery, rose petals and then frozen. Peel off the carton and set iced Bourbon on a cocktail napkin to prevent slipping, and then in a deep tray to catch the melting ice. Surround the iced Bourbon with greenery. Serve mint juleps in silver julep cups or silver-coated plastic julep cups.

Instead of the traditional red for roses, perhaps you would prefer to use another color theme, such as your favorite racing silks. Use local Kentucky pottery for favors, containers or as serving pieces.

Fill a silver wine cooler with red roses or red carnations. Make an infield centerpiece by lining a large tray with foil. Cut a piece of grass sod to fit the tray, arrange a grouping of ceramic or wooden horses. Build a fence around the entire piece with popsicle sticks or roping. Add small flowers if you wish. Horse head place mats could be cut from felt and wood carved horse head napkin rings are available at some stores. Place a large, handsome horse sculpture in the center of a table and surround with greenery and a garland of roses for the horse's neck. Grapevine and straw wreaths can be decorated with betting tickets, racing forms, miniature horses, silk roses and ribbons as door decorations. Corn husk or wood roses also may be used as door decorations.

Edible centerpieces, such as fresh fruit, vegetables and even scooped-out loaves of bread make interesting containers for many foods.

Because one of the Kentucky Derby's main events is the Balloon Race, balloons make colorful decorations. Purchase oversized balloons, fill with helium, tape ribbons over each balloon, tie straw baskets underneath balloons and fill with flowers.

If entertaining informally, use signs to decorate your home. Tape a sign on the closet door market "Paddock", on the bar marked "Watering Hole", on the kitchen door marked "Infield", to the dining area as the "Club House" and the television room as the "Grandstand". Racing posters are available at the "Finish Line" shop in the Museum (as are many other party favors, napkins, glasses, books, etc.) Many people collect the annual Derby poster to add to their collection and to display at Derby party time. The sound track from "The Greatest Race" is available on a 15 minute cassette tape. Played about a half an hour before the race, it would add to the excitement. This may inspire everyone at the party to join in with the television crowd and sing "My Old Kentucky Home".

"Weighing In", the day of the party. First impressions! Greet your guests for a festive day by decorating and carrying out your theme throughout your home. Decorate a mailbox or lamp post with large red bows or balloons. Line a walkway or front stoop with masses of red geraniums. Wreath your front door or cover the entire door with a horse poster.

'Off and Running" Your guests have arrived and you are "off and running" for a spectacular day. The "watering hole" is stocked to serve all kinds of refreshments, including the traditional mint julep with Kentucky's famous Bourbon. Make sure there is ample seating and television viewing available for the number of guests invited. Many people use two or three televisions in separate areas of the house.

"Better's Choice". To add to the excitement of the day, everyone enjoys a friendly wager, be it matchsticks or money. For your pari-mutuel pool, first set a price for each ticket. A dollar is usually the simplest. Slips of paper can be passed around and each guest can write his or her name and choice for the winning horse in the Derby. Betting only to "win", a guest may buy as many tickets as he or she wants. As soon as the race results are official, count the winning tickets, divide that number into the total money bet, and you have the payoff for each winning entry. Another idea is to have a large sheet of paper and list in order the post positions of all the horses running in the Derby on the left side of the paper. Across the top of the sheet write "Win," "Place" and "Show" and draw lines to form squares. The guests betting write their names in the square of their horse and whether they want to win, place or show. They may bet as many times as they wish at one dollar per bet. After the official results, the money is totaled in the "Win" column and divided among the winners. Do the same with "Place" and "Show". With this method you can bet "across the board".

"Winner's Circle". All winning wagers are paid. A long stemmed rose or lei of red flowers can be given to the winners. You may wish to present any of the favors mentioned in the favor suggestions that are traditional for Derby Day.

"Daily Double". Desserts and dessert wines. At the end of the evening, serve a sparkling wine or port with traditional desserts such as Kentucky Derby Museum Pie, Cadiz Fudge Cake, Idie's Schaum Torte, Chess Pie, Mint Julep Kisses, Bourbon Balls or Truffles. Miniature meringue dessert shells filled with fresh strawberries and whipped cream are especially appealing and attractive. Fill a large serving tray or china platter with homemade cookies and candies garnished with a rose or mint. These can be served from your buffet table or passed among your guests.

"Finish Line" Favors. Favors add to a memorable day. These may be given at the start of your party or saved for an extra treat as your guests depart. Some thoughts from our Kentucky home are:

Derby Glasses
Silver Julep Cups
Mint or Bourbon jellies
Small boxes filled with candies and tied with a ribbon
Kentucky Ham
Henry Bain Sauce
Lapel pins or tie tacks
Posters
T-shirts with the Derby motif
Small baskets filled with assorted Homemade Kentucky goodies
Bourbon Ball Candies
Small items from our own Kentucky potteries

Table of Contents

Appetizers..Page 21

Beverages...43

Soups 53

Salads...63

Cheese and Eggs 83

Poultry...91

Meats 109

Seafood.. 133

Vegetables.. 149

Sauces 169

Breads 181

Desserts 201

Cookies/Candies 231

Index 249

Menus for Derby Week

Saturday Before Derby Balloon Race

Freshly-squeezed Orange Juice
Strawberries
Kuchen*
Apricot Bread with Cream Cheese*
Granola*
Wonderful Hot Chocolate*
Hot Coffee

Sunday Evening Barbecue

Kentucky Barbecue* and Burgoo*
Bauer's Hot Slaw*
Glenis's Egg Cornbread*
Mildred's Chess Pie*

Monday Supper

Chicken Dijonnaise*
Wild Rice Salad*
Pretty Party Peas*
Yeast Rolls with Butter*

Tuesday's Derby Trial Cold Supper

Chevre and Leek Flan*
Molded Gazpacho*
Sausage Balls*
Marinated Vegetable Salad*
Homemade Crackers*
Orange Date Cake* with Liberty Hall Pudding
    Sauce*

Wednesday's Boat Race Picnic

Some Stardust Wine Cooler*
Zucchini Torta*
Quick Brioche*
Broccoli Salad*
Fried Chicken*
Stretch Brownie Squares*

Thursday Pegasus Parade Grill-out

Rebel Yell Sours*
Cold Cucumber Soup*
Marinated Leg of Lamb*
Barley Pilaf*
Green Bean Salad*
Processor French Bread*
Meringues* with Strawberries and Whipped
    Cream

Friday Kentucky Oaks Formal Dinner

Stuffed Cocktail Tomatoes with Watercress
    Spread*
Caviar Beggar's Purses*
Pendennis Champagne Punch*
Veal Filets with Mushroom Cream Sauce*
Stuffed Carrots*
Fresh Asparagus
Hot Kentucky Goat Cheese Salad on Bibb
    Lettuce*
Beaten Biscuits*
French Lace Cookie Baskets with Ganache*

Saturday Derby Day Brunch

Mint Juleps*
Country Ham*
Biscuits
Turkey Hash* over Corn Cakes*
Grits Casserole*
Bibb Lettuce with Herbed Vinaigrette
   Dressing*
Fried Apples
Chocolate Macaroon Cookies*

Saturday Box Lunch

Crudites
Beaten Biscuits with Country Ham and
   Mighty Mustard*
Benedictine on Whole Wheat Bread*
Grapes
Museum Winner's Pie (Tarts)*

Box Lunch for the Infield

Kentucky Fried Chicken
Submarine Sandwiches
Beer Cheese* and Homemade Crackers*
Shade Seeker Lemonade*
Mrs. Field's Faux Chocolate Chip Cookies*

Derby Day Evening Cocktail Supper

Ophelia's One-step Open-faced Tomato
   Sandwiches*
Onion Rounds*
Salmon*
Diamond Beef Filet in Aspic*
Henry Bain Sauce*
Adeline and Jane's Corn Pudding*
Julia's Spinach Casserole*
Derby Salad*
Helen's Mint Julep Kisses*
Cheesecake* with Strawberries and Whipped
   Cream
Chocolate Truffles*

Sunday After Derby Breakfast

Bloody Mary's
Freshly-squeezed Orange Juice
Houseguest Eggs*
Sausage and Bacon
Mini-Cinnamon Wheels*
Ginger and Honey Fruit Salad*
Hot Coffee

*Kentucky Derby Museum Cookbook recipes

Notes

FIRST RACE

APPETIZERS

COMMITTEE'S HANDICAP

1	MUSHROOMS NORMANDY	SERVES 8
2	SHRIMP TOAST	SERVES 20
3	BEER CHEESE	SERVES 12-15
4	BAKED STUFFED BRIE	SERVES 10
5	MARK'S SPREAD	SERVES 4-6
6	HOT CRAB CASSEROLE	SERVES 8
7	CURRIED CHICKEN PATÉ	SERVES 8
8	NAPLES NIBBLES	SERVES 12

Committee Selections   4-7-6

Kentucky bred entry 3,

Tasty Trivia
Drain freshly cooked bacon on paper towels atop wax paper. The drippings won't soak through onto the range or counter top, and the paper towels can be folded inside the wax paper and used later to grease casseroles.

APPETIZERS

Artichoke Nibbles

2	6-oz. jars marinated hearts
1	small onion, chopped
1	clove garlic, diced
4	eggs
¼	cup fine dry bread crumbs
¼	tsp. salt
⅛	tsp. pepper
⅛	tsp. oregano
⅛	tsp. liquid hot pepper seasoning
½	lb. sharp shredded cheese
2	T. minced parsley

Drain marinade from one jar of artichokes into skillet. Chop artichokes and set aside. Add onion and garlic to artichoke liquid and simmer five minutes. Let cool. In a bowl beat eggs on high speed until frothy. Add crumbs, salt, pepper, oregano, and hot pepper seasoning. Stir in cheese, parsley and artichokes. Then add onion mixture.

Turn into greased 7-inch by 11-inch pan and bake 325 degrees for about 30 minutes or until set when lightly touched. Let cool in pan 5 minutes and then cut into squares and serve.

Artichoke Dip

yields 1½ cups

1	16-oz. can artichoke hearts, drained (not marinated)
2	T. chopped yellow onion
⅓	cup mayonnaise
	juice of ½ lemon
¼	tsp. cayenne, or more
6	slices bacon
	salt and pepper to taste

Drain and chop the artichoke hearts to a pulp; combine well with the onion, mayonnaise, lemon juice, and cayenne pepper. Cook the bacon until crisp. Drain bacon and crumble. Add the bacon to the artichoke mixture. Correct seasoning with salt and pepper as desired. Chill this mixture before serving.

This can be refrigerated as much as three days before serving. This dip may be served in hollowed out, steamed fresh artichoke and presented with crisp toast points.

Asparagus Rounds

yields 7 dozen rounds

20	slices soft white bread
3	oz. Blue cheese, softened
8	oz. cream cheese, softened
1	large egg
20	stalks freshly cooked asparagus or frozen
2	sticks butter

Trim the crust off the bread, and flatten each slice with a rolling pin. Blend together the Blue and cream cheeses, along with the egg. Spread the cheese mixture on each slice of bread. Place asparagus on bread; roll up. Melt butter in a small rectangular pan. Dip each asparagus roll in the butter then put on a cookie sheet. Freeze for 8 hours or overnight. Remove from freezer and slice each roll into 4 pieces. Put in plastic freezer bags. Remove when needed and bake in 400 degree oven for 15 minutes or until golden brown. Serve warm.

Cafe Musée's Caramelized Bacon

yields 75 pieces

4	T. mustard
6	T. brown sugar
1	lb. bacon

Combine mustard and brown sugar; brush over one side of bacon strips. Place on oven rack with a pan directly under bacon to catch the grease. Bake at 325 degrees for 15 minutes or more, until bacon is crisp and shiny. Cool bacon and cut with scissors into serving pieces, about 4 to 5 pieces per strip.

Beer Cheese

serves 12-16

1	lb. sharp Cheddar, finely ground
1	lb. mild Cheddar
1	clove garlic, minced
1	tsp. salt
1	12 oz. can beer
3	T. Worcestershire sauce
4-5	drops hot pepper sauce, to taste
1	tsp. dry mustard

Combine all ingredients, except beer, and beat with electric mixer. Pour in beer slowly and beat until cheese is very smooth. Store in covered jar. Remove from refrigerator at least 30 minutes before serving. Beat once more.

Boursin Cheese Wafers

yields 3 dozen

½	cup Mock Boursin Cheese*
1	stick unsalted butter
	scant cup unbleached flour
	cayenne pepper to taste

Preheat oven to 400 degrees. Blend ingredients in food processor. Shape in a log about 8" long using waxed paper. Chill several hours. Slice ¼-inch thick and bake for approximately 10 to 12 minutes.

Mock Boursin Cheese

yields 3 cups

3	8-oz. pkgs. cream cheese
1	medium clove garlic, finely minced
3	tsp. finely chopped, fresh parsley
½	tsp. salt
½	tsp. basil
½	tsp. chives
¼	tsp. tarragon
¼	tsp. sage
	pepper to taste
1½	T. white vermouth

Beat all ingredients in mixer until well blended. If using fresh herbs, double or triple proportions. Serve with Bremner Wafers.

Baked-Stuffed Brie

serves 15-20

1	2.2 lb. wheel of Brie
1	medium carrot, diced
¼	cup minced scallions
2	T. minced shallots
½	cup sliced mushrooms
2	tsp. minced garlic
½	cup sweet butter
	Pinch saffron
	Pepper to taste
3	T. grated Parmesan cheese
2	sheets puff pastry
1	egg wash (1 egg mixed with 2 tsp. water)

Preheat oven to 425 degrees. Place Brie in freezer about 20 minutes to firm; remove and slice in half horizontally to create two layers.

Sauté carrots, scallions, shallots, mushrooms and garlic in butter until tender. Add saffron and pepper; cool. Fold in Parmesan cheese. Place 1 layer of Brie, rind down, on puff pastry. Spoon on filling and press firmly. Place second layer of Brie on top. Brush with egg wash. Pull puff pastry up around, covering Brie with pastry. Pinch edges to seal, then brush with egg wash. Decorate with pastry dough and egg wash decoration. Chill in refrigerator for 20 minutes. Bake for 15 minutes or until golden brown.

Chili Con Queso

yields 3 cups

¼	cup chopped onions
1	T. butter
½	cup mild salsa
¼	cup diced green chilies
2	cup shredded mild Cheddar cheese
⅓	cup heavy cream

In skillet, cook onions in butter until tender. Add salsa, chilies and cheese. When cheese is almost melted, stir in the cream. Heat thoroughly, but do not let boil. Serve warm with tortilla chips.
Variation: may use hot salsa and sharp Cheddar.

Ed's Salsa

yields 2-2½ cups

1	28-oz. can tomatoes
2	medium onions, chopped
½	green pepper, chopped
2	cloves garlic, minced
1	can green chilies, chopped
3	fresh, chopped jalepenos
⅔	bunch fresh chopped cilantro leaves or 3 tsp. dried
1-2	tsp. cumin
1	tsp. dried oregano
1	tsp. olive oil
1	T. red wine vinegar
½	tsp. pepper
1	tsp. salt
2	dashes cayenne

Use plastic blade in processor. Whiz all ingredients for 8-10 seconds. Use as a dip with corn chips.

Savory Cheese Bites

yields 60 Bites

Microwave
4	**eggs**
½	**cup whipping cream**
1	**jar (2 oz.) sliced pimiento, drained**
¼	**tsp. hot pepper sauce (Tabasco)**
1	**can (4 oz.) chopped green chiles, drained**
2	**cups (8 oz.) shredded Cheddar cheese**
2	**cups (8 oz.) shredded Swiss cheese**
1	**can (3 oz.) French fried onions, coarsely chopped**

From grocery bag or heavy brown wrapping paper, cut a piece of brown paper to fit bottom of 12 x 8 x 2-inch dish. Grease well. In large mixing bowl, beat together eggs and cream. Stir in pimiento, green chilies, pepper sauce and cheeses, mixing well. Pour into prepared dish. Microwave at Medium (50% power) for 10 minutes.

Sprinkle onions evenly over partially-cooked mixture. Rotate dish ½ turn and *microwave uncovered at medium for 12 to 15 minutes,* until center is almost set. Let stand 10 minutes to set. Invert onto cutting board, peel off brown paper then turn right side up on serving platter, Cut into squares. Serve on crackers or king-size corn chips.

For spicy flavor, substutute Pepper cheese for Swiss cheese.

Bourbon-Glazed Ham Balls

yields 24 Balls

Microwave
1	**lb. ground cooked ham**
½	**lb. ground pork**
3	**slices soft bread, cubed (about 1½ cups)**
2	**T. water**
2	**T. Bourbon**
1	**egg**
¼	**cup minced celery**
2	**T. minced onion**
2	**T. minced green pepper**
½	**tsp. dry mustard**
¼	**tsp. freshly ground black pepper**
⅛	**tsp. ground cloves**
⅓	**cup brown sugar, packed**
1	**T. prepared mustard**
½	**T. vinegar**

Combine ham, pork, bread, 1 tablespoon Bourbon, water, egg, celery, onion, green pepper, dry mustard, pepper and cloves in large bowl. Shape mixture into about 24 meatballs, using a heaping tablespoon mixture for each. Evenly space meatballs in 12x8x2-inch micro-wave oblong dish. Cover with waxed paper.

Microwave on High 9 to 11 minutes, rearranging ham balls so that less-cooked ones are to outside of dish after about 5 minutes. Be sure that all balls are fully cooked.

Stir together brown sugar, prepared mustard, vinegar and remaining 1 tablespoon of Bourbon. Drizzle glaze over balls and return to microwave oven for about 2-4 minutes longer, gently stirring after 2 minutes, until lightly glazed. To serve, transfer finished balls to serving platter and serve with wood picks.

APPETIZERS

Chutney Cheese Canape

yields 1½ cup

1	8-oz. pkg. cream cheese
¼	cup chutney
¼	tsp. dry mustard
1	tsp. curry powder
1	small pineapple half, cut lengthwise
½	cup sliced, toasted almonds

In a processor, blend cream cheese, chutney, mustard and curry powder until well mixed. Scoop out the inside of the pineapple half and fill with cream cheese mixture. Refrigerate until ready to serve. Sprinkle with almonds.

Crusty Havarti

serves 8-10

1	7-oz. round Cream Havarti cheese
1	T. Dijon mustard
¼	cup chopped fresh herbs*
4	frozen puff pastry shells, thawed
1	egg, slightly beaten with 2 tsp. water

*suggested herbs: basil, dill, fennel, chives, parsley, watercress or combination.

Preheat oven to 375 degrees. Spread top of cheese with mustard and herbs. Set aside. Roll puff pastry dough out into one large piece. Put cheese in center, herb side down. Gather edges of pastry over cheese, pinching together with water. Place on greased foil on cookie sheet, seam side down. Brush with beaten egg. Chill 30 minutes. Brush again with egg. Roll foil up closely around sides of cheese.
Bake for 15 minutes. Brush again with egg. Bake another 15 minutes or until well browned. Cool 30 minutes and serve with or without crackers.

Green Chilies Hors d'oeuvres

serves 12

5	small cans chopped green chilies (to make it extra spicy, add 3 T. Jalepeno peppers to the green chilies.)
1	lb. very sharp Cheddar cheese, grated
5	eggs
5	T. milk

Preheat oven to 325 degrees. Thoroughly drain cans of chilies. Put in a strainer and press all of juices out of chilies (this is important). Place drained chilies in a greased 13 x 9 baking dish. Grate Cheddar cheese and sprinkle over mixture. Mix in a blender 5 eggs and 5 tablespoons milk and pour over cheese and chilies. Bake for 25 minutes or until chilies, cheese and eggs are firm. Serve in baking dish with sesame or rye crackers.

Herbal Cheesecake

serves 20

Crust:
½   cup cold butter, cut in 1 T. slices
1   cup plain flour
½   tsp. salt
1   egg yolk
    grated rind of 1 lemon

To make crust combine butter, flour, salt, egg yolk and lemon rind in processor. Pulse until mixture crumbles. Press into a springform pan, bringing crust up ½ on side. Place in freezer.

Filling:
1   small onion, chopped
3   T. butter
3   oz. Parmesan cheese (1 ¼ cups)
3   8-oz. pkgs. soft cream cheese
3   T. flour
4   eggs
    juice of 1 lemon
⅓   cup chopped parsley
½   tsp. each of oregano, basil,
        tarragon, rosemary
2   tsp. salt
    dash Tabasco

Preheat oven to 400 degrees. Saute onion in 3 tablespoons of butter but do not brown. In a processor blend cheeses, flour and eggs until smooth. Add remaining ingredients, including onions. Pour filling into crust and bake 10 minutes at 400 degrees. Reduce heat to 325 degrees and cook 50 minutes. Remove from oven and let sit for 1 hour. Refrigerate 5 hours. Remove from pan and let sit one hour at room temperature before serving.

Serve with crackers or serve in a wedge with fresh fruit as a dessert.

Best made at least 3 days before serving. Keeps in refrigerator about 2 weeks. Freezes well.

Holly's Mexican Appetizer

yields 3-4 dozen

1   pkg. flour tortillas
1   carton whipped Philadelphia
        Cream Cheese
    chopped green onions (to taste)
    dash Worcestershire
    dash seasoned salt
    mayonnaise (only if needed to
        make spreadable)

Mix all but tortillas and correct seasoning. Spread on tortillas and roll as a burrito (jelly roll style). Place seam side down. Cut each into crosswise slices to make bite-size pieces. Serve with bowl of picante sauce for dipping. (Paceś picante is delicious). Use "medium" if you like it hot.

APPETIZERS

Mark's Spread

yields 1¼ cup

2	T. Chut-nut (Raffeto's)
1	8-oz. pkg. cream cheese
2	tsp. curry powder
2	tsp. mustard powder
	juice of one slice of lemon

Chop Chut-nut and mix with all other ingredients. Refrigerate 2-3 hours to bring out curry flavor.

Serve with crackers or fresh, chopped vegetables.

Pineapple Cheese Ball

serves 8

1	8-oz. pkg. cream cheese (softened)
4	oz. crushed pineaple (drained)
1	cup finely chopped pecans
½	cup finely chopped green pepper
1	T. finely chopped onion
¼	tsp. seasoned salt

Place all ingredients in a bowl, except half of the pecans. Mix and mash. Form into a ball. Roll ball in the remaining pecans. Chill and serve with your favorite crackers.

Post Time Cheese Mold

serves 8

1st Layer:
½	lb. sharp Cheddar cheese, grated
½	cup chopped pecans
¼	cup mayonnaise

2nd Layer:
1	10 oz. pkg. frozen, chopped spinach, drained
1	8-oz. pkg. cream cheese
	salt and pepper to taste

3rd Layer:
4	T. Chut-nut Chutney
1	8-oz. pkg. cream cheese
1	tsp. nutmeg

4th Layer:
½	lb. Cheddar cheese, grated
¼	cup pecans, chopped
¼	cup mayonnaise

Combine ingredients of each layer. Spray a 5 inch deep mold with vegetable oil. Place first layer firmly in bowl and follow with remaining layers. Refrigerate several hours and unmold.

Note: May be frozen. For variety use: pepper jelly and cream cheese, or eggs and caviar.

Roquefort Walnut Spread

yields ¾ cup

¼   cup walnuts
2   oz. Roquefort cheese, chilled
2   T. sour cream or heavy cream
4   oz. farmer's or pot-style cottage
    cheese

Process nuts in processor with on-off motions until nuts are coarsely chopped. Remove from work bowl. Place Roquefort and sour cream in work bowl and process until smooth. Add farmer's cheese and process until completely incorporated.

Shantung Torte

serves 15-20

1   cup water
4   T. gelatin
1   cup Smearcase (recipe in salad
    section)
1   cup Beer cheese (recipe in
    appetizer section)
1   cup Benedictine (recipe in
    cheese section)
1   cup Red Pepper Sauce (recipe in
    sauce section)

Dissolve gelatin in water. Heat mixture over hot water until clear. Add ¼ cup gelatin mixture to each individual layer: Smearcase, Beer cheese, Benedictine and Red Pepper sauce.

When each layer is partially chilled, begin putting into a greased 1-quart round mold. Put Red Pepper sauce in mold first, then Benedictine, then Beer cheese, lastly Smearcase. When unmolded, red layer is on top. Garnish with scored cucumber slices.

Tarragon Dip

serves 20

1   pint sour cream
1⅓ T. horseradish
1   T. paprika
1   T. minced green onion
½   tsp. salt
1   tsp. tarragon
1   clove garlic, minced
⅛   tsp. pepper

Mix all ingredients. Allow to stand for a few hours, refrigerated. Serve with crudités.

Watercress Spread

yields 1½ cups

1   8-oz. pkg. cream cheese, softened
1   3-oz. pkg. cream cheese, softened
1   bunch watercress, leaves only
1½ tsp. horseradish
    dash of Worcestershire

Whip cream cheese in container of food processor. Add watercress and blend until smooth. Add seasonings. Place in pastry bag and pipe filling into cherry tomatoes.

Tasty Trivia
Bury avocados in a bowl of flour to ripen.

APPETIZERS

Baby Hot Browns

Cafe Musée

yields 18

1	chicken bouillon cube
¼	cup hot water
¾	cup half and half
3	T. unsalted butter
2	T. flour
1	cup grated Swiss cheese
5	strips bacon, cooked, crumbled
1	onion, sliced thin
6	oz. cooked turkey, thinly sliced
18	slices of party rye or small french bread
	parsley

Dissolve bouillon cube in hot water, add half and half. In a saucepan, melt butter and add flour. Whisk and cook until mixture is frothy and raw flour taste is gone. While stirring, add the bouillon mixture. Stir constantly with a whisk until the sauce thickens and begins to bubble. Add Swiss cheese and stir until smooth. (If sauce needs to be thinned, heat and add a little water.)

Assemble hot browns by placing turkey and onion on each bread slice. Top with sauce and crumbled bacon. Heat at 350 degrees for 10 minutes. Garnish with parsley.

Curried Chicken Paté

yields 2 cups

1	whole chicken breast, skinned, poached and cut in 1 inch pieces
1	shallot, quartered
¼	medium Delicious apple, peeled, seeded, cored, quartered
¼	lb. unsalted butter, cut into pieces
1	tsp. lemon juice
½	tsp. salt
¼	tsp. curry powder, or to taste
1	T. mango chutney

Add chicken, shallots and apple to work bowl of processor and process until finely chopped. Add remaining ingredients and process until mixture is very smooth. Taste for seasonings. Spread on beaten biscuit halves and dip tops in chopped parsley, toasted chopped almonds or place sliced pitted black olives on top.

Garnishes: fresh parsley, chopped almonds, toasted and chopped black olives, pitted and thinly sliced

Ham and Green Peppercorn Paté

serves 24

3	cups ground, baked country ham
2	cups ground, fully cooked ham
2	shallots, chopped
2	T. butter
2	T. bottled green peppercorns, drained
2	T. Dijon mustard
2	T. Balsamic or other good wine vinegar
1⅓	sticks unsalted butter, slightly softened

Purée ground ham in processor until smooth. Remove to bowl. Sauté shallots in 2 tablespoons butter until soft. Process peppercorns until fine. Add mustard, vinegar and butter and continue processing until well blended. Combine processed ingredients with ham and shallots and mix thoroughly.

Place a piece of cheesecloth the width of the bottom of a 6-cup terrine long enough to extend up the ends and a bit beyond, if the paté is to be unmolded. Pack the ham down firmly. Cover and refrigerate several hours or overnight. Unmold and decorate with slivered black olives.

Glazed Chicken Wings

serves 10-12

3	lbs. plump chicken wings
⅔	cup soy sauce
2	T. vegetable oil
2	cloves garlic, crushed
½	cup honey
2	tsp. Five Spice powder
½	tsp. onion powder

Cut each chicken wing at joint, making 3 pieces. Discard tips. Place wings in a shallow pan. Mix remaining ingredients and pour over chicken. Cover and refrigerate, turning once. Keep refrigerated for a minimum of an hour. Drain marinade and save. Preheat oven to 350 degrees and using marinade, baste wings once and bake 15 minutes. Turn wings and baste again and return to oven for 15 more minutes.

Party Chicken Livers

serves 6-8

¼	cup white wine
1	lb. chicken livers, trimmed of fat
10-12	slices bacon-cut in half
3	T. French mustard
¾	cup cracker crumbs or toasted bread crumbs

Preheat oven to 425 degrees.

Pour white wine over chicken livers; let sit for 10 minutes. Drain.

Microwave the bacon 3-4 minutes, or parboil for 1 minute in boiling water; drain on paper towels.

Dip the livers lightly in mustard. Wrap a half slice bacon around each liver and secure with a wooden toothpick. Sprinkle the livers with cracker or bread crumbs. Place in a buttered baking dish. Bake for 20-25 minutes, or until the livers have almost lost their pink interior.

Ham Balls with Sweet-Sour Pineapple Sauce

serves 30

2	cans (14 oz.) pineapple tidbits
1½	cups brown sugar
2	tsp. dry mustard
½	cup cider vinegar
1	cup orange marmalade
2	T. molasses
2	T. chili sauce
¼	cup cornstarch
½	cup water
2	lb. cooked lean ham, ground
2½	cups uncooked ground lean pork
4	cups soft bread crumbs
2	cups milk
2	tsp. salt
1	green pepper
1	small jar pimientos, cut into strips

Turn pineapple, with syrup, into saucepan. Blend in sugar, mustard, vinegar and marmalade. Heat mixture to a boil, stirring constantly. Mix in molasses and chili sauce. Mix the cornstarch and water; stir into the sauce. Cook and stir until sauce is thick and clear; set aside.

Mix the ham, pork, bread crumbs, milk and salt. Divide the mixture into fourths. Press each fourth into a rectangle 8-inches by 6-inches. Cut into 40 pieces and shape into balls. Arrange in 2 shallow jelly roll pans (in one layer). Pour sauce over meat. Bake uncovered at 350 degrees for 30 minutes. Turn the meatballs and add the green pepper and pimiento strips. Bake 15 minutes longer. Serve at once. Meatballs and sauce may be frozen after baking (preferably without green pepper and pimiento strips).

APPETIZERS

Sausage Balls

serves 16-20

2   lbs. hot sausage
      flour
1   cup sour cream
      large bottle Major Grey's chutney, chopped
½   cup sherry

Form sausage into 1 ½ inch balls. Roll balls in flour. Fry sausage balls in skillet until thoroughly cooked. (Can be done ahead). Mix together sour cream, chutney and sherry and put in a chafing dish. Drain sausage balls and put in mixture. Serve warm.

Steak Tartare

serves 6-8

1   lb. ground round (ground 2-3 times)
½   cup finely chopped onions
1   clove garlic, minced fine
1½   tsp. salt
1   tsp. pepper
1   raw egg
¼   tsp. dry mustard
      capers

Mix several hours before serving. Top with capers and serve with pumpernickel bread and whipped unsalted butter.

Meatballs in Creamy Dill Sauce

yields 72 Meatballs

1½   lb. ground beef
1   lb. ground veal
1   4½ oz. can deviled ham
1   small can evaporated milk (⅔ cup)
2   eggs
1   T. grated onion
3   slices whole wheat bread, crumbled
½   tsp. salt
½   tsp. all spice
¼   tsp. pepper
¼   cup shortening, for frying

Combine all ingredients, except shortening, in a large bowl. Mix thoroughly with a fork. Shape into 72 small meatballs. In a large frying pan brown a few at a time. Refrigerate overnight.

Creamy Dill Sauce
2   T. butter or margarine
2   T. flour
½   tsp. salt
1   cup water
1   cup sour cream
1   T. catsup
1   T. dill weed

Melt butter in small saucepan and blend in flour and salt. Cook, stirring constantly, until mixtures bubbles. Stir in water slowly and continue cooking and stirring until sauce thickens and boils for one minute. Stir in sour cream, catsup and dill weed. Heat just to boiling.

To serve: Heat meatballs in ¼ cup water in frying pan. Place meatballs in chafing dish and pour sauce over them. Keep hot. This could also be a main dish.

Mushrooms

serves 12

1	lb. fresh mushrooms, uniform size, washed and dried
¼	cup butter
2-3	green onions, sliced
½	cup bread crumbs
1	T. chopped parsley
1	T. lemon juice
½	tsp. salt

Preheat oven to 450 degrees. To prepare mushrooms, remove stems trom caps and chop stem. Sauté stems in butter with onions. Add remaining ingredients and blend. Place filling in mushroom caps, and put caps on a cookie sheet, stuffing side up.

Bake about 8 minutes, or until brown.

Hot Mushroom Dip

serves 12

1	lb. fresh mushrooms
3	T. butter
1½	T. flour
1	cup sour cream
½	tsp. lemon juice

Wash mushrooms, trim off stems and slice. Then sauté in skillet with butter for a few minutes, add flour and stir until thickened. Add sour cream and lemon juice. Cook 15 minutes on medium heat. Do not allow to boil.

Serve warm in a chafing dish with melba rounds.

Museum Mushrooms

serves 8-10

3	oz. pkg. cream cheese
2	tsp. chopped chives
6	strips crisp bacon, crumbled
16	to 20 fresh mushrooms

Preheat oven to 350 degrees. Mix cream cheese, chives, and bacon. Remove stems from mushrooms and stuff with cheese mixture. Bake 15 minutes, then broil until brown.

Cheese Puffs

yields 4-5 dozen

1	cup sharp cheese, grated
1	stick butter
1	cup flour
1	cup Rice Krispies
	pinch salt
½	tsp. Tabasco

Preheat oven to 350 degrees. Let cheese and butter come to room temperature. Blend well. Add flour, rice cereal, salt and Tabasco. Mix well. Pinch off marble-sized pieces and place on lightly greased cookie sheet. Bake for 10-15 minutes.

Keeps well in an airtight container.

APPETIZERS

Mushroom Mousse

yields 2 cups

1	clove garlic, minced
1	T. butter
½	lb. mushrooms, chopped
1½	tsp. unflavored gelatin
1	T. dry Sherry
¼	cup cold chicken broth
1	egg, separated
1½	drops Tabasco
¼	cup mayonnaise
1	tsp. capers, drained
1½	T. chopped green onion
½	tsp. lemon juice
1½	T. fresh chopped parsley
	pinch of white pepper
½	cup heavy cream

Sauté the chopped garlic in the butter over low heat for a minute. Add the mushrooms and brown in butter, stirring often for 10-15 minutes. Drain in a sieve and discard juices.

Soften the gelatin in the Sherry and chicken broth in a blender or processor. Blend briefly. Add the remainder of the ingredients, except the cream and egg white. Blend until smooth, then add the cream; blend again.

In a small bowl, beat the egg white until stiff, then fold into the mushroom mixture. Pour into a 2-3 cup mold and refrigerate until ready to serve.

To serve, unmold and garnish with watercress or parsley sprigs and radish roses. Spread on melba toast points (freshly made) or water biscuits.

Mushrooms Normandy

serves 12

1	lb. mushrooms, diced in ⅜ inch cubes
1	medium tart, crisp apple, cut into 1 inch matchsticks
2	T. butter
2	tsp. Applejack
⅔	cup heavy cream
¼	tsp. ground cardamon
2-3	grinds of pepper
	salt
2	T. sour cream
2	T. ground walnuts

Sauté mushrooms in 1½ tablespoons butter over moderately high heat until juice is evaporated and they begin to brown. Partially cook julienned apple in ½ tablespoon butter a minute or two until pieces become a pale yellow yet crisp. Sprinkle with Applejack and toss lightly.

Boil cream until reduced by about one-third. Add mushrooms, cardamon, salt and pepper and continue cooking, stirring to coat mushrooms, until almost all the cream is absorbed. Stir the sour cream a bit first then add to the mushrooms. Stir in apples and walnuts. Keep warm over hot water. Serve in crustades*or puff pastry shells and top with parsley cluster.

*Recipe below

*Crustades

6	long French rolls, cut in half crosswise, crusts trimmed
1-1½	sticks butter, melted (margarine may be used)

Preheat oven to 450 degrees. Cut out center of each rectangle with grapefruit knife, leaving about ⅜ inch sides and bottom. Press inside with fingers to form even shell. Toast in oven for four minutes. Brush with butter inside and out and toast two to three minutes more. Reheat to serve. Freezes well.

Caviar Mousse

yields 4 cups

1	envelope unflavored gelatin
2	T. cold water
½	cup boiling water
16	oz. commercial sour cream
1	3½ oz. jar black or red caviar
2	T. mayonnaise
2	T. lemon juice
	Dash of tabasco

Soften gelatin in cold water; add boiling water, stirring until gelatin is dissolved. Stir in remaining ingredients; spoon into a lightly oiled 4 cup mold. Cover and chill several hours or until set. Serve with crackers.

Caviar Beggar's Purses
Quilted Giraffe Restaurant, New York

serves 12

12	crêpes (recipe follows)
12	long chives
4	T. Beluga caviar
1½	T. crème fraîche (sour cream is an acceptable substitute)
¼	cup clarified butter
2	lemons

Trim the crêpes to a diameter of 4½ inches. Blanch the chives in hot water from the tap for 10 seconds so that they become limp. Lay the trimmed crêpes out on a table. Spoon 1 teaspoon of caviar onto the center of each one. Spoon a small dollop of crème fraîche onto each mound of caviar. If you are right-handed, grasp the edge of a crêpe in-between the thumb and forefinger of your left hand and then, using your right hand pleat the crêpe in the fashion of a medieval leather purse. Tie a chive around the gathers about ½ inch from the top of the purse. Trim away the excess chives. Heat the clarified butter gently until warm. Dip the beggar's purses into it to warm them ever so slightly and serve them, each on top of a slice of lemon. (If you decide to make the beggar's purses earlier in the day, refrigerate them in a tightly sealed container, and take them out an hour before serving them to allow them to reach room temperature.)

crêpe recipe continued on next page

Crèpes
Quilted Giraffe Restaurant

yields 40 6-inch crèpes.

4	oz. pastry flour
	pinch of salt
4	eggs
1¾	cups milk
1	T. clarified or melted whole butter

In a mixing bowl combine the pastry flour, salt and eggs, stirring them with a wooden spoon until you obtain a very smooth paste. Gradually add 1½ cups of the milk. Once it is properly mixed, strain the batter and let it stand at room temperature for an hour. At the end of an hour, stir in the butter with a whisk. Heat your crèpe pan over a moderate flame. Using a paper towel moistened with a bit of melted butter, lightly grease the pan. Pour just enough batter into the pan to lightly coat the bottom. Pour the excess batter into the uncooked batter immediately. The proper amount of batter will cling to the pan. Cook the crèpe until it is lightly browned on the first side. Then lift the crèpe with a small spatula or a knife point and flip it over. Cook it for 15 seconds more. (If you find your first crèpe to be too thick, use some of the additional milk to thin the batter to the proper consistency.) Stack the finished crèpes on a piece of wax paper. If you are not planning to use the crèpes immediately, wrap them carefully in plastic wrap to keep them from drying out.

Winingham Farm's Baked Clam Dip

yields 3 cups

2	8 oz. cans clams, drained
1	tsp. lemon juice
1	medium onion, chopped
1	clove garlic, minced
½	green pepper, chopped
1	stick butter
	dash of Tabasco
	salt and pepper to taste
1	tsp. oregano
1	tsp. parsley
¼	cup grated Cheddar cheese
3	T. grated Parmesan cheese
½	cup bread crumbs
	Italian seasonings

Simmer clams with lemon juice for 15 minutes. Sauté all other ingredients in butter in another pan (except bread crumbs and cheese). When onion mixture is soft, add clams and bread crumbs. Sprinkle with Italian seasoning. Put mixture in a small baking dish, top with cheeses. Bake 20 minutes in a 350 degree oven.

Serve with party rye bread or crackers

Hot Crab Casserole

yields 2½ cups

1	8-oz. pkg. cream cheese
1	T. milk
1	lb. fresh crab meat, picked over for bones and cartilage
1½	tsp. onion, chopped
½	tsp. horseradish
¼	tsp. salt
	freshly ground pepper
⅓	cup slivered almonds, toasted lightly

Soften the cream cheese. Mix in the milk until creamy. Add the remaining ingredients, except the almonds. Refrigerate for one day.

Put the mixture into a small casserole. Sprinkle with the slivered almonds. Bake at 375 degrees for 15 minutes. Serve while warm with unsalted crackers.

Oysters Rockefeller Spread

serves 12

2	10 oz. packages frozen chopped spinach
1	pint fresh oysters, with liquor
⅓	cup butter, melted
1	clove garlic, minced
⅓	cup flour
⅓	cup chopped green onions
⅓	cup chopped fresh parsley
1	tsp. salt
¼	tsp. cayenne
1	tsp. anchovy paste or mashed anchovies (optional)
1	inch cubes dark onion rye bread

Cook the spinach only until thawed. Drain well. Cook the oysters in their liquor for 3 minutes or just until their edges curl. Drain the oysters, saving the liquor, and chop.

Melt the butter and add the garlic. Sauté briefly and add the flour. Stirring constantly, cook 5 minutes over low heat. Remove from heat and blend in 1 cup oyster liquor. Simmer, stirring constantly, until thickened. Add the green onions, parsley and spinach. Add the seasonings of salt, cayenne and anchovy paste. Adjust the seasonings, if needed, and the thickness. If thinning is necessary add more oyster liquor or milk. It should be somewhat thick for dipping. Add the chopped oysters. Serve in a chafing dish, surrounded with dark onion rye bread for dipping.

Oyster Roll

serves 8-10

1	can broken smoked oysters
1	tsp. lemon juice
1	tsp. Worcestershire sauce
1	8 oz. pkg. cream cheese

Drain oil from smoked oysters; cut into small pieces, then drain more. Mix with lemon juice and Worcestershire sauce. Put cheese between 2 layers of wax paper. Roll to form a rectangle (approximately 10-inches x 6-7-inches). Remove top layer of wax paper. Put oysters in a strip down the center length of the cream cheese. Carefully roll up, jelly-roll fashion; remove paper. Decorate top with paprika and parsley. Serve with party rye bread or crackers.

APPETIZERS

Smokey Salmon Spread

yields 2 cups

1   T. fresh dill or ¼ tsp. dried dill
     weed
12   oz. cream cheese, room
     temperature, cut into pieces
1   7¾ oz. can red salmon, thoroughly
     drained
1   tsp. liquid smoke
2   tsp. lemon juice
7-9 drops Tabasco
     chopped parsley

If using fresh dill, process first in the processor. Add the cream cheese and process until smooth. Add remaining ingredients and process until smooth.

Variation: Pipe Smoked Salmon Spread into cherry tomatoes or in miniature cream puffs.

Seafood Mold

yields 2½ cups

1   8 oz. pkg. cream cheese, room
     temperature
1   cup chopped, cooked shrimp or
     crabmeat, or both
1   T. horseradish
½   cup finely chopped celery
1   small jar pimiento, drained well
     and diced
½   small onion, minced
½   small clove garlic, minced
1   scant tsp. Seafood Seasoning

Mix all ingredients together and put in an oiled 3 cup mold. Chill overnight.

Note: Mold may be "iced" with sour cream.

Junie's Marinated Shrimp

serves 15-20

2½   lbs. raw shrimp, shelled and
     cleaned
½   cup celery tops
¼   cup mixed pickling spices
1   tsp. salt
2   cups sliced sweet onions
     (Bermuda or Vidalia)
6-8 Bay leaves
2   lemons, thinly sliced

Marinade:
¼   cup vegetable oil
¾   cup vinegar
3   T. capers (optional)
2½   tsp. celery seed
     dash of Tabasco

Cover shrimp with boiling water; add celery tops, spices and salt. Cover and low simmer 5 minutes. Rinse immediately in cold water. In a large glass dish alternate layers of shrimp with raw onions, bay leaves and lemon slices. Mix marinade ingredients and pour over shrimp. Cover and refrigerate at least 24 hours (stir several times). Drain partially.

Serve with cocktail forks and crackers

Cheesey Shrimp Mold

serves 8

1	12 oz. Cheddar cheese
1	3-oz. pkg. cream cheese
3	green onions, cut in 1 inch pieces
¾	lb. shrimp, cooked
1	cup mayonnaise
½	tsp. Worcestershire sauce
	salt and pepper
	garlic powder to taste (or crushed clove of garlic)

Grate cheese in food processor; add cream cheese and finely chopped onion. Mix well. Add shrimp and remaining ingredients and process until smooth. Put in a greased mold and cover with plastic wrap. Chill for 4-5 hours or overnight. May be used as a spread, if desired.

Shrimp Cocktail Ball

yields 2 cups

2	8 oz. pkgs. cream cheese
2	4 ½-oz. cans baby shrimp, drained
1	T. lemon juice
1	tsp. Worcestershire sauce
1	clove of garlic, minced
	cocktail sauce

Mix thoroughly the cream cheese, shrimp, lemon juice, Worcestershire sauce and garlic. Form into a ball and place on serving platter. Cover with cocktail sauce. Serve with crackers.

Shrimpers Party Spread

yields 2 cups

1	8 oz. pkg. cream cheese, softened
2	T. chili sauce
2	T. chopped onion
1	tsp. prepared horseradish
¼	tsp Tabasco
2	T. chopped fresh parsley
1	tsp. salt
¼	tsp. finely chopped garlic
½	lb. shrimp, cooked and chopped

Combine all ingredients, except shrimp, and mix thoroughly. Stir in shrimp. Cover and refrigerate at least one hour before serving. Garnish with parsley sprigs and serve with crackers.

Shrimp Toast

yields 2 dozen

1	3 oz. pkg. cream cheese, room temperature
1	stick butter, room temperature
1	small can shrimp, drained
1	loaf thin sliced white bread

Preheat oven to 350 degrees. Combine cream cheese and butter well; mix in shrimp. Trim crusts from thin, white bread and spread generously with mixture. (These may be frozen at this point). When ready to serve, cut in quarters and bake for approximately 20 minutes.

Shrimp Toast to Show

yields 56

14	slices day old sandwich bread (Pepperidge Farm)
¾	pound frozen uncooked shrimp
¼	cup finely chopped onion
1½	tsp. salt
1	tsp. sugar
1½	T. cornstarch
1	T. chives
1	egg, beaten
1	can water chestnuts, drained
	Dry, unflavored bread crumbs
	Oil for frying

Trim crusts off bread. Lay out slices to dry. Chop shrimp finely in food processor. Mix shrimp, chopped onions, salt, sugar, cornstarch and chives. Beat egg well and stir into shrimp mixture. Finely chop water chestnuts in food processor and add to shrimp mixture. Spread mixture over bread slices and sprinkle each with unflavored bread crumbs. Cut each piece of bread into four triangles.

Set electric frying pan at 375 degrees and deep fry each triangle, shrimp side down until brown. Drain on paper towels. Put on cookie sheet and freeze. When ready to serve, bake at 400 degrees for about 10 minutes, watching carefully not to burn.

Tuna Paté

serves 8-10

1	8-oz. pkg. cream cheese, softened
2	T. chili sauce
2	T. chopped fresh parsley
1	cup chopped onion
1	T. Worcestershire sauce
½	tsp. Tabasco
2	7-oz. cans water-pack, white tuna, drained

Blend together the ingredients, except tuna. Add the tuna and mix well. Refrigerate at least 3 hours before serving.

Serve with assorted crackers.

Note: Leftover paté may be sliced for sandwiches.

Naples Nibbles

yields 24 ounces

2	pkgs. oyster crackers (12 oz. each)
2	pkgs. Hidden Valley Dry Original Ranch Salad Dressing (1 oz. each)
1	12-oz. bottle Orville Redenbacher's popping oil

Mix all of the ingredients in a large airtight container and shake well. Let sit for 24 hours. Store in container.

APPETIZERS

Onion Rounds

serves 12

12	rounds of white bread cut in 2 inch diameter
12	slices of onion, thinly sliced in 2 inch rounds
12	T. mayonnaise
	paprika

Toast bread rounds. Place slice of onion on toast, then spoon mayonnaise on top. Broil until mayonnaise begins to bubble. Sprinkle with paprika.

Indian Feast Popcorn

⅓	cup popcorn
1	T. oil
1	T. butter
⅓	cup butter, melted
1	tsp. dried dillweed
1	tsp. lemon pepper
1	tsp. Worcestershire sauce
½	tsp. garlic powder
½	tsp. onion powder
	salt
2	cups shoestring potatoes
1	cup mixed nuts

Preheat oven to 250 degrees. Pop the popcorn in 1 tablespoon oil and 1 tablespoon butter. Mix the melted butter, dillweed, lemon pepper, Worcestershire sauce, garlic powder, onion powder and salt, to taste. Toss with the remaining ingredients. Spread the mixture on a jelly roll pan. Bake for 6-8 minutes.

Ophelia's Derbytime One-Step Tomato Sandwiches

yields 45 open face canapes

1	cup commercial mayonnaise (Hellman's)
½	tsp. chopped onion
½	tsp. freshly ground pepper
¼	tsp. salt
½	tsp. dried basil or thyme
¼	tsp. paprika
¼	tsp. vinegar
	tomatoes, 3 inches in diameter, sliced approximately ¼ inch thick
2	loaves fresh, soft white bread Parsley, chopped for garnished

Ophelia Ellis, a well-known cateress in Louisville, has an assembly-line approach to making open-faced tomato sandwiches for a cocktail party.

Season the mayonnaise with chopped onion, freshly ground pepper, salt, basil, paprika and vinegar the day before you plan to use the sandwiches. Store in a jar in the refrigerator. As you get ready to assemble the sandwiches, slice the tomatoes and store in a deep dish. Cut the bread into bread rounds; cut with a cutter the same size as the tomatoes. Spread the bread rounds with the seasoned mayonnaise. Make "mayonnaise sandwiches" and stack them in a deep dish or box and cover with a layer of wax paper and with a wet towel to keep bread fresh. Closer to the time of the party get your trays ready and open the sandwiches, put a slice of tomato on each and sprinkle with chopped parsley.

Notes

SECOND RACE

BEVERAGES

COMMITTEE'S HANDICAP

1	RINGER		SERVES 1
2	SHADE SEEKER LEMONADE		SERVES 36
3	MOCK CHAMPAGNE PUNCH		SERVES 10
4	BLINKER		SERVES 1
5	MOTHER'S OLD FASHIONED CUSTARD		SERVES 8-10
6	REBEL PARTY SOUR		SERVES 6
7	MR. CLOISSON'S MINT JULEP		SERVES 8-10
8	BOURBON SLUSH		SERVES 16-20

Committee Selections   7-3-5

Kentucky bred entry 1, 5, 6, 7, 8

Tasty Trivia
Mr. George Garvin Brown gave this recipe for a Ringer to his daughter, Laura Lee Deters. It was developed by Brown-Forman Distillers using Old Forrester bourbon instead of brandy.

Apricot Liqueur

yield 1 quart

1	lb. dried apricots
15	oz. rock candy (crystal)
1	qt. Vodka

Put all ingredients in 2 quart jar or bottle. Shake daily for 2 weeks. Let stand 90 days. Strain through fine cloth into bottles. Save the apricots! They are delicious over ice cream, on cereal, in cut up fruit or just plain.

Banana Daiquiri

serves one

1 ½	jiggers Rum
½	large banana
½	lime, squeezed
1	tsp. sugar
2	ice cubes

Put all ingredients in a blender, and blend until well mixed (5 seconds). Pour into a short, fat glass.

Blinker

serves 1

1	jigger Kentucky Bourbon (1½ oz.)
¾	jigger grapefruit juice
¼	jigger Grenadine
	cracked ice

Shake well and strain into a cocktail glass. (Try it and you'll know where it gets its name).

Coffee Liqueur

makes 1¼ quarts

4	cups sugar
2	oz. jar instant coffee
1½	cups boiling water
2	cups Vodka
1-2	fresh vanilla beans

Mix sugar and coffee. Add boiling water. Stir quickly until dissolved. Let cool. Add Vodka. Pour into a gallon jug. Tie string to vanilla bean or beans so it can be removed; add to mixture, leaving string outside the bottle. Close bottle tightly. Shake mixture vigorously every day for 30 days. Remove vanilla from jug. Rebottle and drink with pleasure.

Cranberry Punch

serves 12

1	lb. can jellied cranberry sauce
8	oz. fresh, bottled or frozen lime juice
1	fifth Vodka
2	qts. cracked ice
	sugar or sugar substitute to taste

Mix cranberry sauce with lime juice in mixer. Sweeten to taste. Pour over ice. Add Vodka and stir rapidly for a minute or so. Strain into jars and store in refrigerator until ready to serve. Serve over cracked ice.

BEVERAGES

Track Talk
The "Fighting Finish" Derby (1933) was won by Broker's Tip
with jockey Don Meade. In the stretch this jockey fought off
Herb Fisher aboard Head Play, who grabbed at anything,
including Meade's boot and his saddlecloth.

Cafe Brulot Diabolique
(Chad Mitchell)

serves 10

	peel of one lemon
	peel of one orange
8	whole cloves
2	cinnamon sticks
1½	T. sugar
3	oz. Brandy (or 2 oz. Brandy and 1 oz. good orange liqueur)
3 to 4	cups strong black coffee, hot

Peel the lemon in one length; peel the orange in one length and stud it with the cloves. Place the peels, cinnamon, sugar and Brandy in a fireproof bowl and heat over open flame. When the Brandy is hot, but not boiling, bring the bowl to the table and ignite it with a long match. Use ladle to stir and pour the liquid around in the bowl for a minute or two. Pour in the hot coffee and ladle it into the demi-tasse cups.

Note: Chad was a student at LaVarenne in Paris, very young and very talented. This is his version of a lovely dessert coffee.

Bimini Planter's Punch

serves 3

1	jigger Bacardi rum
2	jiggers Jamaica dark rum
1	jigger Port
½	jigger Drambuie
2	cups pineapple juice
	cinnamon
3	slices pineapple
3	slices orange
3	slices grapefruit

Whip all ingredients, except fruit, in a blender or shake 2 minutes in a cocktail shaker. You may pour mixture into 3 16-ounce or 18-ounce iced tea glasses. Double Old Fashioned glasses work well. Add fruit and fill glasses with ice. Put the fresh fruit in each. Muddle and serve.

Bourbon Slush

yield 3 quarts

2½	cups tea (2½ cups water and 2 small tea bags)
1	12-oz. can frozen lemonade, thawed
1	6-oz. can frozen orange juice
2	cups Makers Mark Bourbon
1	cup sugar
6	cups water

Let tea cool, then mix all together and freeze in a plastic container. When ready to serve, scoop into a glass. Garnish with pineapple chunks or a cherry on a toothpick, or mint.

Cricket

serves 2

2	jiggers brown Crème de Cacao
1	jigger Brandy
½	pt. vanilla ice cream, cut in pieces
1	cup crushed ice, or 4 whole cubes

Put all ingredients into blender and frappé until sherbet-like consistency. Serve in cocktail glasses.

Daiquiri

serves 2

1½   jiggers strong, dark Rum
      juice of 1 lime
½   tsp. powdered sugar
¼   cup pineapple juice
      cracked ice

Shake well and strain into bowl type Champagne glass filled with finely shaved ice.

Derby Fizz

serves 1

1   jigger Kentucky Bourbon (1½ oz.)
5   dashes lemon juice
1   tsp. powdered sugar
1   egg
3   dashes Curacao
      cracked ice
      carbonated water

Mix ingredients in cocktail shaker. Shake well. Strain into small highball glasses. Fill with carbonated water.

Dixie Whiskey

serves 6

4   glasses (3-4 oz. each) Kentucky
         Bourbon
¼   tsp. Angostura bitters
½   tsp. Curacao
2   tsp. Créme de Menthe
2   small tsp. sugar
      cracked ice

Shake well and strain into glasses and serve.

Golden Cadillac

serves 1

1   oz. Liquore Galliano
2   oz. white Crème de Cacao
1   oz. cream
3   oz. crushed ice

Put ingredients in blender at slow speed for 10 seconds. Strain or pour directly into glass. (For more body, substitute 1 oz. vanilla ice cream for cream).

Kentucky Derby Cranberry Punch

serves 8-10

20   oz. cranbery juice
10   oz. Kentucky Bourbon
6   oz. frozen lemonade
20   ice cubes

Blend all ingredients until frothy. Place in freezer until slushy. Serve in champagne glasses or sherbet glasses, topped with a cherry.

BEVERAGES

Track Talk
*THE JULEP CUP — A special tradition is observed after each
Kentucky Derby — the winning owner drinks a toast to his
horse from a sterling julep cup. The winner's name and the
year won is engraved on the cup and it is then added to the
collection owned by Churchill Downs.*

About the Mint Julep

Few people agree on the way in which a "proper" mint julep should be made, many contending that theirs is the one and only way it should be concocted. Following are several versions so the imbiber can determine for himself.

Irvin Cobb's Mint Julep

Take from the cold spring, some water, pure as the angels are; mix it with sugar till it seems like oil. Then take a glass and crush your mint in it with a spoon—crush it around the border of the glass and leave no place untouched. Then throw the mint away—it is a sacrifice. Fill the glass with cracked ice; pour in the quantity of Bourbon you want. It trickles slowly through the ice. Let it have time to cool, then pour your sugared water over it. No spoon is needed, no stirring allowed. Just let it stand a moment. Then around the brim place sprigs of mint, so that one who drinks may find taste and odor at one draught.
"And that, my friend, is one hell of a fine mint julep.'"

Mint Juleps
serves 8-10

1	cup sugar
1	cup water
1	bunch fresh mint sprigs
	crushed ice
	Kentucky Bourbon

Combine sugar and water and boil for 5 minutes, without stirring. Cool. Pour over a handful of mint. Refrigerate over night in a closed jar. Remove mint leaves and continue to refrigerate. This will keep several weeks and individual juleps may be made as desired.

For each serving, fill an 8 ounce glass with crushed ice. Add one tablespoon syrup and one tablespoon water. Add 2 ounces Bourbon. Stir gently until glass is frosted. Insert straw and garnish with a sprig of mint.

Mr. Closson's Mint Julep

(This recipe comes fom Burton Closson of Cincinnati. The technique of steeping mint leaves in Bourbon caught the attention of cookbook committee members.)
Fill julep glass with crushed ice. Pour 1 to 1½ tablespoons of simple syrup (see recipe) over ice. Fill glass with mint-flavored Bourbon (see recipe). Stir. Garnish with sprig of mint.

Simple Syrup:
Boil equal amounts of sugar and water. Cool and refrigerate.

Mint-Flavored Bourbon:
1 quart Bourbon - Old Rip Van Winkle
Fresh mint leaves (enough to stuff the bottle)
Wash and dry mint leaves. Add to Bourbon and let steep in the bottle for 3 days. Remove leaves and discard them. To serve, mix Bourbon with simple syrup and crushed ice.

Nancy's Mint Juleps

serves 8-10

1   egg white
        granulated sugar
4   cups sugar
2   cups water
1   bunch mint (1½ cups firmly
          packed, with stems)
½   cup chopped fresh mint
        lots of crushed ice
1   qt. Kentucky Bourbon
8-10 sprigs fresh mint

Lightly whip, with fork, one egg white. Dip the rims of silver mint julep cups, if available, in the egg white, then in a dish of granulated sugar. Frost in the freezer 1 hour or more. Boil the sugar and water in a heavy pot, stirring at first until the sugar melts, and washing down the sugar from the sides with a wet pastry brush dipped in water. Let boil 5 minutes. Meanwhile, wash and dry the mint and place in a heat-proof bowl. Pour in the sugar syrup, stir well and let cool overnight in the refrigerator. Strain the syrup.

Just before serving, stir the chopped mint into the sugar syrup. Fill the mint julep cups with crushed ice, pour in 3-4 tablespoons mint syrup, and fill the cup the rest of the way with Bourbon, adding ice as needed. Garnish with a sprig of mint, and serve immediately.

Mock Champagne Punch

yield 11 cups

1   6-oz. can frozen lemonade
          concentrate
1   6-oz. can frozen pineapple juice
          concentrate
2   cups cold water
2   7-oz. bottles ginger ale, chilled
2   7-oz. bottles sparkling water,
          chilled
1   large bottle sparkling Catawba
          grapejuice
        ice ring or cubes containing mint
          leaves and cherries

Pour concentrates and water into a punch bowl. Float ice ring on top. Carefully pour ginger ale, sparkling water and grape juice down inside of bowl.

Pendennis Champagne Punch

servings approx. 35

        juice of 12 lemons
        powdered sugar
1   qt. carbonated water
½   pt. Maraschino liqueur
½   pt. Curacao
1   pt. Brandy
2   qts. Champagne

Sweeten the lemon juice to taste with powdered sugar. Add carbonated water. Place a large block of ice in punch bowl and add juice mixture. Stir well. Add remaining ingredients. Stir. Decorate with fruits in season.

Serve in 4 ounce punch glasses.

BEVERAGES

Polar Bear

(beverage or dessert)

serves 2

⅓   **cup vanilla ice cream**
⅓   **cup Kahlua**
⅓   **cup Vodka**

Mix ingredients in blender until frothy. Serve as after-dinner drink or dessert.

"Ringer"

serves 1

     Like a Stinger, but use Old Forrester Bourbon instead of Brandy
⅓   **white Creme de Menthe**
⅔   **Old Forrester Bourbon**
     cracked ice

Mix ingredients in cocktail shaker. Shake together and strain into a pretty glass. The River Valley Club made these popular.

Sherry Bolo

serves 4

9   **oz. good quality Sherry**
2   **limes, juice and some grated rind**
     sugar to taste

Mix all ingredients and serve in chilled glasses.

Some Stardust Wine Cooler

serves 20

2   **cups orange juice**
1   **6-oz. can frozen lemonade concentrate, thawed**
1   **cup orange liqueur**
1   **fifth dry white wine**
1   **28-oz. bottle carbonated water, chilled**

In large pitcher or punch bowl combine orange juice, lemonade concentrate, orange liqueur and wine. When ready to serve, add carbonated water and ice.
You can add fresh sliced fruit if desired-peaches, oranges, limes, etc.

White Wine Sangria
serves 6

1   **bottle white wine**
¼   **cup Cointreau**
½   **cup sugar**
1   **10-oz. bottle club soda**
     ice cubes 12-13
     lime slices for garnish

Mix all ingredients in large clear pitcher, add lime (or other citrus slices) and serve.

Mother's Old Fashioned Custard (or Eggnog)
serves 6-8

2   **eggs, separated**
½   **cup sugar**
1   **qt. milk**
     sugar to taste
     vanilla to taste
8   **oz. Rum or Bourbon (optional)**

Cook egg yolks, sugar and milk in a double boiler until thick (coats a spoon). Beat egg whites, add sugar and vanilla to taste. Add to custard while still hot and beat thoroughly. Add Rum or Bourbon.

Mint Grape Punch
serves 10

2   **cups boiling water**
⅔   **cup sugar**
½   **cup packed fresh mint**
2   **cups red grape juice, chilled**
2   **cups fresh orange juice, chilled**
¾   **cup fresh lime juice, chilled**
     crushed ice
     fresh mint sprigs - garnish

Combine sugar, mint and 2 cups boiling water. Stir until sugar dissolves. Let cool. Strain. Stir in rest of ingredients and serve over crushed ice with a garnish of a mint sprig.

Rebel Party Sour
(Old Fitzgerald Distillery)
serves 6

6   **oz. can frozen concentrated**
     lemonade, thawed
6   **oz. Rebel Yell Bourbon**
6   **oz. beer**

Blend or shake with crushed ice and serve in whiskey sour glass. Garnish with maraschino cherry and orange slice.

BEVERAGES

Track Talk
*1968's winner, Dancer's Image was disqualified for the use
of an illegal drug. Forward Pass was declared the winner.*

Shade Seeker Lemonade
serves 36

1   lb. sugar
3   qts. water
12   lemons, juiced
1   fresh pineapple, sliced and juiced
      in food processor or blender
2   qts. club soda
12   lemons, sliced very thin
36   cubes of fresh pineapple
36   fresh, ripe strawberries

Place sugar, water, lemon juice and pineapple juice into a large punch bowl. Mix well. When ready to serve, place, a large block of ice in the punch bowl and stir in the club soda. Add lemon slices.

Place some crushed ice in each punch cup; fill with lemonade and garnish with the strawberries and pineapple cubes which have been placed on party pics.

Spanish Chocolate
serves 1

¾   cup milk
1   oz. bitter chocolate
½   inch stick of vanilla bean or ½ tsp.
      vanilla extract
1   T. sugar or more to taste

Put milk, chocolate and vanilla bean, if used, in top of double boiler; heat until chocolate is soft. Beat with a wooden spoon until chocolate has completely dissolved. Add sugar and sweeten to taste. (Saccharine may be used instead of sugar in proper amounts, if preferred; add at table.) Add vanilla extract now, if vanilla bean was not used. Serve plain. Thin with extra hot milk, if desired. The Spaniards like their chocolate with milk for breakfast, thick as above for late afternoon.

Wonderful Hot Chocolate
serves 8

2½   squares Baker's unsweetened
      chocolate
½   cup cold water
¾   cup sugar
      dash of salt
½   cup heavy cream, whipped
      hot milk

Combine chocolate and water and cook about 4 minutes or until blended, stirring constantly. Beat until smooth and add the sugar and salt. Cook for 4 minutes. Stir. Cool and fold in whipped cream. Place a rounded tablespoon of syrup in a cup and pour in hot milk. Garnish with whipped cream.

The Cookbook Committee's Favorite Countertop Tea

1   gallon glass jar with lid
6   tea bags, small, or 3 family size
1   gallon tap water

Place tea bags in jar. Fill with water and leave on kitchen counter for an hour. Remove bags. Refrigerate or not. Guaranteed clear tea!

Notes

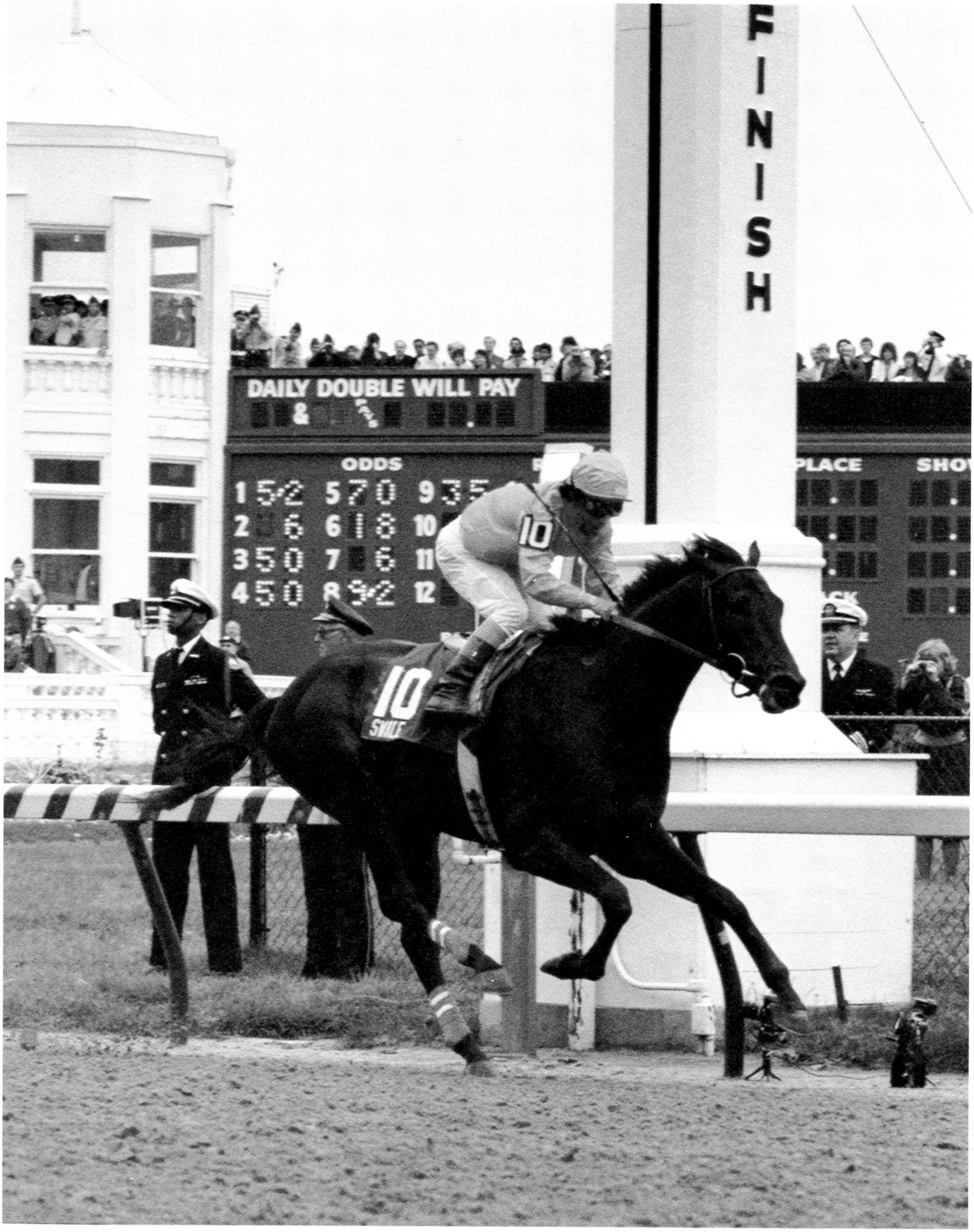
FINISH
DAILY DOUBLE WILL PAY
ODDS
PLACE
SHOW

THIRD RACE

SOUPS

COMMITTEE'S HANDICAP

1	CREAM OF CUCUMBER SOUP	SERVES 4
2	LOBSTER BISQUE (MAISONETTE)	SERVES 6
3	CHEESE SOUP	SERVES 6
4	THE CLARK HANDICAP	SERVES 8
5	CURRY CREAM OF CORN SOUP	SERVES 4
6	SPINACH SOUP	SERVES 10-12
7	DUCK SOUP	SERVES 50
8	JELLIED BEET SOUP	SERVES 6

Committee Selections   2-8-6
Kentucky bred entry 5, 7, 8

53

Run for the Roses

serves 4

3   **cups fresh tomatoes, peeled and chopped**
¾   **cup milk**
¾   **cup half and half**
1   **T. fresh chopped parsley**
1   **T. fresh chopped basil**
2   **T. catsup**
1   **tsp. salt**
¼   **tsp. white pepper**

Garnish: thin slices of lemon or lime

Place all ingredients (except the garnish) in the blender or processor: purée well. This step may have to be done in 2 smaller batches if there is too great a quantity for the machine. Serve chilled in cold bowls. Garnish with a thin slice of lemon or lime.

"As a change from gazpacho."

Asparagus Soup with Tarragon

serves 8-10

2   **lbs. asparagus, 1 inch of all tips cut off and reserved**
1   **lg. leek, including 2 inches of green top**
1   **sm. potato (4 oz.), peeled and sliced**
4-6   **cups chicken broth**
1   **cup light cream**
2   **tsp. dried tarragon, or 2 T. fresh, minced**
     salt and freshly ground pepper
     fresh tarragon leaves for garnish

Blanch the reserved asparagus tips in boiling water, chill immediately in cold water and set aside.

In a large saucepan, combine the asparagus stalks, sliced and washed leek, peeled and sliced potato and 4 cups of the chicken broth. Bring to a boil, cover partially and simmer for 20 minutes or until the vegetables are soft. Transfer to a food processor, fitted with the steel blade; purée the mixture in batches and return it to the saucepan.

Stir in the cream, tarragon, and reserved asparagus tips, (cut in ½ inch pieces) salt and pepper to taste, and add enough broth to thin the soup to the desired consistency. Simmer, but do not let boil, for 6-7 minutes. Serve warm or chilled, garnished with fresh tarragon leaves or a sprinkling of fresh chopped parsley. A dollop of fresh whipped unsweetened cream may be added as a special garnish.

Variation: Curried Asparagus Soup: Proceed as for the asparagus soup above, omitting the tarragon and substituting ¾ teaspoon curry powder and ½ teaspoon dill weed. Garnish with chopped fresh cilantro or fresh parsley.

Track Talk
The "Run for the Roses" was coined by Bill Corum in 1925.
He was later president of Churchill Downs from 1950 to
1958.

Jellied Beet Soup

serves 6

1	lb. beets
1	onion
6	cups chicken broth
1-2	T. lemon juice
2	T. gelatin (dissolved in ½ cup heated tomato juice

Garnish: dill and sour cream

Dice and cook beets and onion in broth until tender, about 15 minutes. Add lemon juice. Dissolve gelatin in warm tomato juice and add to beet mixture. Put in a food processor and blend until smooth. Chill until jellied.

Serve garnished with sour cream and dill.

Mrs. Potter's Borscht

serves 7

1	16.5-oz. glass jar Aunt Nellie's pickled beets
½	glass jar plain beets
2	(10½-oz.) cans beef bouillon
	sour cream with chives

Put beets in blender and blend. Add beef bouillon. Refrigerate overnight. Serve cold with a dollop of sour cream.

Makes 7 one-cup servings.

Cream of Cucumber Soup

serves 4

2	cups cucumbers, peeled and coarsely chopped
1	cup chicken broth (fat skimmed off)
1	cup light cream or rich milk
¼	cup fresh chopped chives
¼	cup chopped celery leaves
3	sprigs fresh parsley
3	T. soft butter
2	T. flour
	salt and pepper to taste

Garnishes: dillweed, cucumbers, chopped and lemon rind, grated

Put all ingredients in a blender or processor, and "whiz" until puréed. Season with salt and pepper, if desired. Serve hot or cold. If hot, garnish with small amount of dill weed. If cold, garnish with finely chopped cucumbers and a bit of grated lemon rind.

SOUPS

Cream of Leek Soup

serves 10

3	large white onions, thinly sliced
8	T. butter
2	qts. homemade chicken stock
4	cups peeled and coarsely chopped potatoes
1	tsp. salt
	freshly ground pepper
1	bunch leeks, sliced, white part only
3	fresh garlic cloves, minced
1	cup heavy cream
3	T. fresh chives or parsley, finely cut

In a heavy saucepan, sauté onions in 4 tablespoons butter. Add chicken stock and potatoes, salt and pepper. Simmer over low heat, partially covered, for 40-50 minutes, or until vegetables are tender. Put mixture in blender or food processor and blend until smooth; return to pot.

Sauté leeks and garlic in remaining butter until transparent. Add this to the soup. Add 1 cup heavy cream. Adjust seasonings to taste. Reheat when ready to serve. Garnish with chopped chives or parsley.

Serve hot or chilled.

Park Cottage Tomato Soup

serves 8

2	lbs. tomatoes
1	onion, sliced
1	carrot, sliced
1	strip lemon rind
1	bay leaf
6	peppercorns
	salt
	chicken bones or 1 chicken cube, for stock
2	pints water, for stock
1½	oz. butter
3-4	T. flour
	rind and juice of ½ orange
	pepper
	sugar, to taste
1½	cups cream

Wipe the tomatoes and cut in half, squeezing to remove seeds. Put tomatoes, onion and carrot into a pan with lemon rind, bay leaf, peppercorns and a good pinch of salt. Then make the stock: put chicken bones or bouillon cube into pan with 2 pints water and a pinch of salt. Bring to boil, and then reduce liquid to approximately 3 cups by simmering. Add stock to tomato mixture, put lid on, and simmer until tomatoes are pulpy (about 30 minutes). Rub mixture through a sieve, and set aside. Clean the pan, melt the butter in it and stir in the flour. Pour in the tomato mixture, blend and bring to boil. Shred the orange rind; blanch by cooking in boiling water for 1 minute then drain, rinse well with cold water, and set aside. Now add the orange juice to the soup, then seasoning and sugar to taste. Stir in the cream at the last moment and finally add the orange rind. Serve at once.

Spinach Soup

serves 10-12

½	cup butter
½	cup flour
½	tsp. pepper
½	tsp. nutmeg
1	tsp. celery salt
½	tsp. garlic powder
½	tsp. Tabasco
4	cups milk (2%)
4	cups chicken broth
2	(10-oz.) pkgs. chopped spinach, thawed and drained well

Make a roux with butter and flour (melt butter in pan over low heat; do not let brown. When melted, add flour, mix well and let simmer for several minutes, stirring constantly.) Add spices and milk. Stir over medium heat until thick and smooth. Add hot chicken broth and stir well. Add spinach and cook over low heat for 30 minutes. Put mixture in a blender and purée.

Serve hot or chilled. If serving cold, add a little white wine to thin, and dot with a dollp of sour cream.

Pot of Gold Squash Soup

serves 8

2	lbs. summer squash (about 6), sliced
1	onion, chopped
4	cups chicken broth (homemade preferred)
½	cup heavy cream
1	cup sour cream
	cinnamon and nutmeg to taste
	salt and pepper to taste

Boil together the squash and onion in chicken broth. If preferred, you may sauté the onion first in a tablespoon of butter. When the vegetables are tender, transfer the broth and vegetables to a food processor or blender, and purée in several batches. Add cream, sour cream and seasonings to taste. May be served hot or chilled.

Cheese Soup

serves 8

4	carrots, cut into 1 in. matchsticks
3	celery stalks, cut into 1 in. matchsticks
1½	cups chicken stock
2	T. onion, minced fine
2	T. butter
¼	cup flour
3	cups hot chicken stock
2½	cups grated Cheddar cheese
1	can tomatoes (28-oz.), chopped and undrained
	Tabasco
	nutmeg
	fresh ground pepper
1½	cups cream, heated
	parsley or chives, minced

Add carrots and celery to stock, and bring to boil. Simmer 15 minutes, until crisp-tender. Set aside.

Sauté onion in butter until transparent, and add flour. Mix well, and cook 5-7 minutes, stirring to keep from turning brown. Stir 3 cups hot stock into flour mixture, and stir until thickened. Blend in cheese; stir until melted. Add tomatoes and undrained cooked vegetables. Season to taste with Tabasco, nutmeg and pepper. Just before serving, stir in hot cream. Garnish with parsley or chives.

The Clark Handicap

serves 8

1	can (16-oz.) pumpkin
4	cups chicken stock
	nutmeg, freshly grated, to taste
½	tsp. salt
⅓	lb. fresh mushrooms, chopped
	cayenne to taste
1	tsp. crushed, dried thyme (optional)
½	cup heavy cream
1	whole pumpkin, seeds and pulp removed

Simmer pumpkin and chicken broth for 20 minutes. Add nutmeg, salt, mushrooms and a dash of cayenne (and thyme, if desired). Bring to a boil, then lower heat to a simmer and cook ten minutes more. Add cream and serve in a fresh pumpkin shell from which you have removed strings and seeds. This may be served hot or chilled.

Curried Cauliflower Asparagus Soup

serves 6

2	lbs. cauliflower, broken into florets
1	potato, (8-oz.), peeled and sliced
4-5	cups chicken broth
½	tsp. curry powder
	salt and freshly ground pepper
1	cup light cream
10-12	stalks fresh asparagus
	Garnish: chopped parsley

In a large saucepan, combine the cauliflower, potato and 4 cups of chicken broth. Bring the stock to a boil, cover partially and simmer the mixture for 20 minutes, or until the vegetables are soft. In a food processor, fitted with the metal blade, purée the mixture in batches; return to the saucepan. Stir in the curry powder, salt and white pepper to taste, the cream and enough stock to produce the desired consistency. Taste for seasoning. Steam the asparagus stalks until crisp-tender and run under cold water. Cut into ¼ inch slices and add to the soup when ready to serve. Serve warm, garnish with chopped parsley.

Curry Cream of Corn Soup

serves 4

1	17-oz. can of cream-style corn
3	T. butter
1	medium slice of onion, chopped
3	T. flour
1	tsp. salt
	white pepper, dash
1	cup chicken broth
1	cup heavy cream
1	tsp. curry powder

Put corn in blender or food processor; blend and reserve. Melt butter in saucepan and add onion. Cook until soft. Stir in flour, salt and pepper and mix until smooth. Add corn, chicken broth, cream and curry. Heat thoroughly, being careful not to scorch.

If serving cold, thin with additional chicken broth and chill.

Track Talk
"*Whatever happens afterward, the Kentucky Derby establishes
the class of the colts and fillies competing.*"
Harvey Woodruff, Chicago Tribune

Duck Soup

serves 50

12	**carcasses of 12 young ducklings**
3	**gallons water**
1	**(28-oz.) jar chicken base**
	necks, skins and back bones from 12 young ducklings
4	**carrots**
6	**celery ribs**
1	**cup flour**
	fat from baked necks, skins and back bones to make roux
1	**gallon chopped celery**
1	**gallon chopped carrots**
½	**gallon chopped Spanish onions**
2	**large boxes barley, cooked**

Put the carcasses into large pot with 3 gallons water and cook at a simmer for 4 hours. Strain and add chicken base.

Take the necks, fat from skins and back bones and bake at 400 degrees with the carrots and celery ribs for 2 hours.

Make a roux by adding enough fat from baked duckling parts to 1 cup flour to make a thick paste; save to use as thickening for soup. In fat from baked duckling parts, sauté the chopped vegetables.

Gradually add roux into stock from carcasses and blend. Cook about an hour. Collect all meat from bones and add to the stock along with the sautéed vegetables and cooked barley. Heat thoroughly.

Maisonette-Lobster Bisque

serves 6

1	**oz. carrot, chopped**
1	**oz. onion, chopped**
2	**parsley stalks**
1	**oz. celery, chopped**
1	**pinch thyme**
½	**bay leaf**
2	**T. butter**
2	**lb. raw lobster**
2	**T. Brandy**
2	**cups dry white wine**
	salt and freshly ground pepper
1½	**qt. fish stock**
2	**T. tomato purée**
1	**T. butter and 1 T. flour, well mixed**
1	**cup heavy cream, hot**
1	**T. Cognac**

Brown the carrot, onion, parsley, celery, thyme and bay leaf in the butter in a saucepan. Add a 2-pound raw lobster that has been cut into small sections, and cook until the shells acquire a red color. Sprinkle with 1 tablespoon Brandy and 1 cup white wine. Season with the salt and pepper. Cook at a low boil to reduce to ½ of its volume. Moisten with 1 quart of fish stock. Cook 10 minutes more. Strain. Remove meat from lobster and set aside.

Crush lobster shells in a mortar. Put back in cooking liquor. Add 2 tablespoons tomato purée, ½ quart fish stock and 1 cup white wine. Cook slowly for 15 minutes. Thicken lightly with as much of the mixture of butter and flour as needed. Strain through a fine strainer.

Before serving, add 1 cup hot heavy cream, the diced lobster meat and 1 tablespoon Cognac.

59

SOUPS

Wild Duck Gumbo

serves 10-12

10	wild duck breasts
8	carrots
4	onions
4	celery stalks and leaves
	bay leaves
	bouillion cubes (4)
2	quarts water
	salt and pepper to taste
½	cup flour
⅔	cup oil
2	cans stewed tomatoes (16-oz. cans)
1	lb. smoked sausage, cut into small pieces
1	cup smoked ham, chopped
½	tsp. thyme
2	T. basil, dried (4 T. fresh basil)
2	cups chopped celery
2	cups chopped onions
1	cup chopped green pepper
2	cloves garlic, minced
¼	cup oil
1	T. salt
1	T. pepper
2	(10-oz.) pkgs. frozen okra, thawed and sliced
½	chopped parsley
½	tsp. Tabasco

Simmer duck breasts with first 6 ingredients in 2 quarts of water, using bay leaves and bouillon to taste. Cook several hours. Strain stock and add water to measure 2 quarts liquid. Brown ½ cup flour in ⅔ cup oil in skillet, making a roux, stirring constantly. Add tomatoes and cook until thick. Add sausage, ham, basil and thyme. Cook for 5 minutes. Bring stock to a boil and add tomato mixture, stirring constantly. Sauté celery, onion, green pepper and garlic in ¼ cup oil until tender. Add sautéed vegetables, 1 tablespoon salt and 1 tablespoon pepper and remaining ingredients. Simmer 1 ½ hours.

Serve with rice and French bread. This freezes well.

Fast Track Soup

serves 10-12

½	cup butter
1	cup chopped onion
1 ½	cups chopped celery
½	cup flour
	salt and pepper to taste
4	cups chicken broth
5	cups milk
4	boxes (10-oz.) frozen Brussels sprouts, cut into halves

Melt butter in saucepan and sauté onion until clear. Add celery and stir a few minutes, but do not brown. Stir in flour, then salt and pepper to taste. Stir until flour is blended. On low heat, gradually add broth and milk. Stir well. Add the sprouts and cook 35 minutes, stirring occasionally.

Mushroom Soup

serves 4-6

½   lb. or more, fresh mushrooms
2   T. olive oil
2   T. butter
1   garlic clove, shallot or onion
1   bay leaf
1   rounded T. flour
1   quart milk, or half and half
1   T. Worcestershire sauce

Grind mushrooms, or mince finely in food processor; add to olive oil and butter in large skillet. Add garlic, crushed, or onion or shallot, bay leaf, salt and pepper; simmer covered for 5 minutes. Add flour and stir until smooth. Gradually add milk, stirring constantly. Add Worcestershire and continue stirring until mixture comes to a boil. Turn off heat, cover and set aside for several hours or refrigerate overnight. Remove garlic (onion or shallot) and bay leaf. Reheat and serve.

Sherried Cream of Mushroom Soup

serves 4

¼   cup butter
½   cup finely chopped onions
½   lb. fresh mushrooms, chopped
5   T. Flour
½   tsp. salt
⅛   tsp. freshly ground pepper
⅛   tsp. freshly ground nutmeg
3   (13-oz.) cans chicken broth (or 5
      cups homemade)
¾   cup light cream
¼   cup dry Sherry
2   T. fresh parsley, chopped, for
      garnish

Melt the butter in a large saucepan. Add the onion, and sauté over medium-low heat for 5 minutes, stirring often. Add the mushrooms and cook 5 minutes more, stirring often. Remove from the heat, and add the flour, salt, pepper and nutmeg. Stir until smooth. Gradually add the chicken broth and over medium heat, stirring constantly, bring just to a boil. Reduce the heat and simmer, covered 5 minutes. Stir in the cream and Sherry. Garnish with chopped parsley.

Cold Spinach-Cucumber Soup

serves 8

1   bunch green onions, chopped
2   T. butter
4½   cups peeled, seeded and chopped
      cucumbers
3   cups chicken broth
¾   cup chopped potato
1   tsp. salt
¼   cup lemon juice
1   cup frozen, chopped spinach,
      defrosted
1   cup cream
      Garnish: lemon slices or
         cucumber slices

Sauté onions in 2 tablespoons butter until soft. Add cucumbers, broth, potato, salt and lemon juice. Simmer until potatoes are tender. Add spinach and barely cook. Put in processor or blender, and purée. Add cream and chill overnight. To serve, garnish with lemon slices or cucumber slices.

Notes

FOURTH RACE
SALADS
COMMITTEE'S HANDICAP

1	**BAUER'S HOT SLAW**	SERVES 6
2	**SPRINTER TURKEY SALAD**	SERVES 6
3	**CORNBREAD SALAD**	SERVES 6-8
4	**FRENCH GREEN BEAN SALAD**	SERVES 8
5	**NORMANDY INN SALAD**	SERVES 6
6	**SMEARCASE**	SERVES 2-4
7	**BROCCOLI SALAD**	SERVES 6
8	**KENTUCKY GOAT CHEESE SALAD**	SERVES 6

Committee Selections   8-4-2

Kentucky bred entry 1, 6, 8

Tasty Trivia
Lettuce and celery keep longer if you store them in the
refrigerator in paper bags instead of cellophane ones. Do not
remove the outside leaves of either until ready to use.

Chicken and Fruit Salad

serves 8

4	chicken breasts, cooked, skinned and boned
1¼	tsp. curry powder
1	tsp. salt
	freshly ground pepper
1	T. lemon juice
½	cup coarsely chopped walnuts
3	T. slivered candied ginger, soaked to remove suger
1	cup one inch cubed cantaloupe or honeydew melon
1	cup seedless grapes
½	cup homemade mayonnaise
¼	cup sour cream

Cut chicken breasts into one inch cubes. Combine curry powder, salt and pepper and stir in lemon juice. Pour over chicken and mix well to coat each cube. Add walnuts and ginger and refrigerate until ready to serve. Mix sour cream with mayonnaise and stir into chicken. Cut melon into one inch cubes, add with grapes and toss until well mixed.

Cold Pasta Salad with Red Peppers, Chicken and Artichoke Hearts

serves 10-12

1	whole frying chicken
1	carrot, cut in chunks
1	leek or half an onion, sliced
1	rib celery, cut in chunks
5	peppercorns
1	bay leaf
2	sprigs fresh parsley
½	tsp. dried thyme (or 1 tsp. fresh if available)
4	sweet red peppers
1	box fusilli (16-oz.)
2	jars artichokes, packed in oil, halved (drain and reserve marinade)
	olive oil
	salt and freshly ground pepper
	herbs of your choice (fresh preferred)

Cover chicken with water. Add next 7 ingredients and simmer about 45 minutes, or until tender. When cool, tear meat from bones, cut in chunks and set aside. Save the stock for another use.

Clean the red peppers, cut into 1½-x1½-inch chunks and cook in boiling water for 1 minute. Remove and refresh under cold running water and set aside.
Cook fusilli al dente stage in boiling water, to which a little salt has been added. Drain well and place in a bowl. Toss with the oil from the artichokes and enough additional olive oil to moisten. Add chicken, red pepper chunks and artichoke halves. Season well with salt, pepper and fresh herbs; such as tarragon, basil and parsley.

SALADS

64

Chicken Salad with Wild Rice

serves 4

½   cup wild rice
1½ cups salted water
2   cups diced poached chicken
1   cup watercress leaves, washed
       and patted dry
½   cup thinly sliced green onion
½   cup diced celery
½   cup toasted blanched almonds,
       chopped

Rinse rice. Bring water to boil in a saucepan. Stir in rice and return to boil. Stir rice with fork and reduce to simmer. Cover and cook until grains puff open and white appears, 30-40 minutes. Rinse rice under cold water; drain well. Transfer to a large bowl. Add chicken, watercress, green onion, celery and almonds.

Tarragon Dressing:
½   cup olive oil
¼   cup white wine vinegar
1   T. chopped fresh tarragon or 1
       tsp. crushed dried tarragon
1   tsp. coarse salt
½   tsp. freshly ground pepper

To make dressing: Whisk oil into vinegar one drop at a time. Stir in tarragon, salt and pepper. Pour small amount of the vinaigrette dressing over chicken salad and toss gently, adding more vinaigrette a little at a time until evenly coated. Serve slightly chilled.

Curried Chicken and Rice Salad

serves 4-6

½   cup mayonnaise
2   tsp. lemon juice
      salt and pepper to taste
      chutney to taste (blueberry or
       mango)
1   tsp. curry powder
4   scallions, chopped
2   celery ribs, chopped (or 1 can
       sliced water chestnuts)
4   oz. slivered almonds, toasted
3   cups cooked chicken breast, cut
       into bite size pieces
2   cups cooked brown rice, cooled

Mix all ingredients in order given adding chicken and rice last. Cover and chill. Serve with tomatoes, sliced avocado or green grapes.

Sprinter Turkey Salad

serves 6

3   cups cubed cooked turkey
1   cup sour cream
⅔   cup Major Grey's chutney
      Bibb lettuce
      toasted almonds, optional

Mix turkey, sour cream and chutney lightly. Serve on chilled lettuce-lined plates. Top with almonds if desired.

Tasty Trivia
Line the bottom of the vegetable compartment with paper toweling. This absorbs the excess moisture and keeps all vegetables and fruits fresher for a longer period of time.

Pasta Seafood Salad

serves 4-6

¼   lb. Rotini
1½   lb. shrimp
1   pkg. frozen peas
8   T. chopped parsley
2-4   T. fresh basil. chopped
1-2   tsp. fresh summer savory or tarragon
¼   cup tarragon vinegar
1¼   cup mayonnaise
½   cup sour cream
   salt and pepper

Cook pasta al dente; wash with cold water and drain. Refrigerate 1 hour. Cook, rinse, peel and devein shrimp and refrigerate. Pour boiling water over frozen peas, drain and chill. Mix peas, pasta and shrimp (cut in pieces if large). Add herbs and mix. Add vinegar and mix. Add mayonnaise and sour cream; mix. Check for seasonings. Serve chilled.

Warm Scallop and Avocado Salad

serves 4

¾   lb. sea scallops
½   cup chicken broth or Court Bouillon (3 cups clam juice, 1 cup white wine, 2 medium onions, minced, ½ a bay leaf, sprig of parsley, pinch of thyme, 3 cracked peppercorns simmered together 30 minutes, cooled and strained)
¼   cup olive oil or corn oil
1½   T. Sherry wine vinegar
1   tsp. Dijon mustard
   salt and freshly ground pepper
20   large spinach leaves (about 6 oz. after stemming)
2   medium avocados, peeled, pitted and thinly sliced lengthwise
25   toasted almond halves

Put scallops in the cold broth or Court Bouillon and bring very slowly to a boil. Turn off the heat immediately and let cool in the broth. (Set pan in ice water to speed up process.)
Just before serving, slice scallops into thin rounds. Combine oil, vinegar, mustard, salt and pepper in small saucepan and bring to a simmer.

Stack spinach leaves and roll up lengthwise. Cut cross-wise into chiffonade. Divide spinach among 4 warm salad plates. Arrange scallops and avocado decoratively atop spinach. Garnish with almond halves. Pour warm dressing over salads and serve immediately.

Sour Cream Cranberry Salad

serves 8

1   cup jellied cranberries
2   cups hot water
2   pkgs. raspberry jello
1   cup sour cream
1   cup pecans, chopped
1   small can crushed pineapple, well drained

Mix jellied cranberries and 1 cup hot water in blender or mixer until liquid and smooth. Dissolve both packages of jello in 1 cup of hot water. Add cranberry mixture, nuts and pineapple. Pour ½ of mixture in an 8 inch square pan. (Reserve remaining ½ of mixture at room temperature.) Chill in the refrigerator until firm. Spread sour cream over top of chilled mixture. Add second half of gelatin, being careful when pouring it over sour cream. Refrigerate until firm.

SALADS

66

Ginger Honey Fruit Salad

serves 16-20

5	grapefruit, peeled and sectioned, reserving juice
½	cup water
¼	cup honey
1	T. julienned fresh ginger
1	T. grated fresh orange peel
5	navel oranges
	sugar syrup (1 cup sugar, 5 T. water, 1 T. corn syrup)
1	quart fresh strawberries
1	ripe medium avocado
	mint sprigs

Combine ½ cup grapefruit juice, ½ cup water, honey, ginger and grated orange peel in small saucepan, Bring to a boil, reduce heat to low and simmer, covered, until ginger is tender, about 20-25 minutes. Remove from heat and cool completely.
Add cooked honey-ginger mixture to grapefruit sections and toss well. Refrigerate 4 hours or overnight.

With a vegetable peeler, remove strips of the orange part of the peel of 3 of the oranges. Cut the peel into very fine julienne - as fine as possible. Drop into 1 quart simmering water and simmer 10-15 minutes or until tender. Drain, rinse in cold water and pat dry.

Meanwhile, bring the sugar syrup ingredients to a boil in another saucepan, twirling the pan by its handle until sugar has dissolved and liquid is clear. Cover pan and boil over high heat for a few minutes, until syrup reaches soft-ball stage (238 degrees). Drop the peel into the syrup and boil slowly for several minutes, until syrup has thickened again. Set aside until ready to use. This may be stored for weeks in the refrigerator.

Trim the oranges of the white pith to expose the flesh. Cut the oranges into neat crosswise slices, and cut into bite-size pieces.

One hour before serving, quickly rinse, drain and hull strawberries; cut lengthwise into ¼-inch slices. Pare and pit avocado; cut into ¾ inch dice.

Remove grapefruit from refrigerator. In a large glass salad bowl or trifle bowl, arrange fruit in layers as neatly as possible as follows: grapefruit, avocado, oranges, strawberries, small amount candied orange peel; follow this order two times, ending with the remaining orange peel. Pour the grapefruit syrup over the top. Garnish with mint sprigs.

A fruit bowl with some new interest.

Island Salad

serves 1

For each salad:
4   **pretty leaves of Bibb lettuce**
3   **slices of avocado**
3   **slices of mango**
3   **slices of papaya**
3   **sections of grapefruit**
2-3 **slices of Kiwi on top**

Arrange decoratively and drizzle with two tablespoons of a good vinaigrette dressing that has been slightly sweetened.

Island Salad Dressing:
2   **T. good white wine vinegar**
6   **T. light oil**
1   **T. Dijon mustard**
½   **tsp. sugar**
     pinch of dried, crushed, green
       peppercorns (optional)

Put ingredients in jar and shake well.

Springtime Fruit Salad

serves 12

1   **fresh pineapple, peeled, cored**
      and cubed
1   **qt. strawberries, washed,**
      stemmed and sliced in half
½   **cup fresh or frozen blueberries**
½   **cup fresh or frozen raspberries**
1   **11-oz. can mandarin oranges,**
      drained
2   **cups orange juice**
½   **cup sugar**
¼   **cup Cream Sherry**
½   **tsp. vanilla**
½   **tsp. almond extract**

     garnish - pineapple rings

Combine the fruit in a large bowl, preferably a glass one. Combine the remaining ingredients in a separate bowl, stirring until the sugar dissolves. Pour over the fruit mixture, tossing lightly. Garnish with pineapple rings. Chill 2-3 hours.

Broccoli Salad

serves 6

1   **cup mayonnaise**
⅓   **cup sugar**
2   **T. wine vinegar**
1   **head uncooked broccoli florets**
½   **red onion, minced**
4   **oz. raisins (about 1 cup)**
1½ **cups Spanish peanuts, unsalted**

Mix mayonnaise, sugar and vinegar; set aside. Mix dressing with broccoli, onion and raisins; add peanuts just before serving.

Strawberry Salad

serves 6-8

¾   **cup fresh water chestnuts, peeled, thinly sliced**
3-4   **shallots, minced**
1   **quart small spinach leaves, stemmed and torn**
1   **quart garden lettuce cut in narrow strips**
3   **T. hazelnut oil**
1   **T. raspberry vinegar**
    salt, freshly ground pepper
1   **pint strawberries, sliced lengthwise**
2   **small navel oranges, peeled, sliced crosswise, cut in half**

Blanch the water chestnuts for two minutes in boiling water and immediately refresh in cold water. Combine with greens and shallots. Add oil and toss; add vinegar, salt and pepper. Add fruit and gently toss again.

Bauer's Hot Slaw

serves 6

1   **small head cabbage**
1   **tsp. finely chopped onion**
6   **slices bacon, fried**
2   **cups apple cider vinegar**
1   **cup water**
¾   **cup sugar**
2   **tsp. salt**
¼   **tsp. white pepper**
    dash garlic powder or bud garlic

Slice cabbage finely as for sauerkraut. Add onion and stir. Fry bacon, drain and reserve grease. Crumble bacon and set aside. Combine bacon grease, vinegar, water, sugar, salt, pepper and garlic. Bring to a boil and stir until sugar dissolves. Pour over cabbage. Toss and top with bacon.

Butter Bean Salad

serves 12-16

2   **10-oz. pkgs. frozen shoe peg corn**
2   **10-oz. pkgs. frozen small butter beans (lima beans)**
1½   **green peppers, chopped**
4   **ribs celery, chopped**
3   **green onions, chopped**
1   **pint cherry tomatoes, chopped**
2   **T. Durkees Famous Sauce**
    mayonnaise to taste
    celery salt and pepper
2   **T. chopped fresh dill**
    paprika for color

Cook corn and beans; drain and cool. Mix all ingredients and serve cold. Put in lettuce cups, mounded in center of tomato aspic or as stuffing in a tomato.

Boyle County Stuffed Tomatoes

serves 6

6	ripe summer tomatoes, peeled, scooped out and drained
8	oz. cottage cheese
3	oz. cream cheese
	green onions, chopped
	cucumber, seeded, diced
	green olives, sliced (optional)
	salt and pepper to taste

Prepare tomatoes and set aside. Mix the remaining ingredients together. Fill the tomatoes with this mixture. Garnish with parsley or watercress.

Chinese Slaw

serves 12

1	can Del Monte seasoned green beans
1	can tiny green peas (Le Seuer)
1	can Chinese vegetables
1	can water chestnuts, sliced
1	onion, sliced thin
1	cup diced celery
1	green pepper, diced
1	cup sugar
¾	cup vinegar
	salt and pepper to taste

Drain all cans of vegetables well. Slice some of the bigger hunks of Chinese vegetables. Mix all together and refrigerate.

Keeps well in refrigerator for 10 days to 2 weeks.

Club Salad

serves 6

¼	cup ripe olives, sliced
1	cup cooked rice
¼	cup sweet pickle, diced
½	cup celery, chopped
1	T. green onion, thinly sliced
½	cup mayonnaise
2	T. tomato catsup
	lettuce
	ripe olives

Combine olives, rice, pickle, celery, onion, mayonnaise and catsup. Press into individual salad molds then unmold carefully on lettuce. Garnish each salad with ripe olives.

SALADS

Confetti Rice Salad

serves 6

4	cups cooked rice
	salt and pepper to taste
½	cup chopped fresh parsley
⅓	cup chopped celery
⅓	cup chopped pimiento
¼	cup chopped black olives
¼	cup chopped shallots
	cherry tomatoes for garnish

Toss all ingredients except tomatoes. Mix lightly with the Vinaigrette Dressing; garnish with tomatoes.

Vinaigrette Dressing:

⅔	cup olive oil
⅓	cup white wine vinegar
1	small clove garlic, finely minced

Place all ingredients in a covered jar and mix well.

Cornbread Salad

serves 6

1	box cornbread mix
6	green onions and tops, chopped
6	radishes, sliced
½	green pepper, chopped
2	tomatoes, peeled and chopped
½	cup mayonnaise
½	cup creamy cucumber dressing
2½	T. prepared mustard.

Bake cornbread according to instructions on package in an 8 x 8 inch pan. When cool, crumble baked cornbread, add vegetables, mayonnaise, dressing, mustard and salt and pepper to taste. Refrigerate.

Dilled Cucumber Slices

yields 5 cups

3	medium cucumbers, sliced
1	medium onion, sliced
2	T. chopped pimiento
¼	cup sugar
⅔	cup white vinegar
1	tsp. dill weed
2	tsp. salt
½	tsp. cream of tartar

In 2½ quart serving dish or casserole, place cucumbers, onion and pimiento. Pour dill marinade over and mix well to coat each piece. Cover and refrigerate overnight.

To make dill marinade: place sugar, vinegar, dill weed, salt and cream of tartar in a pint glass measuring cup or small microwave-safe bowl. Microwave until hot and sugar is dissolved, about 1½ to 3 minutes. Use High power.

Fettucine Freddo al Pronto

serves 4-6

6	T. olive oil
2	garlic cloves, chopped
2	oz. pine nuts, chopped
1	lb. fettucine noodles
1	cup fresh tomatoes, peeled and chopped
½	red pimiento, cut in strips
12	black olives, chopped
2	T. parsley, chopped
4	T. chopped fresh basil
2	T. red wine vinegar
	salt and pepper to taste
	Italian-style tuna (optional)

Heat olive oil in large skillet. Add garlic and pine nuts. Sauté 5 minutes, or until nuts are golden; pour into a large salad bowl. Cook fettucine noodles in boiling water 8-10 minutes or al dente; drain. Add pasta to salad bowl, and toss gently to coat. Add tomatoes, pimiento, olives, parsley, basil, vinegar, salt and pepper. You may add tuna, if you desire. Toss with salad forks. Sprinkle top with more parsley and serve at room temperature.

French Green Bean Salad

serves 8-10

1	lg. garlic clove
1	tsp. salt
2	lbs. green beans (tiny and as uniform as possible)
6	T. walnut oil
2	T. vinegar
1	T. Dijon mustard
	salt, freshly gound pepper
½	lb. Gruyére cheese, cut in ½" square dice
2-3	T. fresh parsley and tarragon, minced

Crush a large head of garlic and rub it well into a large wooden salad bowl, along with 1 teaspoon of salt. Discard the garlic. Remove stems of green beans and cook for 5-7 minutes, or until crisp-tender. Run under cold water, drain well, dry and chill.

Make a dressing of the walnut oil, vinegar, mustard, salt and pepper in the processor or by hand with a whisk. Pour the dressing over the beans in the wooden bowl, add the Gruyére, and the minced fresh parsley and tarragon. Toss well and serve.

Frozen Tomato Salad

serves 6-8

4	cups canned tomatoes, drain juice
2	stalks celery, finely diced
2	green onions, minced
1	tsp. Worcestershire sauce
2	tsp. lemon juice
2	tsp. dry green peppercorns, crushed
	mayonnaise to garnish

Put all ingredients in processor and pulse for 2 seconds. Freeze in a non-metallic bowl. Serve partially frozen with a garnish of mayonnaise (and a fresh basil leaf if you have one.)

SALADS

Marinated Vegetable Salad

serves 12-16

1	cup vinegar
1	T. sugar
1	T. dill seed
1	tsp. garlic salt
1	tsp. black pepper
1	tsp. salt
1½	cups oil
½	cup Zesty Italian dressing
1	head cauliflower, cut into florets, blanched
2	bunches broccoli, cut into florets, blanched
1	lb. mushrooms, cut in half
1	large carrot, sliced thin, blanched
1	can artichoke hearts, drained, cut in half
1	pint cherry tomatoes
1	jar green olives
1	can pitted black olives

Mix the marinade ingredients thoroughly and pour over the bite-size pieces of the vegetables and olives. Let marinate 24 hours in the refrigerator. Drain before serving.

Pumpkin Salad

serves 8-10

1	small pumpkin, peeled, cut into cubes about ¾ inch size
3	heads Bibb lettuce
6	green onions, minced
1½	cups vinaigrette dressing

Steam the cubes of pumpkin in a colander over simmering water, covered, until just barely fork tender. If necessary to keep pumpkin from overcooking, refresh under cold water. Cool and chill in refrigerator.

Serve over Bibb lettuce. Sprinkle with minced green onion and a clear vinaigrette dressing.

Smearcase

yield 1½ cups

1	cup cottage cheese
½	cup sour cream
	garnish with chopped chives or chopped onion

Mix well in processor or blender until smooth and serve with sliced tomatoes. Excellent with steak.

Molded Gazpacho

serves 10-12

2	envelopes gelatin
⅓	cup water
3	T. olive oil
1	clove garlic, minced
½	cup minced scallions
⅓	cup minced red pepper
⅓	cup minced celery
1	tsp. crushed dried green peppercorns
	dash Tabasco
1	tsp. dill
1½	tsp. lemon juice
1	quart tomatoes, slightly chopped
½	cup grated cucumber

Soak gelatin in water; reserve. Heat olive oil in 2 quart saucepan. Sauté garlic and scallions in oil until wilted. Add red pepper and celery and cook briefly, leaving crunchy. Add green peppercorns, Tabasco, dill, lemon juice and tomatoes; heat thoroughly. Add gelatin, stirring until dissolved. Pour 1 cup into 6-cup greased mold; refrigerate until it begins to set. Spread grated cucumber on this aspic and cover with the other half of gazpacho. Congeal in refrigerator. Serve with homemade mayonnaise or smearcase.

Refreshing Asparagus Salad

serves 8

2	pkgs. unflavored gelatin
1½	cups plus 2 T. water
⅓	cup champagne vinegar
1	2-oz. jar of pimientos, chopped
1	10.5-oz. can asparagus tips, drained
	juice of ½ lemon
2	tsp. grated onion
1	cup chopped celery

Soften gelatin in ½ cup plus 2 tablespoons cold water. Mix sugar, one cup water and vinegar in a saucepan; bring to a boil. Add gelatin and stir until dissolved. Cool. Stir in remaining ingredients and pour into a 4 cup mold. Chill until firm. Unmold and serve with dressing on the side.

Molded Salad Dresing

1	cup sour cream
¼	cup lemon juice
2	T. sugar
1	tsp. salt
	cayenne pepper to taste
½	tsp. paprika
1	tsp. dry mustard
½	tsp. garlic (optional)

Combine all ingredients in a bowl and blend with a whisk until smooth and thick.

Summer Orzo Salad

serves 6

2	cups cooked orzo (1 cup uncooked)
4	carrots, coarsely chopped
2	zucchini, coarsely chopped
2	tomatoes, peeled, seeded, diced
1	large onion, chopped
1	can chickpeas, rinsed and drained
½	cup golden raisins
½	cup dates, pitted, chopped
½	cup slivered almonds, toasted

Combine all ingredients, except almonds, and toss with dressing (below).

Dressing:

6	T. olive oil
¼	cup lemon juice
½	tsp. salt
½	tsp. pepper
¼	tsp. ground ginger
¼	tsp. turmeric
¼	tsp. cinnamon

To make dressing, combine all ingredients in a jar and shake well.

Sprinkle salad with almonds and serve at room temperature.

Tabouli—Cold Vegetable Salad

serves 6

1	cup boiling water
1	cup bulgar wheat
2-3	tomatoes, peeled, seeded and diced
1	green pepper, seeded and cut in 1-inch strips
1	cucumber, peeled, seeded, cut in half circles
1-2	stalks celery, diced
4-5	radishes, sliced
¼	cup fresh parsley, minced
⅓	cup fresh mint, minced
⅓	cup scallions, chopped
½	cup lemon juice
¼	cup olive oil
	salt to taste

Pour boiling water over bulgar and let stand in a bowl for 1 hour. Drain off excess water. Combine bulgar and all vegetables and toss with olive oil and lemon juice. Salt to taste. Refrigerate. Serve on a bed of lettuce.

Tomato and Dill Salad

serves 6

5	tomatoes, peeled
	pinch of sugar
2	T. chopped fresh dill
1	egg yolk
	salt
	cayenne pepper, dash
½	tsp. dry mustard
⅛	tsp. chili powder
	rind of 1 lemon, grated
1	clove garlic, crushed
½	cup oil
3	T. cream
1	egg white, stiffly beaten

Cut tomatoes in thick slices and sprinkle with sugar; let stand for a few minutes. Add chopped dill. Make the following dressing:

Put 1 egg yolk, salt, pepper, mustard, chili powder, grated lemon rind and garlic in a bowl. Mix well and add oil slowly. Mix in cream, then egg white. Mix lightly with tomatoes and serve chilled.

Tortellini Vegetable Salad

serves 6-8

16	oz. frozen cheese tortellini, cooked 'al dente', drained
½	cup extra virgin olive oil
½	cup lemon juice
½	tsp. basil
½	tsp. dill weed
½	tsp. salt
¼	tsp. pepper
⅛	tsp. crushed red pepper
2	cloves garlic, minced
1	T. chives, minced
1	lb. broccoli florets, blanched
6	oz. snow peas, blanched
1	lg. green or red bell pepper, cut into thin strips
2	oz. pimiento, drained, cut into thin strips (omit if you use red pepper)
2	T. fresh parsley, minced - garnish

Mix the olive oil, lemon juice, basil, dill weed, salt, pepper, red pepper, garlic and chives thoroughly. Add the cooked tortellini and marinate up to 2 hours.

Pour boiling water over broccoli and let stand one minute. Drain and refresh immediately in cold water and dry thoroughly. (May be done a day ahead and stored in a Ziploc bag in refrigerator.) Repeat the process for the snow peas. Toss the four vegetables with the marinated pasta just before serving. Serve at room temperature on Bibb lettuce. Garnish with minced parsley. This salad is good also with other types of pasta. If desired, extra lemon juice may be added just before serving.

SALADS

Track Talk
"I'll tell you what the Derby's got that makes it special. It's got the first Saturday in May."
-Matt J. Winn, creator of the modern Kentucky Derby.

Wild Rice Salad

serves 24

Wild Rice Salad Dressing:

⅔	cup olive oil (Extra Virgin)
⅓	cup Safflower oil
¼	cup Pear vinegar
1	tsp. lemon curd (found in specialty stores)
1	tsp. prepared mustard
2	tsp. garlic pepper
2	tsp. ground coriander
2	tsp. cilantro (dried or fresh)
2	T. thyme, dried (fresh-1-1½ T.)
4	T. parsley, dried (fresh-3 T. Italian variety)

To make dressing blend all ingredients above; let dressing sit at room temperature to gain in flavor.

Salad:

3	cups wild rice, uncooked
1	cup sunflower kernels, roasted and salted
½	cup freshly grated Parmesan cheese
2	bunches spring onions, finely chopped in processor
6	ribs celery, cut into ¼" cross sections
1	small basket cocktail tomatoes, red or yellow
1	cup ripe Greek black olives, soaked in olive oil and Herbs of Provence or plain black olives, chopped
	Optional: ⅓ cup fresh basil, chopped (use only if using plain black olives)

Boil rice in large pot of cold water until just tender (about 30-40 minutes). Kernels will just be opening. Drain. Add ½ cup dressing; add more later if desired. Add all the other salad ingredients, tossing thoroughly.

This dish is excellent served with dove or any other game or poultry. This salad may be stuffed in a tomato (leave out cocktail tomatoes), or served on a leaf of red radiccio. It may be served warm, cold or at room temperature.

Wilted Lettuce Salad

serves 4

4	heads Bibb lettuce (or leaf lettuce)
3	T. bacon or ham drippings
4	T. vinegar
3	T. sugar
	salt and pepper to taste

Cut lettuce up. Heat bacon grease; add sugar, salt and pepper. Add vinegar carefully, as it will splatter. Pour over lettuce while hot.

Hot German Potato Salad

(Microwave)   serves 4-6

4	medium potatoes
6	strips bacon
2	T. flour
¼	cup sugar
1½	tsp. salt
½	tsp. celery seed
⅛	tsp. pepper
1	cup water
½	cup vinegar

Wash and pierce potatoes with fork. Place on paper towel in microwave oven. Cook at High for 10-12 minutes, until tender. Remove from oven, cool slightly, peel and cut in ⅛ inch slices

In 2 quart casserole cut bacon in small pieces. Cover with paper towel. Cook at High about 6 minutes, until crisp. With slotted spoon remove bacon to paper towels to drain. Set aside.

Stir flour, sugar and seasonings into fat until smooth. Cook at High for 1-2 minutes, until bubbly.

Add water and vinegar to flour mixture. Cook on High for 4 minutes, until mixture boils and thickens. Remove from oven and stir until smooth. Add potatoes and bacon; stir gently so potatoes hold their shape. Cover casserole and let stand until ready to serve.

Blue Boar's Lettuce
with Cottage Cheese Dressing

serves 9

16	oz. creamed cottage cheese
8	oz. (1 cup) mayonnaise
½	T. grated onion or juice
½	tsp. salt
⅓	tsp. white pepper
	sprinkle of paprika
1	large head iceberg lettuce, or equivalent amount other lettuce

Combine the cottage cheese, mayonnaise, grated onion, salt and white pepper; mix well.

Line the salad plate with lettuce that has been cut into 2½ ounce slices. Top with 2½ ounces of cottage cheese dressing, to cover the slice of lettuce. Sprinkle lightly with paprika.

"This is our most requested recipe. Easy to prepare and from items most often found in the 'frig' ".

Guadeloupe Vinaigrette

yields 1½ cups

⅓	cup good quality white vinegar (malt, if possible)
⅔	cup good quality vegetable oil (light variety)
⅔	cup Dijon mustard
2	T. finely minced scallions
1	tsp. whole, dry green peppercorns, crushed

Put all ingredients in a glass jar, cover and shake well.

Serve at room temperature over Chef Salad, sliced tomatoes, tossed green salad or salad of your choice.

SALADS

Track Talk
*Calumet Farms has bred the most Derby winners. Whirlaway,
in 1941 and Citation in 1948, the most famous of the eight
horses.*

Derby Salad

serves 12-15

3½ T. fresh lime juice
½ tsp. grated lime rind
¾ cup olive oil or combination with vegetable oil
1-2 tsp. chopped fresh mint
salt and pepper
Boston lettuce-1 large head
Iceberg lettuce-1 small head
Romaine lettuce-1 large head
12 stalks asparagus, blanched
2 avocados, optional
2 medium carrots, grated

Dressing: Slowly whisk the oil into the lime juice and lime rind until well mixed. Season to taste with fresh mint, salt and pepper.

Wash and pat dry the lettuce; tear up into 2 inch pieces in a large salad bowl. Refrigerate, covered with a damp towel an hour or more. Plunge the asparagus stalks into boiling water or steam 3 minutes until crisp tender; immediately run under cold water. Cut into 1-inch diagonal pieces. Cut the avocado and toss in a tablespoon or more of dressing. Just before serving, toss the vegetables with the greens and toss with enough dressing to lightly coat the greens.

Dijon Dressing

serves 6-8

Makes 1¼ cups
½ tsp. sugar
½ tsp. dry mustard
1 tsp. Dijon mustard
1 tsp. lemon juice
1 clove garlic, crushed
5 T. tarragon vinegar
2 T. olive oil
10 T. vegetable oil
1 raw egg
½ cup light cream
salt and freshly ground pepper

8 cups favorite greens, well-chilled

Mix all dressing ingredients and shake well in a jar or mix in a food processor. Toss the greens with enough dressing to lightly coat leaves. The dressing will keep for up to a week in the refrigerator.

Walnut-Cheese Salad

serves 6-8

Walnut Cheese Vinaigrette:
6 T. oil (4 T. olive oil and 2 T. corn oil)
2 T. raspberry or wine vinegar
1 tsp. salt, or less
⅛ tsp. freshly ground black pepper
⅛ tsp. dry mustard
1 head Romaine lettuce, washed and dried
¼ cup Stilton cheese, crumbled
¼ cup English walnuts, broken

Mix the vinaigrette dressing in the salad bowl and whisk until the oil is emulsified. Tear the Romaine into bite-size pieces. To the lettuce, cheese and walnuts add enough dressing to coat the greens and toss well.

Kentucky Goat Cheese Salad

serves 6

8	oz. Kentucky Bibb lettuce
	Kentucky Vinaigrette Dressing
3	4-oz. pieces of Kentucky Goat Cheese from Subtle, Ky. (or other mild goat cheese)
1	T. freeze dried green peppercorns, crushed or
3	T. toasted walnut pieces

Kentucky Vinaigrette Dressing:

2	T. vinegar
6	T. oil
1	T. Dijon mustard
	salt and pepper to taste

Grease a baking sheet. Preheat broiler. Place shelf 2 inches to 3 inches below broiler. Line salad plates with lettuce. Divide horizontally each round of goat cheese into 2 inch pieces. Place all six pieces on baking sheet and broil for 30 seconds to 1 minute (enough to heat but not melt cheese). Quickly place on lettuce on each salad plate and top with dressing. Sprinkle with either crushed green peppercorns or toasted walnuts. Serve immediately.

Herbed Vinaigrette Dressing

yields 2 ½ cups

2	tsp. salt
1	tsp. pepper
2	tsp. crushed black and white peppercorns
1	tsp. dry mustard
½	tsp. sugar
1	small clove garlic, crushed
1	tsp. lemon juice
¼	tsp. Worcestershire sauce
6	T. vinegar
2	cups oil
1	hard-boiled egg, chopped fine
1	T. chopped capers
3	green olives, chopped
1	T. fresh chives
½	T. fresh thyme
½	T. fresh basil

Into a 1 quart, screwtop jar put salt, pepper, peppercorns, mustard, sugar, garlic, lemon juice, Worcestershire sauce, vinegar and oil. Screw top on securely and shake until thoroughly mixed. Add chopped egg, capers, olives and herbs; mix well and pour over greens or cold, cooked vegetables.

SALADS

Track Talk
Carry Back (1961) and Swaps (1955) are buried on the
grounds of The Kentucky Derby Museum.

Mushroom-Spinach Salad
with Parmesan Dressing

serves 4

¼	**lb. mushrooms, washed and sliced**
	Parmesan Dressing*
4	**cups packed spinach, washed, dried and torn**
¾	**cups slivered almonds, blanched and toasted**
⅓	**cup sliced green onions**

Marinate mushrooms in Parmesan Dressing for 2 to 3 hours. Just before serving, combine spinach, almonds and onions. Toss with mushrooms and dressing.

*Parmesan Dressing

½	**cup raspberry vinegar**
½	**cup olive oil**
3	**T. grated Parmesan cheese**
1	**tsp. dried basil, crushed**
1	**clove garlic, finely minced**
¼	**tsp. salt**
⅛	**tsp. freshly ground pepper**

Place all ingredients in blender, processor or bowl and mix thoroughly.

Normandy Inn Salad

serves 4

3	**T. tarragon vinegar**
2	**small cloves garlic, minced**
6	**T. olive oil**
1	**tsp. salt**
	freshly ground pepper
1	**small head Boston lettuce**
1	**small head Bibb lettuce**
½	**small head Romaine lettuce**
1	**head Belgian endive**
2	**T. sesame seeds, toasted**
	croutons
	Provolone cheese, grated

To mix the dressing, place vinegar and garlic in a bowl. Slowly whisk in the olive oil and season with salt and pepper to taste. This may also be mixed in the processor. Let dressing sit at least 2 hours.

Wash, dry and tear lettuce; place in a salad bowl, along with sliced endive. Add sesame seeds and croutons and pour on desired amount of dressing. Sprinkle generously with Provolone cheese.

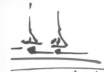

Kentucky Spring Salad

Kentucky Boiled Dressing:

2   eggs
1   tsp. dry mustard
1   tsp. salt
½   cup sugar or less
1   tsp. flour
½   cup vinegar
½   cup cream (or ½ cup milk and 3 T. butter)
1   large head leaf lettuce
2   hard-boiled eggs, sliced
½   cup green onions, sliced thin (white and green part)

In top of double boiler, beat eggs; add mustard, salt, sugar, flour and vinegar. Cook over water until mixture thickens, then add cream. Cook until thickened. Cool, then chill. Serve the dressing over greens and garnish with egg slices and green onions.

Watercress-Orange Salad

serves 4

2   bunches watercress, washed and dried
3   heads Beligan endive, washed and dried
2   oranges, peeled and sectioned
1   shallot, finely chopped
⅓   cup olive oil
2   T. lemon juice
      salt, freshly ground pepper
½   cup slivered almonds, toasted - optional garnish

Cut off the large stems of the watercress; cut the rest of the watercress into smaller pieces. Cut off ends of endive and cut into ½-inch pieces. In a salad bowl, mix the orange and endive sections with the watercress.

Mix well in the processor, or with a whisk, the shallots, olive oil, lemon juice, salt and pepper to taste. Pour the dressing over the salad and toss gently. Sprinkle with toasted slivered almonds, if desired.

Blue Cheese Dressing

yields 2 cups

¼   tsp. salt
½   tsp. garlic, minced or ⅛ tsp. garlic powder.
¼   tsp. prepared mustard
3   oz. pkg. cream cheese, room temperature
½   cup mayonnaise
½   cup milk
¾   cup Blue Cheese, crumbled

Blend salt, garlic and mustard with cream cheese. Add mayonnaise alternately with milk. Whip until smooth. Add Blue Cheese. Chill.

Good with Bibb lettuce and sliced fresh tomatoes.

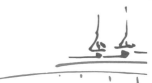

Notes

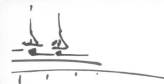

Notes

FIFTH RACE
CHEESE AND EGGS
COMMITTEE'S HANDICAP

1	**EGG AND BACON SOUFFLÉ**	SERVES **8**
2	**CHÈVRE AND LEEK FLAN**	SERVES **8-10**
3	**HOUSEGUEST EGGS**	SERVES **8**
4	**BENEDICTINE**	SERVES **6-8**
5	**EGG AND WATERCRESS SANDWICHES**	SERVES **3**
6	**GRITS CASSEROLE**	SERVES **6**
7	**PIMIENTO CHEESE**	SERVES **16-20**
8	**BREAKFAST RAMEKINS**	SERVES **8**

Committee Selections   8-5-2

Kentucky bred entry 4, 6, 7

Tasty Trivia
Benedictine is a spread made famous by Miss Jennie Benedict, a Louisville caterer and restauranteur at the turn of the century. Bacon crumbled on a benedictine sandwich is a wonderful variation.

Benedictine

yields 2 cups

1   cucumber, peeled
1   medium onion
1   lb. cream cheese
2-3 drops green food coloring

Grate cucumber and onions (may use a food processor) and drain well in a strainer, pressing down with spoon to remove all liquid. Discard liquid. Add drained cucumbers and onion to cream cheese and mix well in food processor. Color with 2-3 drops of green food coloring.

Use as a sandwich spread or as a dip.

Cheese Sandwiches

3 cups

2   cups finely grated New York sharp
       Cheddar cheese
¾   cup mayonnaise
¼   cup chili sauce
¼   cup finely chopped stuffed olives
½   cup finely chopped pecans
½   tsp. salt
1   tsp. Worcestershire sauce

Mix all ingredients well and chill. This can be used as a dip, a stuffing for celery or for sandwiches.

Five Color Frittata
(Microwave)

serves 1

3   cherry tomatoes, cut in eighths
3   medium green onions, including
       part of green top, sliced thinly
¼   tsp. salt
⅛   tsp. pepper
¼   tsp. prepared mustard
1   T. butter
¼   cup chopped green pepper
2   eggs
1   tsp. water
¼   cup shredded sharp Cheddar
       cheese

In a small bowl, stir together the cut-up tomatoes, sliced green onions, salt, pepper and mustard. Let topping stand while preparing frittata.

In 7 or 8-inch microwave pie plate, place butter and green pepper. Microwave at High for 2 minutes, until pepper has softened. Meanwhile, in small bowl, whip with a fork the eggs, water and cheese. Add egg mixture to precooked pepper, stirring well to mix all ingredients in pie plate. Microwave at High for 1½ to 2½ minutes more, stirring after 1 minute to push the cooked areas from edges to center. When done, all areas will be set but soft; egg mixture continues to firm up during brief standing period.

Remove frittata from oven and spoon on tomato topping, spreading evenly over top. Serve hot.

Cheese Timbales with Spinach Sauce

serves 9-10

6	oz. cream cheese
3	whole eggs
3	egg yolks
½	cup heavy cream
4	oz. Gorgonzola cheese, or good quality Blue cheese
4	T. butter
2	T. freshly grated Parmesan cheese salt, if needed, and freshly ground pepper

Sauce:

3	T. butter
1½	T. heavy cream
2	cups fresh spinach, cooked, well-drained and chopped sprinkling of flour
3	T. Parmesan cheese
2	T. minced fresh chives or dill (or 2 tsp. dried dill) salt and freshly ground pepper

optional: bits of beurre manié (2 T. flour creamed with 2 T. butter)

Preheat oven to 350 degrees. Butter the ramekins or custard cups. Line the bottoms with buttered waxed paper. Set aside.

In food processor or blender, combine the cream cheese, eggs, yolks, and cream; blend well. Mash the Gorgonzola together with the butter until smooth; add to the processor with the Parmesan. Blend well and season to taste.

Pour the mixture into the buttered, paper-lined ramekins, and then place them in a large baking pan. Pour boiling water into the pan until it reaches halfway up the sides of the ramekins. Place the pan in the oven, and cover it with a sheet of buttered parchment. Bake for 20-25 minutes, or until the tops are lightly browned and a knife, when inserted in the middle, comes out clean.

While the ramekins are baking, make the sauce. Melt 3 tablespoons butter in a heavy skillet. Add cream and cook until butter is incorporated into the cream, about 3-5 minutes over medium heat. Sprinkle drained, chopped spinach with a small amount of flour. Add spinach, Parmesan, chives or dill, salt and freshly ground pepper to taste. Cook until thickened enough to coat the back of a spoon. If needed, add bits of buerre manié to get desired thickening.

When ready to serve, unmold ramekins onto serving dish, spoon the spinach sauce over them and serve hot as an appetizer or for brunch or lunch. Garnish with a sprig of dill or small spinach leaf.

The sauce and timbales may be made a day ahead. Cover the timbales with foil and refrigerate. Reheat in a 200 degree oven until heated through, about 20-25 minutes.

Pimiento Cheese

4 cups

1	lb. sharp Cheddar cheese, grated
2	green onions, finely chopped
1	medium green pepper, diced
1	(4 oz.) jar pimientos, chopped
½	cup mayonnaise

Mix together all of the ingredients. Chill for several hours before serving. Serve with thin wheat crackers, or corn chips, or as a sandwich spread.

Tasty Trivia
Egg shells can be removed easily from hot hard-boiled eggs
if they are quickly rinsed in cold water first.

CHEESE and EGGS

Grits Casserole

serves 6

1	cup quick grits
4	cups boiling water
1	tsp. salt
¾	cup grated Cheddar cheese
1	small roll garlic cheese
¼	stick butter
2	eggs
⅔	cup milk
	dash Tabasco
	salt to taste
	corn flakes, buttered, crushed
	paprika

Preheat oven to 350 degrees. Cook grits in boiling, salted water until done (about 5 - 7 minutes). Add Cheddar cheese, garlic cheese and butter and stir until melted. Beat eggs with milk, add Tabasco and salt and mix together with grits mixture. Pour into a well-greased 2 quart casserole and sprinkle with buttered, crushed corn flakes and paprika.

Bake about 45 minutes.

Breakfast Ramekins

butter
mushrooms, sliced
bacon, ham or sausage, cooked and
  cut into small pieces
cheese (almost any kind), cut into
  fine cubes
eggs
salt and freshly ground pepper to taste
heavy cream

Preheat oven to 350 degrees. The amounts of ingredients needed for this recipe depend on the number of servings desired. One 3 inch ramekin per serving.

Butter ramekins well. Layer bottom of each ramekin with mushrooms, meat, cheese, one egg, salt and pepper, another layer of mushroom slices and top with cream to completely cover the ingredients.

These ramekins can be prepared and refrigerated the evening before. Fifteen to thirty minutes before serving time, place ramekins in a baking pan with one inch of boiling water. Place in a 350 degree oven for 15-30 minutes, depending on the number of ramekins made. This dish can be served with points of toast which may be dipped in the soft egg center.

Houseguest Eggs

serves 8

8	eggs
4	oz. cream cheese, diced
4	oz. sharp Cheddar cheese, grated
2	cups cream
3	T. butter

Preheat oven to 350 degrees. Grease a 10-inch round (or similar size) casserole. Carefully break eggs into it, without breaking yolks. Arrange the cream cheese and Cheddar cheese over eggs. Pour cream over all. Dot with butter and bake for 30 minutes. This can be halved, doubled or tripled.

Egg and Bacon Soufflé

serves 4 to 6

6	thick slices bacon, diced
6	slices white bread
6	slightly beaten eggs
2	cups milk
½	tsp. dry mustard
½	tsp. paprika
½	tsp. pepper

Preheat oven to 350 degrees. Fry bacon until light brown.

Brush bread with bacon dripping, cut slices in pieces to fit 3 quart casserole; arrange in layers; sprinkle each with bacon.

Combine eggs, milk and seasonings: pour over bread. Refrigerate overnight. Bake one hour or until knife inserted in center comes out clean.

Egg and Watercress Sandwiches

6 tea sandwiches

2	hard-cooked eggs, peeled
2	T. mayonnaise
1	T. Dijon mustard
½	tsp. dried dill
	salt, white pepper to taste
12	sprigs watercress, stems removed
6	thin slices fresh white bread

Finely chop the hard-cooked eggs. Add the mayonnaise, mustard, dill, salt and pepper; mash well with a fork. Coarsely chop the watercress and set aside.

Spread 3 slices of bread with the egg mixture and sprinkle with watercress. Place the other 3 slices on top; trim crusts, if desired, and cut on the diagonal into triangles.

Governor's Egg Casserole

serves 8

½	cup chopped onion
2	T. butter
2	T. flour
1 ¼	cups milk
1	cup sharp shredded cheese
6	hard-cooked eggs, sliced or quartered
1½	cups crushed potato chips
10-12	slices of bacon, fried crisp and crumbled

Preheat oven to 350 degrees. Cook onion in butter till tender, but not brown. Blend in flour; add milk; cook, stirring constantly till mixture thickens. Add cheese; stir till melted. Place layer of egg slices in 10 x 6 x 1 ½ inch baking dish. Cover with half of the cheese sauce, half the potato chips and half the bacon. Repeat layer.

Bake about 30 minutes.

Serve this with country ham, bacon, sausage, grits, fresh fruit and hot biscuits.

Tasty Trivia
To determine whether an egg is hard-boiled, spin it. If it spins round and round, it is hard-boiled. If it wobbles and will not spin, it is raw.

Jennie Benedict's Eggs Baked in Tomatoes

serves 4

4   tomatoes
     salt and pepper
4   eggs
4   slices bread
2   T. butter

Preheat oven to 350 degrees. Select round tomatoes of uniform size. Cut off stem ends and remove enough of pulp to leave a space as large as an egg. Sprinkle with salt and pepper. Drop an egg into each tomato. Place the filled tomatoes in a baking dish with a little hot water and bake them about 15 minutes, or until the eggs are set and the tomatoes are a little softened.

Cut out 3-inch rounds of bread and brown them in butter. Serve the tomatoes on rounds of bread. No sauce is required with this dish.

Chevre and Leek Flan

serves 8-10

½   log (6 oz.) goat cheese
        (Montrachet)
4   T. butter (divided)
3   leeks, cleaned, (white plus 1 in. of
        green)
     salt
1¼   T. flour
1   cup heated milk
½   cup cream
2   egg yolks
     pepper
     few grains nutmeg
     cayenne pepper
1   9 inch pie shell, partially baked

Preheat oven to 325 degrees. Crumble the Montrachet and set aside. Heat 3 tablespoons butter in skillet. Cut leeks on the diagonal, making very thin strips. Sauté in butter over low heat for about 10 minutes; salt to taste. Let cool slightly. Heat 1 tablespoon butter until foaming in a heavy saucepan. Whisk in flour to make a roux and cook a minute. Slowly whisk in milk and stir until thickened, 3-4 minutes. Whisk cream and egg yolks into roux and cook for several minutes; do not boil. Season with salt, pepper, nutmeg and cayenne.

Spread leeks in bottom of pie crust. Sprinkle goat cheese over them. Pour roux mixture over leeks and cheese and bake until custard sets, about 35 minutes.

Brunch Eggs, Taco Style
(Microwave)

serves 6

2   T. butter
2   green onions plus part of the
        green tops, chopped
6   eggs
⅓   cup milk
½   tsp. salt
⅛   tsp. pepper
¼   cup canned chopped mild green
        chilies
6   medium taco shells

     Toppings: chopped tomatoes,
     grated mild Cheddar cheese,
     shredded lettuce

In 2 quart microwave casserole, place butter and green onions. Microwave at High for about a minute until butter is melted. Add eggs, milk, salt and pepper. Beat well. Microwave at High for 4 to 6 minutes, stirring every minute, until eggs are softly scrambled. Lightly stir in chopped chilies just before eggs are set. Spoon eggs into taco shells, then cover with tomatoes, cheese and lettuce. Serve immediately.

Make-Ahead Quiche

serves 6

6	sausage links
1	cup shredded sharp Cheddar cheese
1	T. flour
½	cup shredded Monterey Jack cheese
6	eggs
½	cup light cream
	dash cayenne
1	tsp. Worcestershire sauce

Preheat oven to 350 degrees. Cook sausage according to package directions and drain. In bottom of an ungreased 1½-quart quiche dish, put Cheddar cheese and flour that have been tossed together. Sprinkle evenly with Monterey Jack cheese. Beat together eggs, cream, cayenne and Worcestershire sauce. When well blended pour over cheese. Arrange sausage in spoke fashion on top. Cover and refrigerate up to 24 hours. About an hour before serving, uncover dish and let stand at room temperature about 30 minutes. Bake 35-40 minutes or until mixture is set. Cut in wedges to serve.

Fettucine Casserole

serves 12-15

1	16-oz. pkg. fettucine
24	oz. cream style cottage cheese
1	8-oz butter, melted
1	16-oz. pkg. Monterey Jack cheese, grated
½	cup chopped green onions
⅓	cup chopped fresh parsley
2	cloves garlic, minced
½	tsp. Tabasco
	Salt and pepper to taste

Preheat oven to 350 degrees. Cook noodles in boiling water "al dente"; drain. Combine rest of ingredients reserving half of Jack cheese. Combine this mixture with noodles. Turn into a buttered 9 x 13 inch casserole; sprinkle remaining cheese on top. Bake for 40 minutes. Cover the casserole the first half of the cooking time.

Fusilli with Chèvre Sauce

serves 4

1	T. olive oil
2	cloves garlic, minced
4	oz. Proscuitto ham, finely chopped
1	cup heavy cream
1	tsp. dried basil
1	tsp. dried oregano
3	whole tomatoes, fresh or canned and peeled, seeded, chopped.
5	oz. goat cheese (Montrachet or Bucheron)
¾	lb. fusilli
½	bunch spinach leaves, washed, dried and jullienned
½	cup Parmesan cheese, freshly grated
¼	cup sun dried tomatoes, julienned

Heat olive oil in large sauté pan. Add garlic and ham; sauté about 5 minutes, but do not brown. Add cream, basil, oregano and tomatoes; cook over medium heat 5 minutes more. Add goat cheese and let melt over low heat.

Cook fusilli; drain and toss with sauce and julienned spinach. Top with Parmesan cheese and sun-dried tomatoes.

Notes

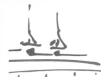

SIXTH RACE

POULTRY

1	STUFFED CHICKEN BREASTS WITH TARRAGON	SERVES 12
2	QUAIL, KENTUCKY STYLE	SERVES 2-4
3	FRENCH PHEASANT	SERVES 4
4	TURKEY HASH	SERVES 6
5	DOVES IN TOMATO SAUCE	SERVES 4-6
6	TRACK TIME PATÉ	SERVES 14-16
7	ROXANNE'S BOURSIN CHICKEN	SERVES 12-16
8	ANITRA MANDARINE	SERVES 2

Committee Selections   1-7-5

Kentucky bred entry 2, 4, 5

Tasty Trivia
Vinegar brought to a boil in a new frying pan will prevent foods from sticking.

Chicken with Artichokes

serves 4

1	2½-3 lb. fryer, cut up
2	T. butter
2	T. finely chopped shallots or green onions
2	T. Cognac or Bourbon
1	10 oz. package frozen artichoke hearts
¼	cup white wine
¼-½	cup cream
	salt and freshly ground pepper

Brown chicken in butter. Remove chicken from pan, and sauté the shallots in the same butter until tender. Deglaze pan with wine, stir to loosen crusty bits. Return chicken to pan. Warm Cognac or Bourbon in small saucepan and pour over chicken. Standing well back, ignite the liquor; when the flame dies down, pour the cream over the chicken, then season to taste with the salt and pepper. Cover pan and simmer gently 15 minutes. Add artichoke hearts, cover again, and cook 10 minutes longer, or until chicken is tender. Place chicken and artichokes on warm platter. Reduce sauce slightly by boiling. Pour over chicken.

Wine: Serve a White Graves or a Chablis

Roxanne's Boursin Chicken

"La Pêche"

serves 12-16

14	whole chicken breasts, skinned, boned and cut into chunks
1	lb. butter
2	medium onions, chopped
8	cloves garlic, chopped fine
1	lb. fresh spinach, chopped
1	lb. cream cheese
1	T. each of the following: basil, marjoram, dill and oregano
2	T. chives
	salt and pepper
	seasoned flour
1	cup cream
3	cups chicken stock
	Gorgonzola cheese

Dredge chicken in flour, seasoned with salt and pepper. Melt part of the butter and sauté the chicken in batches, adding more butter as needed over medium. heat. Set aside. Add onions and garlic to pan and more butter if needed. Cook until onions are soft. Add enough flour to absorb excess butter. Add cream cheese and herbs. Whisk until smooth. Slowly add 3 cups strong chicken stock and 1 cup cream. Add ½ of the spinach to the sauce and cook until wilted. Pour sauce over chicken and wilt remaining spinach in pan. Garnish with this. Crumble Gorgonzola cheese over the top and serve.

Wine: Serve with a white Burgandy or a Chardonnay

POULTRY

Track Talk
*The first flight of an airplane in Kentucky was made from the
infield at Churchill Downs on June 18, 1910.*

Chicken with Cashews and Pineapple
serves 2-4

1	lb. chicken breast, skinned, boned and cut into bite sized pieces
	small clove of garlic, pressed
1	T. cornstarch
¼	tsp. salt
	pepper to taste
1	T. peanut oil
1	T. soy sauce
2	tsp. corn starch
¼	cup water
¼	tsp. MSG
4	slices canned pineapple, cut in wedges or canned pineapple chunks; save juice
	unsalted cashew nuts (available at health food stores)

Mix the garlic, cornstarch, salt, pepper, oil and soy sauce. A few hours before cooking, or even the night before, marinate the chicken in this mixture; cover and refrigerate. Before cooking, mix the next 4 ingredients in a small glass.

Heat a little oil and quick fry chicken until just under-done and just turned white. Add pineapple and juice from can. Mix and stir well. Add the mixture in glass and stir until sauce thickens. Keep warm, but do not boil.

Put a little oil into a separate frying pan. Heat. Add cashew nuts. Brown, but be careful not to burn. Keep stirring. Pour chicken onto serving platter. Top with cashews.

Note: This recipe can be varied greatly. Add wedges of green pepper and onion to be braised with the pineapple. Add a can of button mushrooms, drained, or try a couple of dashes of catsup to add flavor and color. You can add cornstarch and water to thicken any variation.

You may alter your recipe according to the amount of chicken used. Double the marinade for 1½ - 2 lbs. of chicken.

Wine: Serve a White Zinfindel, a Chenin Blanc or a Sparkling Wine

Chicken Breasts with Dressing
serves 8

4	chicken breasts, halved
2	cans chicken broth or homemade
2	3-oz. pkgs. cream cheese
¼	cup mayonnaise
2	T. fresh dill
3	T. lemon juice
1	tsp. grated lemon rind
¼	tsp. seasoned salt
	Romaine or red leaf lettuce
8	tomato slices
	avocado slices
	toasted almonds.
	Homemade Italian or French dressing

Poach chicken breasts in broth 30 minutes. Debone and skin. Cover each breast with paste made of cream cheese, mayonnaise, dill, lemon juice, lemon rind and salt. Chill.

To assemble, place on plate in the following order: lettuce, tomato, chicken, avocado, sprinkling of almonds and drizzle dressing over top.

Wine: Serve a light Italian or a Spanish red or a fruity Chardonnay

Chicken and Green Grapes

serves 6

6	boned and skinned chicken breasts
1	T. butter
1	T. olive oil
1	cup chicken broth
⅔	stick butter
⅓	cup flour
3	cups fresh chicken broth, heated
1	cup dry Vermouth
1	can green grapes (fresh may be used)

Brown chicken breasts in butter and olive oil. Add chicken broth and simmer until tender, about 10-15 minutes. Remove chicken from broth and serve with grape sauce. To make sauce, melt butter and stir in flour. When blended, add hot chicken broth; cook until thick. Add Vermouth and green grapes. Season to taste and serve with buttered rice.

Wine: Serve with a Chenin Blanc

Stir-fry Chicken with Snow Peas

serves 2-4

2	chicken breasts, about ¾ lb. each
3	tsp. cornstarch, divided
1	T. dry Sherry
¼	tsp. MSG, optional
1	tsp. salt
5	T. cold water
4	oz. fresh snow peas
6	T. corn or peanut oil
½	cup fresh mushrooms, quartered (or canned, drained mushrooms)
1	clove garlic finely minced
½	cup water chestnuts, quartered
½	cup bamboo shoots, diced
¼	cup almonds, blanched and toasted

Skin, bone and dice chicken. Mix 1 teaspoon cornstarch, Sherry, MSG and salt. Mix with the chicken and set aside, but for no more than ½ hour. Mix the remaining 2 teaspoons cornstarch with cold water; set aside. Snap off the stems and string the snow peas. Place them in a bowl and cover with boiling water for no more than 45 seconds. Drain immediately and cool under cold water; shake out water and set aside.

Heat a large skillet or wok. When hot, add 2 tablespoons oil and quickly sauté the fresh mushrooms a minute or two. Remove them from the pan with a slotted spoon and set aside. (This step can be omitted if canned mushrooms are used.) Add enough additional oil to the skillet to make 4 tablespoons. To the hot oil, add the minced garlic and diced chicken. Stir-fry until almost done, about 2-3 minutes, but do not allow the chicken to brown. Add the water chestnuts, bamboo shoots, mushrooms, and snow peas. Continue to stir-fry until the vegetables are hot. Add the cornstarch mixture and stir until thickened. Garnish with toasted almonds and serve immediately. Fresh or frozen green peas may be used instead of snow peas, in which case they should be cooked until just tender beforehand. This also may be made as a pork dish using diced pork and omitting the salt. However, add 2 tablespoons soy sauce to the raw pork.

Wine: Serve with a white Zinfandel or a Chenin Blanc

Track Talk
In the 1948 Derby "win" wagering was permitted only
because there were just 6 horses entered. Citation won.

Chicken Piccata

serves 4

4	chicken breasts, skinned and boned
	salt and pepper
½	cup flour
4	T. olive oil
½	stick butter
½	cup dry Vermouth
2	T. lemon juice
4	T. capers, drained
¼	sliced almonds, toasted

Slice breasts ½ inch thick and pound very thin between wax paper. Salt and pepper each breast and dredge in flour. Heat oil, and butter in skillet until mixture bubbles. Sauté chicken 2½ minutes on each side; drain and place on a warm platter. Keep 3 tablespoons cooking oil in pan, add Vermouth and scrape pan to loosen brown bits. Add lemon juice and capers. If sauce is too thin add a little flour. Pour sauce over meat and add almonds, lemon slices, parsley and paprika.

Garnish: paper thin lemon slices, chopped parsley and paprika.

Wine: Serve with a Soave, a Trebbiano or a Gavi

Chicken Suprêmes in Toasted Almond Sauce

serves 6-8

4	whole chicken breasts, skinned, boned, cut in half lengthwise
	salt and pepper
	flour
2	T. butter
2	T. vegetable oil
1	recipe Toasted Almond Sauce

Remove the white tendons on the underside of each breast and flatten the chicken slightly between two sheets of wax paper. Trim any ragged edges. Season with salt and pepper and dust lightly with flour. Heat half the butter and oil in a heavy skillet. When very hot, sauté four of the breast halves. Cook 4 minutes on one side, turn over and cook 2 minutes longer. The breast should be springy to the touch when done. Do not overcook. Remove at once to a heated serving platter, cover loosely with foil and keep warm. Wipe skillet with paper towel, add remaining half of butter and oil to skillet and repeat the process with the other four breast halves. Cover each breast with the sauce, garnish with parsley and serve at once.

Toasted Almond Sauce

3	1-inch thick slices of French bread, crusts removed
2	tsp. wine vinegar
3	T. olive oil
¼	cup shelled, whole, unblanched almonds
1	bay leaf, crumbled
1	clove garlic, peeled
1	cup hot chicken stock
1	T. lemon juice
2-3	T. commercial mayonnaise
	salt, freshly ground pepper

Sprinkle bread with vinegar. Heat oil in a heavy skillet and add bread, almonds, bay leaf and garlic. Turn bread on both sides and stir almonds and bay leaf until all are golden brown. Do not allow the garlic to brown, however. Transfer mixture to a food processor and purée. Gradually add the hot chicken stock and lemon juice. Keep mixture warm. When ready to serve, stir in the mayonnaise. Taste and add salt and pepper, if necessary.

Wine: Serve with a Chablis or a White Mâcon

Elegant Chicken

Serves 4

4	chicken breast halves, boned and skinned
1½	cups cooked wild rice
½	lb. mushrooms, chopped and cooked
2	oz. pâté, chopped
4	T. flour
2	T. butter
	salt and pepper to taste

Preheat oven to 325 degrees. Pound chicken breasts between waxed paper until thin. Combine ½ cup wild rice, mushrooms and pâté. Put ¼ of this mixture on each chicken breast; roll up and secure with a toothpick. Pat with flour and brown in butter in skillet until brown on all sides. Place in an oven-proof dish and bake for 30 minutes. Serve surrounded by remaining wild rice and side dish of Madeira Sauce.

Madeira Sauce:

2	T. browned flour
2	T. butter
1	cup chicken broth
¼	cup Madeira wine
	pinch of thyme
	salt and pepper to taste

Melt butter in skillet or saucepan; add flour and stir well. Slowly add chicken stock and seasonings. Bring to a boil and simmer gently until thickened. Add Madeira, simmer 2-3 minutes and serve.

Wine: Serve with a red Bordeaux or a California Cabernet

Grandstand Chicken Casserole

Serves 8

2	2½ lb. chickens, poached, skinned, boned
1½	lbs. mushrooms, sliced
1	stick butter
8	slices white bread, cut in rounds
1	cup sliced ripe olives
2	cups chicken stock, strained (use poaching liquid)
3	T. flour
1	cup grated Cheddar cheese

Preheat oven to 350 degrees. Cut chicken into bite-size pieces. Sauté mushrooms in ¾ of the butter. Remove from pan, add remainder of butter and sauté the bread rounds until brown on both sides and they have absorbed all ot the mushroom essence.

Layer the chicken, mushrooms and black olives in a casserole. Make a sauce by gradually beating the chicken stock into the flour. When there are no lumps, cook until thickened. Pour over the chicken, mushrooms and olives, top with sautéed bread rounds and sprinkle with the cheese. Bake until cheese is bubbly and beginning to brown on top.

Wine: Serve with a chilled Beaujolais, a light Rhone or a good table White

POULTRY

Hawaiian Chicken

Serves 4-6

4	lbs. chicken pieces
2	cups boiling water
2	T. chili powder
¼	tsp. pepper
½	tsp. cinnamon
2	T. grated onion
1	tsp. salt
¼	cup fat drippings or butter
2	cups pineapple juice
2	cups pineapple chunks
1	tsp. sugar
	paprika
2	bananas, sliced lengthwise
1	ripe avocado, sliced
½	lb. white grapes
1	cantaloupe, cut up

Preheat oven to 350 degrees. Place chicken in deep kettle. Add boiling water, chili powder, pepper, cinnamon, onion and salt. Cover and simmer until tender. Drain, saving broth. Brown chicken in drippings or butter; arrange in a baking dish. Add pineaple juice to broth; heat and pour over chicken. Arrange pineapple chunks over chicken. Sprinkle with sugar and paprika. Bake for 30 minutes.

To serve: Thicken broth and juice for gravy and serve in a separate bowl. Place chicken in center of platter with sliced bananas, avocado, grapes and cantaloupe surrounding it. Serve with rice.

Wine: Serve with a Chenin Blanc or a Blanc de Noir.

Hot Chicken Salad

serves 40

16	cups chicken, cooked and diced
2½	quarts diced celery
4	cans water chestnuts, sliced
2	cups diced almonds
9	T. grated onion
9	T. lemon juice
4	cups grated sharp Cheddar cheese
8	tsp salt
	Tabasco, to taste
4	cups mayonnaise
1	cup mushroom, optional

Preheat oven to 350 degrees. Place diced chicked in large mixing bowl. Add celery, chestnuts, almonds, onion, lemon juice, cheese, salt and Tabasco; toss together. Add mayonnaise, and mix until coated. Fill 2 3-quart casseroles with chicken salad. Bake for 20-30 minutes. May be served in center of a rice ring.

Wine: Serve a Vouvray, a Chenin Blanc or a White Zinfandel

Kelaguen Mannok (Chicken Kelaguen)

serves 6-10

1	chicken, fryer or broiler (or 6 chicken breast halves)
5-6	lemons, juice only
	salt, to taste
2-4	handfuls (1-2 cups) fresh coconut, grated
½	medium onion, chopped
1-3	fresh hot red peppers, chopped (optional to taste)

Cut up chicken at the joints. Grill or broil the pieces. (Grilling gives more flavor.) Cool, bone and chop the meat.

Using a ceramic, glass or stainless steel bowl (never an aluminum bowl), mix the chicken with the lemon juice. Salt to taste. Mix in chopped onion, coconut and peppers. If peppers aren't used, sprinkle paprika on top for color. Chill until ready to serve. Serve on a bed of lettuce. May be put on crackers, party rye, pita bread or served plain.

This recipe is easy to make in multiple quanties for large crowds.

Wine: Serve a chilled Beaujolais, a white Graves or a Chenin Blanc

Poulet en Papillote with Fresh Ginger, Lemon and Butter

serves 4

1	2-inch piece of fresh ginger root
2	chicken breasts, split in half
	salt
	freshly ground pepper
4	slices lemon
2	T. butter

Preheat oven to 450 degrees. Prepare 8 pieces of aluminum foil about 12 inches long. Set aside.

Peel the ginger root and mince finely by hand or in a processor.

Place a piece of chicken on a sheet of foil. Sprinkle with salt and pepper and a teaspoon of ginger. Top with a slice of lemon and about ½ tablespoon of butter, or more to taste. Place a second sheet of foil over the chicken and seal in an airtight package by first folding over the edges and then crimping them together. Prepare the other three packages in the same way. Arrange the packages on a baking sheet. Bake for 25 minutes.

To serve, place the papillote on a plate and cut open with a knife.

Wine: Serve a Fumé Blanc or a Chenin Blanc

Track Talk
Pari-mutuel betting was first offered at Churchill Downs in
1878. Bookmaking and auction pools were outlawed in
1908. Since then only pari-mutuel betting has been allowed.

Mancho Manteles

serves 10-12

1½	lbs. pork loin, cut in 1½-inch cubes
1	2½-3-lb. chicken, cut up
¼	cup vegetable oil
1	15-oz. can tomato sauce
2	T. chili powder
	salt and freshly ground pepper
	flour
1	jalapeno pepper, seeded, diced (use a fork and sharp knife)
3	tomatoes, peeled, seeded, quartered
2	onions, peeled, cut in wedges
2	green peppers, seeded, cut in thin strips
2	large sweet potatoes, boiled, peeled, cut in thick slices
1	pineapple, peeled, cored, cut in chunks
2	tart apples, peeled, sliced
3	bananas, peeled, sliced diagonally, sprinkled with lemon juice

Sprinkle pork and chicken with salt and pepper and dust with flour. Heat oil in a heavy skillet and brown the pork in it. Remove pork to a large pot. Brown the chicken the same way and place on top of pork. Stir the tomato sauce into the chili powder, season with about ½ teaspoon salt and several grinds of pepper; pour over the chicken and pork. Add jalapeno, tomatoes and onions. Cover pot, and simmer slowly for about 30 minutes. Add sweet potatoes and green peppers; simmer 10 minutes or longer. Remove chicken, and when cool enough to handle, skin, debone and cut into chunks; return to pot. Add pineapple and apples just long enough to warm through. Ladle mixture into a large serving dish, and make a border of banana slices around the edges. Serve with the rice on the side and a small bowl of bottled hot chili peppers or jalapenos, seeded and cut into slivers (use fork and sharp knife). A plain green salad and crusty bread, plus a simple dessert, such as a flan, would complete the menu. This reheats well, except for the bananas, of course. To freeze, omit the pineapple and apple, and add these when ready to use.

Garnish: Bottled hot chili peppers or jalapenos, cut in slivers.

Wine: Serve with a Gewürztraminer, a Zinfandel or a good table white

---

Lemon Roasted Chicken

serves 2-4

1	3 lb. chicken
2	lemons
	garlic
	salt, pepper
	crushed rosemary

Preheat oven 350 degrees. Wash 2 whole lemons. Roll on counter to release juices. Poke 20 holes, or more, in each lemon. Put lemons inside chicken and sew closed. Rub on garlic, salt, pepper and crushed rosemary. Roast breast side down 30 minutes. Turn over and roast 20 minutes more. Turn oven to 400 degrees and roast 15 minutes or until nicely brown.

Good cold too.

Wine: Serve a Pinot Noir or a Pinot Blanc

Tasty Trivia
When to add salt:
   Soups and stews: Add early
   Meats: Sprinkle just before taking off the stove.
   Vegetables: Cook in salted water.

Duckling or Cornish Hens Far East Style

Microwave

serves 2-4

2	Cornish Hens, about 1 lb. each or 1 duckling, about 3 lbs., defrosted
¼	cup soy sauce
¼	Sherry wine
¼	cup pineapple juice
1	clove garlic, crushed, or ⅛ tsp garlic powder
½	tsp. curry powder
¼	tsp. dry mustard

Split birds in halves, using kitchen shears or a sharp knife. Place in 12 x 8 x 2-inch dish, skin side down.

In small bowl mix together soy sauce, Sherry, pineapple juice, garlic, curry powder and mustard. Stir to blend well and pour over meat in dish. Refrigerate 4 to 6 hours, or overnight.

Remove from marinade and place in dish, skin side up and baste with marinade. Cover dish with wax paper. Microwave at High for 8 minutes. Brush with marinade and rotate dish ½ turn. Recover. Microwave at high for 10 to 12 minutes more, until meat is tender. Serve immediately.

Turkey Hash

serves 12-15

8	T. butter
½	cup chopped onions
½	cup flour
½	tsp. salt
¼	tsp. pepper
4	cups chicken or turkey stock
4	cups cooked, diced turkey
4	cups cooked, diced potatoes
½	lb. fresh mushrooms, sliced (optional)
½	cup heavy cream (optional)

In a heavy Dutch oven sauté onions and mushrooms in butter until soft. Stir in flour and cook over low heat until well blended. Slowly add stock, stirring constantly until thickened. Add turkey and potatoes, season and simmer 15-20 minutes. Add cream if desired.

Serve over griddle cakes or corn cakes.

Left-over turkey gravy is a good addition to the hash.

Chicken Dijonnaise

serves 4

4	chicken breast halves, skinned and boned
	ground black pepper
⅓	cup dry White wine
⅓	cup Dijon mustard
½	cup heavy cream

Cut chicken breasts into bite-size cubes. Season with pepper. Place chicken in a enamel-lined or non-stick skillet. Pour wine over it and poach, uncovered, on medium-high heat until chicken turns white and opaque. Remove chicken from pan and keep warm. Whisk mustard into juices, then add cream. Simmer for 5-10 minutes to reduce and thicken the sauce. Spoon over the chicken.

Wine: Serve with a Chardonnay, a white Mâcon or a Burgandy.

POULTRY

100

Track Talk
Steeplechase racing was common in the infield at Churchill
Downs in the early 1900's.

Brandied Chicken

serves 4-6

4	chicken breasts, cut in half
¼	cup flour
2	T. oil
1	6-oz. can frozen orange juice. thawed
¾	tsp. garlic powder
1	tsp. onion powder
1	tsp. ground ginger
¼	cup Brandy

Lightly dust chicken in flour and brown slowly in skillet in a small amount of oil. Place thawed orange juice in a bowl; add spices and mix thoroughly. Pour over chicken; add Brandy and simmer slowly until chicken is tender. Add a little water if needed while cooking. Serve over rice.

Wine: serve a Gewürztraminer, a Riesling or a white Zinfandel

Track Time Paté

serves 14-16

2	medium carrots, peeled
¾	lb. fresh spinach
1	lb. boneless chicken breasts, coarsely ground
¼	lb. bacon, ground (about 6 slices)
1	medium carrot
1	large clove garlic, minced
2	eggs, lightly beaten
¼	cup milk
½	tsp. salt
1	tsp. dried herbes de Provence
2	tsp. finely minced, fresh thyme
½	tsp. freshly ground pepper
	carrot curls, optional

Cook 2 carrots in a small amount of boiling water 8 minutes or until tender. Drain and set aside.

Trim stems from spinach; cook leaves in boiling water 1 minute or until pliable. Remove spinach with slotted spoon. Carefully spread on paper towel and pat dry; set aside. Line bottom and sides of an oiled 9 x 5 x 3-inch loaf pan with enough spinach to cover pan, placing spinach smooth side down and allowing some leaves to hang over side of pan. Coarsely chop remaining spinach and squeeze until barely moist. Combine spinach with next 11 ingredients; mix well. Spoon half of meat mixture; into spinach-lined pan. Place whole carrots lengthwise over meat mixture; top with the remaining meat mixture, packing firmly. Fold overhanging spinach leaves over meat mixture. Cover loafpan tightly with aluminum foil.

Set loaf pan in a larger baking pan. Pour enough hot water into larger pan to reach one-third the way up the sides of loafpan. Bake 325 degrees for 1 hour or until done. Do not overcook.

Remove dish from water. Set another loafpan on top of paté and fill loafpan with pastry weights or pans to pack paté as it cools. Drain off pan drippings.

When cool, remove top pan and weights; wrap paté securely and refrigerate at least 8 hours. unmold paté onto serving dish. Garnish with carrot curls, if desired. Slice and serve with crackers or bread for a luncheon, a picnic or as a first course.

Snow on the Mountain

serves 12

Creamed Chicken:

6	chicken breasts
1	bay leaf
½	onion, sliced
½	tsp. salt
4	cups water
9	T. butter
12	T. flour
4	cups chicken stock
4	cups half and half
1½	tsp. salt
½	tsp. freshly ground black pepper
8	oz. fresh mushrooms, sliced, sautéed in 2 T. butter 10 minutes

Accompaniments:

6-7	cups uncooked white rice
4	medium fresh tomatoes, peeled, seeded, chopped
3	bunches green onions, sliced
2	medium cans, chow mein noodles
8	stalks celery, thinly sliced
2	jars stuffed olives, sliced
¾	lb. Longhorn cheese, shredded
2	medium cans crushed pineapple, drained
3	small pkgs. sliced almonds, lightly toasted
2	small pkgs. shredded coconut, lightly toasted

Place the chicken breasts in a large saucepan and add the bay leaf, onion, salt and water. Bring to a boil, skim the foam off the surface and simmer for 10-15 minutes, or until the meat next to the bones just loses its pink color. Cool in the pan. Remove chicken, saving and straining the stock and degrease the stock. (If done the day before, it may be chilled to harden the fat.) Discard skin from the breast, take meat off the bones and cut up the meat in ¾-inch pieces. Set aside.

To make a white sauce, melt the butter in a medium saucepan, add the flour and cook over medium heat for 2 minutes. Off the heat, add the reserved chicken stock (measure for 4 cups-add bouillon, if needed) and stir constantly until the mixture is smooth and creamy. Add 2 cups of half and half, then add more, as needed, to produce the correct consistency of white sauce. Add salt and pepper to taste and cook over low heat, stirring occasionally, for 5 minutes. Add the mushrooms (add juices only if sauce needs thinning) and chicken meat. Taste for seasoning. Heat until hot, but do not let boil.

To serve: Place the creamed chicken in a chafing dish and the cooked rice in a large casserole. Place all the accompaniments on a large tray in individual serving bowls (such as soup bowls). Arrange on buffet table for guest to serve themselves. On a large dinner plate, guests first place rice in the center of the plate, then creamed chicken on top, then sprinkle the various accompaniments over the top, ending with the coconut, or "Snow on the Mountain".

Wine: Serve with a Riesling or a Vouvray

Chicken with Taj Mahal Barbecue Sauce

serves 8

2	cups orange juice
½	cup (firmly packed) brown sugar
½	cup sugar
½	tsp. ground ginger
1	tsp. curry powder
2	T. Sherry
8	whole chicken breasts

Preheat oven to 350 degrees. Combine orange juice, brown sugar, white sugar, ginger, curry and Sherry in large suacepan. Bring mixture to a boil. Add chicken. Simmer 10 minutes and remove to a large baking dish, along with the sauce. Bake for 20 minutes, basting occasionally with remaining sauce.

Wine: Serve with a California Blanc de Noir, a white Zinfandel or Cabernet, or a German Riesling

Track Talk
*Count Fleet won the "Streetcar" Derby in 1943; so named
because of the severe limitations of travel during W.W.II.*

Stuffed Chicken Breasts
with Tarragon Cream   serves 12

6	whole large chicken breasts
6	oz. box of onion and garlic seasoned croutons
8	oz. walnuts coarsely chopped, reserve 12 whole for garnish (optional)
	dry Vermouth
½	cup minced onion
1	clove garlic, minced
5	T. butter
¼	cup minced parsley
1	tsp. dried French tarragon
	salt and freshly ground pepper
	paprika

Preheat oven to 350 degrees. Skin, split and bone the chicken breasts. Place chicken breasts in a glass or ceramic bowl and pour enough Vermouth to just cover. Set aside. Roughly crush croutons to large course crumbs. Combine croutons and walnuts (if using) in a bowl. Sauté minced onion and garlic in 2 tablespoons butter just until onion is soft. Add to the crumb mixture; toss well. Add parsley, tarragon, salt and pepper to taste. Add just enough dry Vermouth to the stuffing so that a handful will hold together when compressed lightly; it should not be wet. Make 12 oval mounds of stuffing in a buttered baking pan and shape a chicken breast half over each. Reserve Vermouth marinade for sauce. Brush each breast very generously with butter, and sprinkle lightly with a little paprika. At this point the chicken can be refrigerated until cooking time.

Bake for 20-30 minutes, or until springy to the touch. If desired, garnish top of each breast with a reserved walnut half. Serve Tarragon Cream on the side.

Tarragon Cream

1	cup dry Vermouth
2	shallots, minced
1	T. French tarragon
3	T. butter, cut in small pieces
3	cups heavy cream
	salt and pepper

In heavy enamel or stainless steel saucepan, boil Vermouth, shallots, and tarragon until reduced to about ⅓ cup. Lower heat and whisk in butter, a few pieces at a time. When all of the butter is incorporated, whisk in the cream a little at a time. Raise the heat and boil gently until sauce is reduced to about 2 cups. If sauce needs to be held over a few hours, add 1 tablespoon flour to sauce and cook an additional few minutes. Cover the sauce with a piece of buttered wax paper.

*An easy way to keep sauce warm up to 2 hours: Pour hot water into a Thermos bottle. When bottle is warmed, pour out the water and replace with sauce for keeping warm.

Wine: Serve with a White Burgandy or Chardonnay

Vitello Tonnato

serves 10-12

1	4-5 lb. turkey breast
1	bottle dry white wine
6-8	cups water
1	tsp. salt
4	onions, peeled and sliced
3	carrots, scraped and sliced
2	tsp. lemon juice
2	7-oz. cans imported tuna in olive oil, drained
4	anchovy filets in olive oil, drained
3	T. capers, rinsed in water
4	cups mayonnaise
2	lemons, juice only
¼	cup parsley leaves, packed

Put turkey breast in large pot; cover with wine and water. Add salt, onions, carrots and lemon juice. Cover partially, bring slowly to a boil, and as it comes to a boil, remove scum that floats to top. Cook until tender, about 2 hours, or until juices run clear when poked with a long fork. Do not overcook. Let cool in broth. This is best done 1-2 days in advance. When turkey is cold, cut into thin slices.

To make Tonnato Sauce, place in processor bowl, the tuna, anchovies, capers, mayonnaise, juice of one lemon and parsley leaves. Process until mixture is of a smooth consistency. Taste for seasoning, adding more lemon juice, if desired. Sauce may be made 2 days in advance and combined with turkey the day before.

To serve, dip slices of turkey in the Tonnato Sauce and overlap on platter. Garnish with one or more of the following: lemon slices, capers, minced parsley, black olives and/or cherry tomatoes. Serve with fettucine.

Wine: Serve with Gavi, or a Beaujolais

Duck Breasts

serves 6-8

4	whole duck breasts (removed from 4 ducks)
1	cup red wine
½	cup oil
½	cup soy sauce
	salt and pepper to taste
	paprika
	flour
2	eggs, beaten
2	T. oil
2	cups bread crumbs
1	stick butter
1	cup or more thinly sliced onions
	chopped parsley

Skin and split duck breasts. Marinate in mixture of wine, oil and soy sauce. Refrigerate for 12-24 hours. Drain, reserving marinade. Pat duck breasts dry with paper towels; flatten between wax paper and season with salt, pepper and paprika. Dredge in flour. Mix eggs and 2 tablespoons oil; dip breasts into this mixture and then bread crumbs. Chill. Brown the breasts in butter in a skillet, then place in a baking dish. Sauté onions in pan drippings, add these, plus marinade to baking dish. Cook at 325 degrees for 25-30 minutes.

Duck may be served thinly sliced or ½ breast per person. Use the remaining part of the duck for a stew, soup or salad.

Wine: Serve with a red Rhone or a light Zinfandel

Track Talk
The Derby was originally a 1½ mile race until it was
shortened to 1¼ mile in 1896.

Doves in Tomato Sauce

serves 4-6

1	beef bouillon cube
1	cup boiling water
3	stalks celery, chopped
1	medium onion, chopped
1	(8 oz.) can tomato sauce
2	T. flour
½	cup water
	salt and pepper to taste
12	dove breasts, skinned
6-7	slices bacon, halved

Preheat oven to 350 degrees. Dissolve bouillon cube in boiling water. Add celery and onion and simmer until soft. Add tomato sauce. Make thickening with 2 tablespoons flour and ½ cup cold water. Season and wrap dove breasts with half slice bacon. Pour sauce over doves. Cook uncovered for an hour. Serve with wild rice.

Wine: Serve with a Rhone or an Italian white

Anitra Mandarine
"Casa Grisanti"

serves 6

6	breasts of duck
1	cup flour
	pinch pepper, freshly ground
¼	cup soy oil
2	T. champagne vinegar
2½	T. granulated sugar
1	pint duck stock (or chicken stock)
¼	cup dry white wine
2⅓	T. arrowroot
2	T. butter
2	oz. mushrooms, sliced
25	capers
¼	honeydew melon, cut into bite-size pieces
¼	cantaloupe, cut into bite-size pieces
2	T. Mandarine Napoleon
6	radicchio leaves, for garnish
6	Mandarine orange sections for garnish

Bone duck breast. Flatten to ¼-inch thickness with mallet. Dredge in flour seasoned with salt and pepper. In a sauté pan, sear duck in hot oil, leaving medium-rare. Set aside. In a small saucepan make a gastrique by melting sugar and vinegar over high heat until sugar is slightly caramelized. Add stock. Simmer. Dissolve arrowroot in white wine. Add to sauce gradually. Keep warm. In a sauté pan melt butter. Sauté sliced mushrooms, capers and melons. Flame with Mandarine Napoleon. Add sauce. Blend. Place duck in a hot oven to re-warm. Remove from oven. Place on warmed plates. Ladle sauce over duck evenly. Garnish plate with radicchio leaf and mandarine orange.

Wine: Serve a champagne, a red Burgundy or a Gewürztraminer

Quail, Kentucky Style

serves 2-4

4-5   quail
4-5   T. butter
2½-3 T. flour
2-2½ cups chicken stock
½   cup Sherry
      salt and pepper to taste

Preheat oven to 350 degrees. Wash and truss quail; tie legs and wings close to body. Brown quail in butter, in skillet. Place quail in casserole, (1½ quart). Add flour to remaining butter in pan. Slowly stir in stock and Sherry. Blend well. Add salt and pepper. Pour over quail. Cover and bake for one hour. Delicious over rice.

Wine: Serve with a light Rhone or California Blanc de Noir

Grape-Stuffed Cornish Game Hens with Orange Butter

serves 4

4   **Cornish Game Hens**
4   **T. butter, room temperature**
2   **T. finely grated orange peel**
2   **tsp. minced fresh ginger**
2   **tsp. minced shallot**

Make a pocket in the breast of each hen by carefully loosening the skin with the fingers. Combine 4 tablespoons butter with orange peel, ginger, shallot in small bowl and mix until smooth. Place half of the butter mixture in each pocket and spread evenly by gently massaging on skin with finger tips. Pushing the mixture along breast and under skin of legs.

Stuffing:
4   **T. butter**
1   **onion, chopped, (about 1 ½ cups)**
4   **slices day-old white bread (crusts trimmed), cubed**
4   **T. minced fresh parsley**
1   **tsp. dried thyme, crumbled**
1½   **cups seedless red or black grapes**
      salt and freshly ground pepper to taste
½-¾ **cup strong chicken broth - optional**
4   **T. melted butter**
2   **T. soy sauce**
1   **T. orange liqueur**
(Grand Marinier,
      Triple Sec or Cointreau)

Stuffing: Melt 4 tablespoons butter in saucepan over low heat. Add onion and sauté until golden, about 7 minutes. Add bread, parsley and thyme and mix well. Blend in grapes. Taste for seasoning. Stuff hens with mixture and truss securely.

Position rack in lower third of oven and preheat to 425 degrees. Combine melted butter, soy sauce and orange liqueur in small bowl. Brush over hens. Arrange hens on sides on rack in roasting pan. Roast 10 minutes. Turn hens to other side and roast 10 minutes. Reduce oven temperature to 375 degrees. Turn hens breast side up and continue roasting until hens test done, sbout 30-40 min., or 180 degrees when probed at the leg joint with an instant thermometer.

Wine: Serve a dry Gewürztraminer or a Riesling

Track Talk
*Colonel Matt Winn became president of Churchill Downs in
1938 even though he had "run" the track since 1902.*

French Pheasant

serves 4-6

2	pheasants, cut into serving pieces
	flour
	hot fat (bacon fat, butter or vegetable oil)
1	clove, garlic, minced
1	small onion, chopped
14	oz. mushrooms, washed, dried, stemmed and sliced
6	pieces rosemary, or 1 tsp. dried
2	sprigs fresh parsley, chopped, or 1 tsp. dried
1½	cups water
2	oz. dry white wine
8	oz. sour cream

Preheat oven to 300 degrees. Dredge pheasants in flour. Brown in hot fat. Place browned pieces in roaster; salt and pepper well. Add the remaining ingredients, except the sour cream. Bake for 2-3 hours, or until the leg joints move easily and the juices run clear when pricked at the thigh. Add sour cream 15 minutes before serving.

Wine: Serve with a St. Emilion or a Chateau-neuf-du-Pape

Chicken a la Roma
(Microwave)

serves 4-6

2	T. olive oil
¾	cup thinly sliced green onion
2	tsp. minced garlic
½	lb. fresh mushrooms, sliced
1	can (6 oz.) tomato paste
1	can (8 oz.) tomato sauce
½	cup dry white wine
1	T. instant chicken bouillon granules
1	tsp. basil
2	tsp. parsley flakes
1	tsp. oregano
½	cup ripe olives, sliced
1	tsp. salt
¼	tsp. pepper
1	chicken, 2 ½ to 3 lbs., cut up
¼	cup grated Parmesan cheese
1	jar (6 oz.) marinated artichoke hearts, well drained

In a 10-inch square glass or ceramic dish, place oil, onion, garlic and mushrooms. Cover. Microwave at High 4-6 minutes. Drain well.

Stir in tomato paste, tomato sauce, wine, bouillon, basil, parsley, oregano, olives, salt and pepper. Add chicken pieces. Spoon sauce over top, making sure all pieces are covered with sauce. Cover dish. Microwave at High 10 minutes. Rotate dish ½ turn and microwave at Medium High (70% power) for 16 minutes.

Rearrange chicken pieces and sprinkle with cheese. Cover. Microwave at Medium High 16-19 minutes.

Arrange artichoke hearts around chicken pieces. Cover. Microwave at High 5 minutes. Let stand covered 5 minutes before serving.

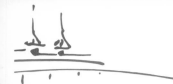

Country Chicken Pie

serves 4-6

2	cups cubed chicken, cooked
1	cup peas, fresh or frozen (thawed)
1	cup chopped artichoke hearts
1	cup carrots, sliced
1	cup corn, fresh or frozen (thawed)
1	6 oz. jar mushrooms or 6 oz. fresh sliced
½	cup butter
½	cup flour
2	cups chicken broth
1	cup white wine or Sherry
1	cup heavy cream
2	T. heavy cream
2	T. chopped parsley

Preheat oven to 350 degrees. Mix first six ingredients. Heat butter, whisk in flour and thicken with stock. Then add wine and bring to a brief boil. Add cream. Arrange vegetables and meat mixture in a shallow casserole (2 quart). Pour sauce over mixture. Place a pie crust (ready made Pillsbury or favorite recipe) over casserole. Bake for 1 hour or until crust is brown.

Wine: Serve a Chardonnay

Crumb Chicken Casserole

serves 8-10

1	8 oz. pkg. Pepperidge Farm cornbread stuffing mix
1	stick melted butter
1	cup cream sauce (can substitute a can of cream of mushroom soup)
1½	cups chicken stock (seasoned with cooked chicken)
1	(4 oz.) can mushrooms with juice (or 4 oz. fresh mushrooms)
4	cups cooked, diced chicken
½	cup chopped onions
½	cup chopped celery
¼	cup mayonnaise
⅛	tsp. cayenne pepper
	salt and pepper to taste
	sliced almonds

Preheat oven to 325 degrees. Blend melted butter and stuffing mix. Line a greased 2 quart, rectangular casserole with half the stuffing mix. Combine all the other ingredients, except almonds, and pour over stuffing mix. It will be soupy. Top with remaining half of stuffing mix and sprinkle with almonds.

Bake for 30 minutes. Do not bake longer, as it will be dry. Freezes well, uncooked.

Wine: Serve with a light California Cabernet or a Chablis

SEVENTH RACE

MEATS

COMMITTEE'S HANDICAP

1	VEAL WITH ORZO	SERVES 8
2	KENTUCKY BURGOO (DEAD HEAT)	SERVES 10
3	ROAST LAMB VINO	SERVES 8
4	DIAMOND BEEF FILET IN ASPIC	SERVES 8
5	COUNTRY HAM	SERVES 20
6	PORK MEDALLIONS IN FIG COULIS	SERVES 6
7	MARINATED PORK ROAST	SERVES 8-10
8	BEEF BRISKET BARBECUE	SERVES 15

Committee Selections   2-7-1

Kentucky bred entry 2, 5, 8

MEATS

Aniello's Braciola
(Stuffed Beef Roll in Tomato Sauce)

serves 4

2	lb. slice beef (top round steak cut about 1¼-inch thick)
	olive oil
1	cup Italian seasoned bread crumbs
4	oz. Italian dry salami, sliced thin
4	oz. Italian Provolone cheese, sliced thin
1	hard-boiled egg, chopped
4	T. vegetable oil
½	cup chopped onions
2	cups crushed tomatoes
2	cloves garlic, minced
1	bay leaf
	pinch salt
	pinch oregano
½	cup red wine

Butterfly steak by cutting almost in half. Open out flat and pound with a kitchen mallet to about ⅜-inch thick. Coat meat with olive oil, both sides; lay flat and spread with seasoned bread crumbs. Arrange salami, Provolone and egg over the crumbs. Roll meat end to end and secure with toothpicks.

In a skillet, heat oil and sear meat until evenly brown on all sides. Remove from pan and set on a plate. In the same skillet, adding more oil if necessary, cook garlic and onion over medium heat until light brown and soft. Add crushed tomatoes, bay leaf, pinch of salt, and pinch of oregano; bring to boil, stirring often. Put beef roll into an oven pan and pour mixture from skillet over it. Cover and place into oven and bake 1½ hours at 375 degrees. Remove cover and pour in wine; recover and return to the oven for about 15 minutes more. Let cool for about 40 minutes, then cut meat into 2-inch strips.

On a dinner plate, place a bed of thin spaghetti with slices of beef over it. Cover with tomato sauce and garnish with fresh parsley.

Wine: Serve with a Barolo, a Barbaresco, or a Nebbiolo.

Beef Brisket Barbecue

serves 15

5-6	lb. brisket
1½-3	oz. liquid smoke (not Wright's)
1	T. ground celery seed
2	T. Lawry's seasoned salt
2	cloves fresh garlic, minced
1	T. onion juice
1	T. paprika
1	small bottle Kraft Plain Barbecue Sauce-optional

2 DAYS AHEAD: Rub meat on both sides with liquid smoke, then the seasonings. Wrap airtight in heavy duty aluminum foil and place in the refrigerator overnight.

Bake in 250 degree oven for 5 hours. Chill thoroughly, preferably overnight. Remove foil and save juices. You should have approximately 1½ cups. Slice meat very thin or shred. Combine juices with Barbecue Sauce or one small bottle of Kraft Barbecue Sauce (plain). Pour over meat slices, cover and bake another ½ hour at 350 degrees. Serve as is or on buns.

Barbecue Sauce

4	T. brown sugar
4	T. vinegar
4	tsp. mustard, dry
1	cup catsup
	Tabasco to taste
	juice from roast

Combine these ingredient thoroughly and pour over meat.

Serve with the following wines: a white Zinfandel or a good table red Burgundy

Ballotine de Boeuf
(Cold Stuffed Flank Steak)   serves 10

2¼	lbs. flank steak (or 2 1 lb. steaks)
1	cup crustless white bread, torn into cubes
½	cup milk
¾	cup carrots, cut into ½ inch cubes
6	oz. Kentucky country ham, cut into ½ inch cubes
6	oz. ground veal
6	oz. ground lean pork
½	cup freshly grated Parmesan cheese
½	cup firmly packed shredded spinach
½	cup minced fresh parsley
2	eggs, lightly beaten
1	T. minced rosemary (or 1 tsp. dried)
1	T. minced fresh thyme (or 1 tsp. dried)
1	tsp. minced fresh sage (or ¼ tsp. dried)
½	tsp. salt
	freshly ground pepper to taste
½	cup chopped onions
¾	cup pistachios, toasted and skinned (or pine nuts)
2	cloves garlic, minced
	butter
4	T. butter
1	T. oil
1	carrot, chopped
1	stalk celery, chopped
1	onion, chopped
1	cup beef broth
½	cup dry red wine
2	tomatoes, chopped
1	bay leaf

Cut a pocket in flank steak, leaving a ¾-inch border on all 3 sides. (Have butcher do this for you.) Trim off fat. Soak bread in milk 15 minutes. Blanch carrots in boiling salted water for 2 minutes. Drain. Squeeze bread dry. In large bowl, combine bread, carrots, ham, veal, pork, cheese, spinach, parsley, eggs, herbs and salt and pepper to taste.

In a small skillet, sauté onions along with pistachios and garlic in butter for 2 minutes, but do not brown. Add to stuffing and mix well. Stuff pocket of flank steak and sew opening closed. Tie meat with string at 1-inch intervals.

Preheat oven to 350 degrees. In a large flameproof casserole, brown the steak in 2 tablespoons butter and 1 tablespoon oil over moderately high heat; remove meat. Add the remaining 2 tablespoons butter and cook carrots, celery and onion 5 minutes. Add beef stock, red wine, tomatoes and bay leaf. Return meat to casserole and bring liquid to boil. Transfer casserole to oven and braise the meat, covered, for 1¼ hours. Transfer meat to platter and allow it to cool; refrigerate. Strain pan juices into saucepan. Bring to a boil and reduce to ½ cup or until it is a thick glaze. When steak is chilled, brush it with this glaze and chill until ready to serve. Remove string and slice ½-inch thick. Arrange slices overlapping on a platter. Spoon a band of Light Tomato Sauce* around rim and place remaining sauce in a sauce boat. Decorate with a few sprigs of watercress.

*Light Tomato Sauce can be found in the Sauce section.

Wine: Serve with a Barolo, a Barbaresco or a Nebbéolo.

Beef Bourguignon

serves 4-6

2	lbs. lean beef, cut in 1 inch cubes
2	T. bacon drippings
4	medium-sized onions, sliced
2	T. flour
½	tsp. thyme
½	tsp. marjoram
1	cup beef bouillon
1	cup red wine
	salt and pepper to taste
1	lb. fresh mushrooms, sliced

Preheat oven to 325 degrees. In a heavy skillet, fry onions in bacon drippings until brown. Remove onions to a dutch oven. Brown beef in drippings until brown on all sides. Remove to dutch oven with onions. Sprinkle meat and onions with flour and seasonings. In skillet add bouillon and wine to deglaze and pour over meat. Cover and cook for 1-2 hours until meat is tender. Stir mixture occasionally while in oven and add more liquid if necessary, as beef should be covered with liquid at all times. Remove from oven and stir in mushrooms. Cool to room temperature and refrigerate overnight. Two hours before serving remove from refrigerator, bring to room temperature and cook approximately 45 minutes or until sauce is thick, dark and bubbling hot.

Serve with rice or noodles, crusty French bread and a tossed salad.

Wine: Burgundy.

Note: This dish is easily doubled or tripled. It may be made ahead and frozen, then thawed and cooked slowly until well heated.

Dead Heat Kentucky Burgoo

serves 10

1	fat hen, at least 4 lbs.
1-2	lbs. lean stew meat (beef, veal and/or lamb)
3-4	pints water
1½	tsp. coarsely ground pepper
½	tsp. cayenne pepper
2	small cans tomato purée
12	potatoes
4	large onions, chopped
1	large head cabbage, finely chopped
6-8	medium tomatoes, peeled and chopped (or 3 1-lb. cans tomatoes)
6-8	ears corn, cut off cob (or 2 cans cut corn)
1	lb. fresh carrots, sliced
1-2	T. salt
1	tsp. pepper
½-1	cup Worcestershire sauce

Cook chicken and other meat in water with coarsely ground pepper and cayenne pepper until chicken will leave the bones and the meat is very tender (about 40 minutes). Remove bones, shred meat and return to the liquid. Add tomato purée, potatoes, onions, cabbage, tomatoes, carrots and corn. Season with salt, pepper and Worcestershire sauce. Cook slowly for 2-3 hours, until consistency of a thick stew, stirring from the bottom to keep from scorching. Add water, if necessary, to keep from sticking. If you like additional vegetables, add 2 cups fresh cut butterbeans, 2 cups fresh sliced okra and/or 2 green peppers, finely chopped.

Wine: serve a Petite Syrah, a Zinfandel, a Rhone red or a Chianti

MEATS

Beef with Broccoli And Black Beans

serves 3-4

1	lb. flank steak
2	T. soy sauce
2	T. cornstarch
1	T. Sherry
1	tsp. sugar
¼	tsp. MSG (optional)
1	bunch broccoli tops (or ½ bunch tops with stems)
5	T. oil (divided)
½	tsp. salt
1	slice ginger root (¼ in. thick)
2	cloves garlic, finely minced
2	T. finely minced black beans (available in Oriental food market)
½	cup chicken broth

Cut flank steak in half or third, (depending on size) down the length of the steak. Slice the steak as thinly as possible, across the grain, holding the knife almost parallel to the cutting board. Mix the sliced steak with soy sauce, cornstarch, Sherry, sugar, and MSG if used and set aside. This may be kept 2 to 3 hours at room temperature or all day in the refrigerator.

Cut the broccoli into 2-inch long florets. If stems are to be used, peel them and slice into lengths about 2-inches long and ½ inch thick. Place broccoli in a large bowl and cover completely with boiling water. Cover the bowl and allow to stand for 2 minutes. Cool immediately by immersing in cold running water. When thoroughly cool, drain and shake out excess water. (If prepared early in the day, store in the refrigerator until needed.)

Heat 2 tablespoons oil in large skillet or wok. Add salt and broccoli and stir-fry for about one minute, or long enough for the broccoli to be coated with oil. Remove broccoli from pan and spread out on a flat plate.

Heat remaining 3 tablespoons oil in same skillet. Add the ginger root (which has been smacked with a heavy knife) and minced garlic; stir-fry a few seconds before adding the steak. Stir-fry the meat until most of the red disappears, then add black beans, broth and broccoil; continue to stir until sauce has thickened slightly and broccoli is heated. Serve at once with white rice.

Variations: Many vegetables may be substituted, such as: cabbage or bok choy, zucchini, onions and mushrooms, peppers, eggplant, green beans, celery, pea pods.

Hint: Fresh ginger root may be peeled, sliced in ¼-inch thick pieces and stored in dry sherry in a jar for months in the refrigerator.

Wine: serve with a light fruity red or a Rosé

113

MEATS

Celide's Meatballs And Sauce

serves 6

1	lb. ground beef
½	lb. sausage or ground pork
8	crackers, finely rolled
3	eggs
½	cup chopped parsley
2	tsp. salt
1	tsp. pepper
1	large clove garlic, minced
1	small tomato, peeled and chopped fine
½	cup grated Romano or Parmesan cheese
	oil

Combine and mix well all of the above ingredients. Form into balls. Lightly coat skillet with a little oil and brown meatballs on all sides. Drop browned meatballs into prepared sauce. Don't stir sauce for the first 20 minutes, or until meatballs rise to the top of the sauce. Then stir sauce and cook for another 40 minutes.

Sauce For Celide's Meatballs

2	cloves garlic, chopped fine
1	large onion
1	lb. fresh mushrooms, sliced
4	T. olive oil
3½	lbs. fresh tomatoes or 2 (1 lb., 13-oz.) cans tomatoes
1	can chicken broth
	pinch red pepper
1	tsp. dried basil, or 1 T. fresh chopped basil
¼	tsp. dried oregano, or ¾ tsp. fresh chopped oregano
1	bay leaf
½	tsp. salt
	pepper to taste
½	cup Vermouth, or any dry wine
1	(6-oz.) can tomato paste

Sauté garlic, onion and mushrooms in oil until soft. Add tomatoes, chicken broth, red pepper, basil, oregano, bay leaf, salt and pepper. Add wine and simmer for 20 minutes. Add tomato paste to simmering sauce and cook for 1 to 2 hours until thick. Add meatballs and cook according to directions for meatballs. Serve over vermicelli.

Wine: Serve with a Chianti, a Barbera, or a Barbaresco

Ribeye Roast

ribeye roast, whole or half
salt and pepper
oregano

Have roast at room temperature. Season ends and top with salt, pepper and oregano. Preheat oven to 550 degrees. Place meat in a flat pan or iron skillet and place in oven, uncovered. If cooking half a roast, turn down to 325 degrees and cook 1 hour. If cooking a whole roast, turn down to 350 degrees and cook 1 hour and 10 minutes. Remove from oven and cover with foil for 1 hour to finish cooking. (Will hold up to two hours)

Track Talk
Burgoo King, the 1932 winner, was named by his owner Col.
E.R. Bradley for his stew made famous by Lexington chef
James T. Looney.

Diamond Beef Filet In Aspic

serves 8

4	lb. filet of beef
2	T. oil
	salt and pepper to taste (optional)

One or two days in advance, roast the beef filet. Preheat oven to 400 degrees. Put beef on a rack in a roasting pan, spoon over the oil and sprinkle with salt and pepper. Roast until meat thermometer inserted in center registers 140 degrees (½ hour). Leave the beef to cool at room temperature. Cover and refrigerate.

Garnish:

4	red peppers
4	green peppers

Blanch the peppers for 45 seconds in boiling water; cool. Cut out in 1-inch diamond shapes (with a canapé cutter if you have one). Place diamonds together to form solid decorative pattern on top of beef, alternating green and red. Secure with toothpicks.

Aspic:

1	oz. gelatin
⅓	cup water
1½	quarts clear beef broth
	salt and pepper to taste

Dissolve gelatin in water. Heat beef broth, add gelatin and stir until smooth. Cool. Pour aspic through a strainer and make ¼ inch layer on a large platter. Chill until set. Place chilled beef on rack over a pan to catch drippings. Pour aspic over decorated beef. Continue pouring aspic slowly over beef until decorative top is well coated. Chill well before serving. Serve with Henry Bain sauce and/or horseradish sauce.

Wine: serve with a Pinot Noir, a Cabernet or a Rhone

Marinated Rolled Rib Roast

serves 10

2	cloves garlic (you may want to use 1 or 2 more)
1	tsp. coarse black pepper
4	T. minced fresh parsley
1	tsp. dried thyme
2	tsp. seasoned salt
3	tsp. grated lemon rind
6	dashes Tabasco sauce
4	T. olive oil
4	T. red wine vinegar
8-10	lb. rib roast (weighed before boning)

Mix garlic, pepper, parsley, thyme, seasoned salt, lemon rind and Tabasco sauce. Add oil slowly to form a paste, then add vinegar. Slash meat in several places and pour marinade in each one. Refrigerate up to 24 hours. Bake at 450 degrees for 30 minutes, reduce heat to 325 degrees and cook 20 minutes per pound for medium. Allow roast to rest 20 minutes. Use meat thermometer for accuracy. Make gravy from drippings using cornstarch, not flour.

Wine: serve with a Burgundy or a St. Emilion Pinot Noir

Eye Of Round Party Platter

serves 6

1½ or 2	lbs. cold cooked eye of round
1	large white onion, peeled, thinly sliced
½	lb. fresh mushrooms, sliced
½	cup red wine vinegar
1	cup salad oil
2	tsp. Dijon mustard
2	T. chopped parsley
1	tsp. salt
¼	tsp. pepper
	dash Worcestershire sauce
	pinch chervil
	pinch marjoram
	Horseradish Sauce:
½	cup sour cream
½	cup mayonnaise
½	cup yogurt
	prepared horseradish to taste

Cook eye of round in 300 degree oven, 20 minutes to the pound, or until cooked medium-done. Cool and refrigerate. Separate the onion into rings and drop into a small amount of boiling water until tender; drain well.

Slice the cooled, cooked eye of round very thin. Arrange the meat, mushrooms and onions in a large flat container. Combine remaining ingredients, for a marinade, and blend well. Pour over meat and let sit in refrigerator for several hours. (Overnight is even better.)

Serve sandwich style with party rye, regular rye bread or buns. Serve with the horesradish sauce.

Wine: serve with a Cabernet or a St. Emilion

Peppered Beef

serves 8 for dinner;
serves 20 for appetizers

¼	cup coarsely ground pepper
1	tsp. ground cardamon
1	4-5 lb. boneless brisket of beef
Marinade;	
⅔	cup soy sauce
½	cup vinegar
1	T. tomato catsup
1	tsp. paprika
3	cloves garlic, crushed

Combine pepper and cardamon, and spread evenly on sheet of waxed paper. Place beef firmly over the mixture, press down and turn beef over. With heel of hand, press pepper mixture firmly down into the meat.

Combine all marinade ingredients. Place meat in shallow dish and pour marinade over it. Cover and refrigerate overnight or for up to two days. The longer the better. Turn meat occasionally.

When ready to cook, remove meat from marinade and wrap in aluminum foil. Either bake in a 300 degree oven for 3 hours or put in smoker and cook about 10 hours, checking periodically so it doesn't dry out. Excellent served cold as hors d'oeuvres. Serve with party rye-bread or small buns.

Wine: serve with a Egni BiKaven, a Spanish Rioja or a good table red.

Germantown Beef

serves 8

5	lbs. or more, rolled rump roast
1	bottle red wine
1-2	bay leaves
1-2	garlic cloves, minced
1	cup beef bouillon
3-4	T. flour
1	jar currant jelly
	salt and pepper to taste
	sour cream mixed with horseradish

Put meat in large oven-proof (non-aluminum or iron) casserole. A heavy one with a heavy lid is best. Pour wine over top of meat and add bay leaves and garlic. Marinate overnight, covered, in refrigerator.

The next day, bring roast to room temperature. Place in a 250 to 300 degree oven and bake, covered with marinade, for 2-3 hours. Remove from oven, let cool and slice. Arrange slices in an oven-proof shallow serving dish.

Take bay leaves and garlic out of marinade. Mix marinade with ¾ cup of bouillon; pour over meat and bake 2-3 hours at 250 degrees. Remove meat and blend remaining ¼ cup bouillon with flour and add to meat juices. Add jelly, salt and pepper to taste. Arrange meat on platter and pour gravy over meat.

Serve with thick pumpernickel bread and side dish of horseradish mixed with sour cream to taste.

Accompaniments: Steamed onions, sautéed in butter with a touch of sugar; broiled mushrooms, baked apple slices; dill pickles and beer.

Wine: serve with a Petite Syrah, a "Bull's Blood" or other full-bodied reds.

Seldom Seen Brisket Hot or Cold

serves 8

4	lb. brisket of beef
	paprika
10	peppercorns
6	whole allspice
1	large onion, quartered
2	cloves garlic, slivered
1	large bay leaf, optional
½	can beef consommé
½	can water

Preheat oven to 375 degrees. Sprinkle top and sides of meat generously with paprika. Roast uncovered at 375 degrees for one hour. Remove from oven and add rest of ingredients. Cover tightly and bake at 325 degrees for two hours.

Slice thin and serve. This is also excellent cold on French bread or pumpernickel bread.

Wine: serve a good California red table wine

117

Tasty Trivia
Add a cup of water to the bottom portion of the broiling pan before sliding into the oven. The water absorbs smoke and grease.

Mike Best's Favorite Ham Glaze

3	heaping T. dark brown sugar
3	heaping T. granulated sugar
1	level T. orange peel, finely grated
½	tsp. ground cloves
½	tsp ground cinnamon

Mix well all ingredients for glaze. Place the ham, fat side up, after it's trimmed, of course, on a cookie sheet in a 200 degree oven. Give it a half hour or so to warm up, and apply about half of the glaze. Let it melt in, then apply the rest of the glaze. Don't let that second coat melt too far. For more penetration, score the ham before you apply the glaze. Word of caution: Not too hot, 200 degrees maximum. Not too long, 1 hour only, you'll dry that ham out if you overdo it.

I'm often asked, "How can I get some of the salt out of a Country ham?" My answer: "You can't!!" At risk of sounding anti-traditional, soaking a ham for 24 hours does not help. Neither does cooking potatoes with the ham or adding cola or 7-Up or vinegar to the water. If it's overly salty when you start, it'll be overly salty when you finish. Mostly, the older a ham is, the saltier and sharper the flavor. For a sweeter, not so salty, not so harsh ham, stick to a sugar cured ham, 8-10 months old.

Let me also give you some tips on how to store a Country ham you have purchased or received as a gift. A heavy paper bag, overlapped at the top and tied tightly, hanging free at room temperature is the best method. Attics are too hot, basements sometimes too humid. If you receive a Country ham in a box, make sure absolutely that the ham is not wrapped in plastic or in a plastic bag, as it will mold excessively and a strong, musty flavor will permeate and ruin the ham. If you have no place to hang it, return the ham to the box, tape it shut, and store it on a shelf in your pantry or closet. Don't refrigerate it, as that also causes mold problems.

Wine: serve with a Riesling or a white Zinfandel

See page 132 for Ham.

Lamb Marinated With Rosemary

serves 6

¼	cup soy sauce
	juice of 1 lemon
2	cloves garlic, minced
1	tsp. dried rosemary
	salt and freshly ground pepper
1	leg of lamb, boned and butterflied with fat and silver skin removed
1	small bag mesquite or hickory chips

Combine soy sauce, lemon juice, garlic, rosemary, salt and pepper. Place lamb in a glass or ceramic dish. Pour mixture over it and rub the marinade over the lamb. Marinate at least 30 minutes. Cook over charcoal (with mesquite or hickory chips added) or in a broiler for about 10-12 minutes on each side. The lamb should be cooked to medium or medium rare.

Wine: serve a Cabernet Sauvignon, a full bodied Zinfandel or a red Bordeaux

Country Ham, Chicken and Mushroom Timbale   serves 8

1	recipe crepes
3	chicken stock
11	T. semolina
2	egg yolks
4	T. butter (optional)
¼	cup Parmesan cheese
4	T. butter
3	T. flour
	salt and cayenne pepper to taste
1	cup chicken stock
2	T. heavy cream
2	egg yolks
1	cup chicken, cooked and diced
1	cup sliced mushrooms, sautéed
1	cup country ham, baked and diced
2	T. parsley

Crepes:

2	cups flour, sifted
½	tsp. salt
4	eggs
1	cup milk
1	cup water
3	T. butter, melted

1. Make crepes. Place all ingredients, except melted butter, into blender and blend at high speed for 1 minute. Add melted butter and blend again, briefly. Stop once or twice to scrape down sides. Let stand for at least 2 hours or overnight in refrigerator. Make crepes, they should be between 7 and 8 inches. Set aside. You may have some left over, freeze for later use.

2. Bring chicken stock to a boil. Add semolina and cook, stirring constantly, till it thickens and begins to pull away from sides of pan. Remove from heat and stir for 30 seconds to cool it a bit. Add egg yolks, stirring briskly and add cheese and blend. Add the optional butter.

3. Melt remaining 4 tablespoons butter in saucepan, add flour and cook a few minutes to eliminate raw taste. Gradually add the 1 cup chicken stock and season to taste with salt and cayenne. Cook until VERY thick, it should coat a spoon heavily. Add cream and then the egg yolks one at a time, stirring briskly. Blend in the country ham, chicken, mushrooms, and parsley. Set aside.

4. To assemble: Butter a soufflé mold (2 quart) cover bottom and sides with the crepes, overlapping them. Let crepes hang over sides. Spread a layer of the semolina mixture over the bottom, cover with another crepe and then spread chicken, ham and mushroom mixture over that and continue, alternating, until filled to top. End with another layer of crepe. Then fold the overhanging crepes over the timbale. CAN BE FROZEN AT THIS POINT. Thaw in the refrigerator overnight and bake in a 350 degree oven in a bain-marie (waterbath) for 60 minutes. Unmold onto platter. Slice as you would a cake. If you don't want to freeze this, but serve it right away, finish by baking in a 350 degree oven for 25 minutes in a bain-marie.

Wine: serve with a Chardonnay, a Riesling, or a Champagne

119

MEATS

Ham And Mushroom Crêpes

serves 4

1	small onion, finely chopped
3	T. butter
¼	lb. fresh mushrooms, sliced (about 1½ cups)
2	T. lemon juice
½	cup chicken broth
½	cup grated Swiss or Gruyere cheese
¼	cup whipping cream
1	T. cornstarch, dissolved in 2 T. cold water
	salt and pepper to taste
8	thin slices country ham
8	crêpes, made by your favorite recipe

Sauté onion in butter until soft. Add mushrooms which have been sprinkled with lemon juice and cook for one minute. Add chicken broth and cook over high heat, uncovered, for one additional minute. Lower heat and slowly add grated cheese and cream. Add dissolved cornstarch and stir until thick and let cool. (When mixture cools it should be thick enough to hold its shape when put on crepe). Add salt and pepper to taste. Preheat oven to 400 degrees. Lay a piece of ham on each crepe. Put about 3 tablespoons of mushroom mixture on top of ham. Roll and turn under ends of crepe. Put in a buttered ovenproof dish and bake about 15 minutes. Serve while warm.

Baked crêpes may be frozen. When taken out of freezer, they should be reheated about 30 minutes in a 400 degree oven.

Wine: serve with a full-bodied Chardonnay or a Chenin Blanc

Roulades de Jambon

serves 4

½	lb. cream cheese
2	T. coarsely chopped filberts, or pecans
4	T. country ham, ground
½	tsp. tarragon
1	tsp. chives, chopped
12	thin slices ham, boiled or baked
½	lb. tomatoes, peeled, seeded and cut in ¾-inch cubes
1-2	cucumbers, peeled, seeded and cut in ¾-inch cubes
½	honeydew melon, cubed in ¾-inch cubes
¼	cup raspberry vinegar or white wine vinegar
½	cup corn oil or olive oil
1	tsp. Dijon mustard
	salt and freshly ground pepper
½	tsp. tarragon
2	T. fresh parsley, chopped

Soften cream cheese and mix in the filberts, country ham, tarragon and chives. Spread in equal amounts on the slices of ham. Roll each slice and place seam side down in a shallow serving dish or platter.

Arrange the cubed tomatoes, cucumbers and honeydew melon over and around the ham roulades.

Mix the raspberry vinegar, oil, mustard, salt and pepper and tarragon in the processor or with a whisk. Pour the desired amount of dressing over the ham, vegetables and fruit. Sprinkle with the chopped parsley and serve.

Wine: serve with a Blanc de Noirs, a Sparkling wine (not too dry) or a Pinot Noir

Moussaka

serves 6-8

3	medium-large eggplants, peeled, cut lengthwise into ¼-in. thick slices
1	cup flour
1-2	cups olive oil
1-1½	cups finely chopped onions
1	tsp. finely chopped garlic
2	lbs. lean ground lamb
3	medium-sized tomatoes, peeled, seeded and finely chopped or 1 large can chopped, drained tomatoes
1	cup canned tomato purée
1	bay leaf
1	tsp. dried oregano, crumbled
½	tsp. cinnamon
2	T. chopped parsley
	salted and freshly ground pepper to taste
1	cup dry red wine or tomato juice
¾	cup freshly grated Kefalotiri cheese or Parmesan cheese

Salsa Besamel (Topping)

2	cups milk
1	T. butter
3	eggs
¼	cup flour
½	tsp. salt

Sprinkle eggplant slices lightly with salt, lay them side by side on paper towels, and weight down with large heavy platter or casserole. Let stand for 20-30 minutes, then dry thoroughly with fresh paper towels. Dip slices in flour and shake vigorously to remove excess.

In a heavy 12-inch skillet, heat ½ cup olive oil almost to smoking point, then brown the eggplant, a few slices at a time, on both sides, regulating the heat so that they color quickly without burning. Drain on paper towels. Add more oil to skillet as necessary.

Add another ½ cup olive oil to skillet and sauté onion and garlic over moderate heat for 8-10 minutes or until soft and golden. Stir in ground lamb and cook until no trace of pink shows. Drain fat and add tomatoes, tomato purée, bay leaf, oregano, cinnamon, parsley, salt, pepper and wine. Blend mixture well and bring to boil over high heat, while stirring frequently. Cook briskly until most of the liquid is absorbed. Taste for seasoning.

To prepare topping, heat 1½ cups milk and the butter in small pan until bubbles begin to form around the rim. Remove pan from the heat. In a heavy 2-3 quart saucepan beat the eggs, the remaining ½ cup milk, the flour and salt together until smooth. Place this saucepan over moderate heat and, stirring constantly with a whisk, slowly add the milk and melted butter mixture in a thin stream. Cook, stirring until sauce comes to a boil and thickens heavily. Set aside off the heat.

ASSEMBLY:
Preheat oven to 325 degrees. Spread half the egg plant slices to cover the bottom of a lightly greased 14 x 9 x 3 inch baking pan. Sprinkle evenly with ¼ cup grated cheese. Pour in meat sauce mixture and spread into corners of dish. Arrange rest of eggplant on top and sprinkle with ¼ cup cheese. Pour salsa besamel evenly over eggplant and sprinkle with remaining cheese. Bake in middle of oven for 30 minutes, then increase heat to 400 degrees and bake 15 minutes longer or until top is golden brown. Remove from oven and let rest 5-10 minutes before serving.

This dish is just as good, if not better, reheated. It also freezes beautifully.

121

M E A T S

Roast Lamb Vino

serves 8

1	**young leg of lamb (6-8 lbs.)**
	flour
1	**T. ground ginger**
	freshly ground pepper
	garlic-optional
1	**can jellied consommé**
2-3	**cups dry red wine**
	lemon, sliced paper thin
	parsley
½	**lb. carrots, quartered**
1½	**cups small whole onions**

Have butcher remove top skin from lamb and score as you would a ham. Dredge with flour, ginger and lots of pepper and garlic, if desired. Pat and smooth mixture over entire leg, seeing that ends and underneath are covered. Preheat oven to 450 degrees and bake for 15 minutes. Reduce heat to 350 degrees. With combination of consommé and wine, baste roast every 15 minutes, adding hot water if more liquid is needed. Sprinkle lightly with flour after each basting. Save about ½ cup basting mixture to add in the last 15 minutes of cooking. When roast is done, it will be very brown. Remove from roaster, and eliminate most of the fat. Add a little flour to absorb remaining fat, stirring constantly over hot fire. Add hot water to obtain desired thickness of gravy, completely scraping pan during process. Add carrots and onions about an hour before roast is done. Allow 25-30 minutes per pound cooking time for the lamb. Garnish roast with lemon slices and parsley.

Wine: serve with a Cabernet Sauvignon, a full bodied Zinfandel or a red Bordeaux

Marinated Lamb Chops

¾	**cup hot water**
½	**cup soy sauce**
¼	**cup honey**
2	**T. olive oil**
2	**T. lemon juice**
4	**cloves garlic, crushed**
1-2	**lamb chops per serving, depending on size**

Mix water, soy sauce, honey, olive oil, lemon juice and garlic. Marinate chops in this mixture for one hour or longer. Grill over charcoal to desired doneness.

Serve with: thinly sliced green peppers, onions and mushrooms steamed in some of the marinade. (Microwave the onions and peppers about 8 minutes on full power, then add whole mushrooms, full power, for 2 minutes.)

Wine: serve with a Cabernet Sauvignon, a full bodied Zinfandel or a red Bordeaux

Spring Veal, Or Lamb Ragout

serves 8

5	lb. boned veal rump roast or leg of lamb
¼	cup flour
2	T. oil
2	large onions, finely chopped
2	garlic cloves, finely minced
1	tsp. sugar
¾	cup white wine
3	medium-sized tomatoes, peeled, seeded, chopped
1	T. tomato paste
2	bay leaves
3½	tsp. rosemary, divided
½	tsp. thyme
1	cup beef broth
1	cup chicken broth
1	T. potato flour or arrowroot, mixed with 2 T. stock
	juice of ½ lemon
½	lb. mushroom caps, sautéed in butter
1	can artichoke hearts, quartered
½	cup small Nicoise black olives (optional)
2	small zucchini, cut into ½ inch cubes, sautéed in butter, or
1	pkg. (10 oz.) frozen peas, defrosted
2	T. finely minced parsley to use as a garnish

Cut the veal or lamb into 1½ inch pieces and trim off all fat, membranes and sinew. Place in an oiled, heavy roasting pan. Sear the meat under a hot broiler, turning each piece until brown on all sides. Toss the meat with the flour and again brown on all sides under the broiler. Transfer the meat to a casserole. Add the 2 tablespoons oil to the roasting pan and toss with the onions and garlic over medium-high heat. When wilted, add the sugar and sauté until the onions are nicely browned, continually scraping the bottom of the pan. Add the wine, bring to a boil and reduce to one half the original volume; add this mixture to the meat.

To a small saucepan, add the tomatoes and tomato paste; bring to a boil and cook for 3 to 4 minutes, or until some of the tomato juices have evaporated. Add the tomato mixture to the meat. Add the bay leaves, 1½ teaspoons rosemary and the thyme to the casserole. Add enough beef and chicken stock to barely cover the meat. Cover the casserole and set in a 350 degree oven for 1½ hours, or until the meat is just tender.

With a slotted spoon, remove the meat to a side dish. Strain juices into a bowl, pressing down on the solids. Return the pan juices to the casserole, or saucepan, and bring to a boil over high heat, reducing the sauce by ⅓ its original volume. Add 2 teaspoons rosemary and enough of the potato flour or arrowroot mixture to thicken the sauce slightly. Add lemon juice, a few drops at a time, until the desired flavor is attained. Add the sautéed mushroom caps, artichoke hearts, black olives and either the zucchini or frozen peas. Return the veal to the sauce, and reheat and serve. Garnish each serving with the chopped parsley. Serve with new potatoes or buttered, parslied noodles.

This is an elegant cousin of the stew that is perfect for large parties and easily prepared ahead and frozen. If prepared ahead or frozen, wait until an hour or two before serving to add the last 2 teaspoons of rosemary, the artichokes, olives and the vegetables.

Wine: serve with a full-bodied Chardonnay or a Cabernet Sauvignon

MEATS

Barbecued Spareribs

serves 4

4	lbs. pork spareribs, cut in serving pieces
1	lemon, thinly sliced
1	large onion, thinly sliced
1	cup catsup
⅓	cup Worcestershire sauce
1	tsp. chili powder
2	dashes Tabasco
2	cups water

Place spareribs in a shallow roasting pan, meaty side up. Place a slice of lemon and a slice of onion on each piece. Bake at 450 degrees for 30 minutes. Combine the remaining ingredients, and bring to a boil. Pour this sauce over the ribs and continue to bake at 350 degrees for 45 minutes to an hour more, basting every 15 minutes. Add more water if sauce gets too thick. Ribs are done when they cut and pull away easily.

Wine: serve with a dry white Zinfandel or a Beaujolais

Bourbon Pork Roast

serves 4-6

3	lbs. pork roast, boneless center cut
	juice of one lemon
2	T. brown sugar
1½	T. flour
1½	tsp. paprika
½	tsp. salt
	pepper to taste
¼	cup water
2	T. Kentucky Bourbon
2	T. dry Sherry
	chopped parsley
	bay leaf
¼	cup Kentucky Bourbon

Rub roast with lemon juice. Blend brown sugar, flour, paprika and salt and rub roast with this mixture. Place fat side up in small uncovered baking dish. Sprinkle with freshly ground pepper.

Combine water with Bourbon and Sherry. Pour over roast. Sprinkle with chopped parsley and place bay leaf in pan. Roast at 350 degrees for 2¼ hours. (or approximately 45 minutes per pound). After 1¼ hours flambé ¼ cup Bourbon and pour over roast. Baste frequently the entire time and add more water, if needed.

Note: The secret to a nice, moist roast is to use a small baking dish so that the liquid surrounds the meat to a higher level. The gravy remaining may be served as an accompaniment for the roast.

Wine: serve with a Blanc de Noir or a Sparkling wine

Mother's Stuffed Pork Chops

serves 4

4	thick pork chops, with pocket cut in middle
4	slices bread, any kind
4	slices onion, sliced thin
2	slices bread, halved
	salt and pepper to taste

Preheat oven to 325 degrees. In a large, flat casserole place whole bread slices. Put slice of onion on top of bread. Insert ½ bread slices in each "pocket" of pork chops. Place in a 325 degree oven, and cook 30 minutes. Turn each chop over (but not the onion and bread slice) and bake for 30 minutes more.

Wine: serve with a white Graves or a light white Italian

Marinated Pork Roast

serves 8-10

2	T. dry mustard
2	tsp. thyme
½	cup Sherry
½	cup soy sauce
2	cloves garlic, minced
1	4-5 lb. pork loin roast, boned, rolled and tied
1	10 oz. jar apricot preserves
1	T. soy sauce
2	T. Sherry

Combine dry mustard, thyme, Sherry, soy sauce and garlic. Marinate the pork in this mixture overnight in refrigerator. Place pork in roasting pan and bake uncovered at 325 degrees for 2½ to 3 hours. Combine apricot preserves, soy sauce and Sherry in saucepan. Heat until preserves melt; serve alongside pork roast.

Wine: serve with a Chenin Blanc, a Riesling or a Blanc de Noir

---

Country Terrine

serves 12-14

1	chicken breast, skinned and boned
¼	cup Brandy
¾	lb. fresh salted pork, sliced or blanched, cured salt pork, or bacon cooked in simmering water for 30 seconds and drained.
¾	cup minced onion
2	T. butter or margarine
1	tsp. green peppercorns in brine, drained
¼	tsp. crumbled dried bay leaf
⅛	tsp. ground allspice
⅛	tsp. ground nutmeg
1½	tsp. salt
¼	tsp. black pepper
¾	lb. veal, ground, excess fat trimmed
1	lb. ground pork
2	eggs
	bay leaves

Place chicken and Brandy in bowl; let stand 30 minutes. Drain and reserve brandy. Line a 6-cup terrine (or loaf pan) with salt pork or bacon, covering bottom and sides with a 2-inch overhang.

Sauté onion in butter until tender. Stir in peppercorns, bay leaf, allspice, nutmeg, salt and pepper. Mix veal, pork, eggs, reserved Brandy and onion mixture thoroughly in medium sized bowl. Pack ½ of mixture firmly in terrine, lay chicken breast down center. Pack remaining mixture in terrine. Fold salt pork or bacon over top. Cover terrine securely with foil. Place in loaf pan. Fill pan with 1 inch boiling water. Bake 350 degrees for 1½ hours. Remove foil and pierce center of meat. If juices are pink, bake another 15-20 minutes, or until juices are clear. Drain excess juices from terrine and cool. Cover and weight with heavy cans or a brick. Refrigerate overnight. Improves if refrigerated 2-3 days. Unmold, garnish with bay leaves. Serve with homemade mustard and thin sliced French bread.

MEATS

Pork Chops In Sauce

serves 6

	Dijon mustard
6	loin pork chops, ½ to ¾-inch thick
4-5	T. butter
1	large onion, thinly sliced
4	T. flour
1	can beef bouillon or consommé (undiluted)
1	cup half and half
	salt, pepper
1	tsp. dill weed

Spread mustard on both sides of chops. Sauté in butter and remove from pan when brown. Sauté onion in same pan. Add flour and stir. Blend in beef broth and stir until thick. Add half and half, salt, pepper and dill. Return chops to sauce. Cover and cook over low heat for 55 minutes. Serve with the sauce over rice.

Wine: serve with a Fumé Blanc or a dry Blanc de Noir

Pork Medallions In Fig Coulis

serves 6

6	dried figs
3	T. Tawny port
8	T. butter, divided
3	T. water
6	pork filets, 1″ thick and trimmed of fat
	salt and pepper to taste
3	T. red wine vinegar or raspberry vinegar
2	T. minced shallots
1	cup cream
1	T. butter

Remove stems from figs and cut figs into pieces and place in a small bowl. Cover with Port and set aside for one hour.

In a small skillet, place the figs and Port, a pinch of salt, 2 tablespoons butter and 3 tablespoons water. Cover and simmer gently for about 20 minutes, or until figs have absorbed most of the liquid. Purée in food processor with 2 tablespoons butter, and set aside.

Season pork medallions lightly with salt and pepper. Melt 4 tablespoons butter in a large skillet, and sauté pork about 5 minutes on each side. Remove to a warm platter. Add vinegar and shallots and 1 tablespoon butter to deglaze the skillet. Add cream and any juices from the pork, and reduce over medium heat 1-3 minutes. Remove from heat and whisk in fig purée. Season with salt and pepper.

Wine: Serve with a Beaujolais or a white Zinfandel

Pork in Phyllo Dough

serves 8-10

5-6 lbs. boneless pork loin

Marinade:
½	cup olive oil
10	cloves garlic, crushed
1	cup thinly sliced onions
¾	cup thinly sliced carrots
2	T. salt
1	cup dry white wine
1	cup white wine vinegar
1	cup dry Vermouth
1	tsp. basil
1	tsp. tarragon
1	tsp. thyme
1	T. peppercorns

Mushroom filling (recipe follows)
Phyllo dough
1-2 sticks butter, melted, for brushing
bread crumbs
egg wash of 1 egg yolk mixed with 1 T. water

Mushroom filling:
1	cup dried mushrooms
4	T. butter
½	cup chopped carrots
½	cup minced onion
½	tsp. minced basil
	salt and pepper

Sauce:
	reserved mushroom liquid
1	cup reserved marinade
3	cloves garlic
3	T. butter
3	T. flour
2	cups brown stock or canned beef stock
1	T. tomato paste
	salt and coarsely ground black pepper, to taste

One week before serving, cut roast neatly in half from fat side, trimming fat. Fold in half. Tie in several places with string. Place in glass or ceramic dish just large enough to hold roast.

In a large skillet, heat olive oil. Add garlic, onions and carrots and sauté until cooked but not brown. Cool. Combine with remaining marinade ingredients. Pour over meat. Cover and refrigerate, turning 3 or 4 times a day for 4 to 7 days.

Pat roast dry, reserving marinade for sauce. Untie and spread mushroom filling in center. Retie, place on rack in roasting pan and brown at 450 degrees for 30 minutes. Remove and cool.

Wrap roast with phyllo leaves on a surface covered with a damp towel. Brush each leaf with melted butter and lightly sprinkle with bread crumbs. If leaves aren't large enough, overlap to completely encase roast. Cover with at least 7 or 8 leaves. Make several small steam slits in dough.Brush with egg wash. Bake at 425 degrees for 20 minutes. Reduce heat to 375 degrees for 40 minutes, or until phyllo is golden brown. Let stand one hour. Return to oven at 300 degrees for 20 minutes. Slice and serve with sauce.

Soak dried mushrooms in hot water for 30 minutes. Drain, saving soaking liquid for sauce. Mince mushrooms. In a sauté pan, melt butter. Add mushrooms, carrots, onion and basil and sauté, stirring, until all moisture evaporates. Taste and adjust seasonings.

Boil mushroom liquid, marinade and garlic until reduced to ½ cup. Remove garlic. Meanwhile, heat butter in another saucepan. Add flour and cook, stirring until golden brown. Add stock, whisking. Stir in marinade-mushroom reduction and tomato paste. Bring to low boil, reduce heat and simmer 30 minutes, stirring occasionally. Add salt and pepper.

MEATS

Pork Tenderloin In Spiced Bourbon Sauce

serve 6

¼　cup Kentucky Bourbon
¼　cup soy sauce
¼　cup brown sugar, packed
3　cloves garlic, minced
¼　cup Dijon mustard
1　tsp. fresh ginger, minced or ¼ tsp.
　　powdered ginger
1　tsp. Worcestershire sauce
¼　cup vegetable oil
2　1-lb. pork tenderloins

Combine all ingredients, except pork with a whisk or in processor. Place tenderloin and marinade in a ziploc bag in the refrigerator overnight. Cook 4 inches from a hot charcoal fire for 15-25 minutes or until the pork has reached 165 degrees internally and has just lost its pinkness. Baste while cooking. Do not overcook or it will be dry. (The meat may also be broiled 6 inches from the heat for 16-18 minutes.) Baste often. Slice in ½-inch thick slices to serve as a main course or slice in ¼-inch slices to put on top of French bread for a picnic.

Wine: Serve with a white Zinfandel, a Sauvignon Blanc or a light red wine

Veal Chops Stuffed With Bel Paese And Sun-Dried Tomatoes
"Casa Grisanti"

serves 2

2　veal chops, 8-oz. each
2　oz. sun-dried tomatoes, packed in
　　olive oil
2　oz. Bel Paese cheese, diced
¼　cup flour
　　salt and pepper to taste
¼　cup olive oil
2　T. unsalted butter
1　tsp. minced garlic
½　tsp. minced shallots
2　T. Madiera wine
½　oz. dried Porcini mushrooms,
　　soaked 30 minutes in hot water
1　cup veal sauce (or ½ cup chicken
　　broth and ½ cup beef broth)

Preheat oven to 350 degrees. Cut a pocket in the meaty portion of each veal chop and set aside. In a food processor, rough chop the sun-dried tomatoes with a little of the packing oil. Add cubed Bel Paese and blend to a paste. Divide mixture into two equal portions and stuff veal pockets. Lay chops on their side and press with palm of hand to expel excess air and distribute stuffing evenly. Dredge chops in flour and season with salt and pepper. Heat olive oil in pan until smoking. Sear chops on both sides until golden brown. Place chops in baking dish; finish cooking in 325 degree oven for 30 minutes.

In a small saucepan, melt 1 tablespoon butter. Cook garlic and shallots without browning. Add Madiera wine to pan away from heat to avoid flaming. Add Porcini mushrooms and simmer 1 minute. Add veal sauce and bring to a boil. Add remaining butter and incorporate into the sauce.

Remove veal chops from oven. Coat with sauce. Garnish plate with medley of winter vegetables and gnocchi.

Wine: serve with a Barola or a Brunello di Montalcino

Veal Filets In Mushroom And Cream Sauce

serves 8

14	oz. fresh mushrooms
⅓	cup oil
1¾	cups heavy cream
¼	cup and 1 T. flour
8	veal filets (about 4 oz. each)
	salt and freshly ground pepper to taste
4½	T. butter
¼	cup chicken broth

Wash mushrooms quickly in cold water. Dry well and slice thinly. Cook in hot oil, in a large skillet, until crisp. Drain oil from pan.

Put cream in a medium saucepan and bring to a boil. Pour cream over crisp mushrooms. Bring to a boil and simmer until mixture is reduced and thickly coats a spoon.

Season flour and coat filets. In a large skillet, heat butter. Over medium heat, sauté veal on both sides, (approximately 5 minutes), until lightly browned. Remove veal to a warm plate. Remove grease from pan and add broth to deglaze. Add juices to cream. Check seasonings. Bring sauce back to a boil and pour over veal.

Wine: serve a full-bodied Chardonnay or a white Burgundy.

Veal with Hazelnut Butter Sauce

serves 6 (4 oz. each)

1½	lbs. veal scallops
	flour
	salt, freshly ground pepper
3	T. oil
4	T. unsalted butter
⅓	cup white wine
1	clove garlic, flattened
¼	tsp. dried sage, or 1 sprig fresh sage
½	finely chopped hazelnuts

Pound veal thin with a meat pounder or side of a plate. Season flour with salt and pepper. Pat veal with flour, shaking off excess. In heavy skillet, heat oil and 1 tablespoon butter. Sauté veal in batches over medium high heat until golden brown on both sides, about 2 minutes on each side. Transfer to serving dish and cover with foil. Keep warm in a 200 degree oven.

Deglaze pan with wine, scraping up browned bits of food. Add garlic, sage, hazelnuts and remaining butter. Stir frequently and cook until nuts are a light golden brown. Discard garlic and sage, if using fresh. Pour hazelnut butter sauce over veal and serve.

Wine: serve a full-bodied Chardonnay

MEATS

Broiled Sweetbreads For Four

4	sweetbreads
2	T. lemon juice
2 or 3	ribs celery with leaves (or sprigs of parsley)
¼	cup chopped onions
	a few peppercorns
½	tsp. salt
¼	cup flour
½	cup butter, melted
	paprika
4	pieces buttered toast
4	tsp. capers
1	T. tarragon vinegar
1	tsp. Worcestershire sauce
	parsley
4	lemon slices

Clean sweebreads under cold running water. Drain them well. Place enough water in a pan to cover the sweetbreads. Add lemon juice, celery or parsley, onion and peppercorns to water and bring to a boil. Drop the sweetbreads into it, lower the heat and simmer them for 10 minutes. Drain, and remove the skin and membrane.

Salt sweetbreads and dust with flour. Put in a shallow pan and pour butter over them. Dust with paprikà. Broil at 350 degrees until golden brown on all sides.

Place sweetbreads on toast and put 1 teaspoon capers on each one. Blend vinegar, Worcestershire in pan juices; mix well and pour over sweetbreads. Garnish with parsley and lemon slice.

Wine: serve a full-bodied Chardonnay or a dry Rosé

Triple Crown Paté

serves 14-16

1	lb. ground pork
¼	lb. boneless veal or ham, cut into ½-inch cubes
¼	lb. boneless pork, cut into ½-inch cubes
¼	lb. calves liver, ground
½	cup finely chopped onion
1	large clove garlic, minced
¼	cup Brandy
2	eggs, beaten
½	tsp. salt
¼	tsp. black pepper or ½ tsp. dried green peppercorns, crushed
8-10	slices bacon
1	bay leaf
1½	lbs. fresh mushrooms, optional

Combine first 10 ingredients (and mushrooms, if desired), mixing until well blended; set aside.

Line the bottom and sides of a casserole or soufflé dish with bacon, letting excess bacon hang over edges of dish. Spoon meat mixture into dish, pressing with the back of a spoon to firmly pack mixture. Place bay leaf on top of paté. Cover paté with overhanging bacon strips; cover dish with foil. Set dish in a larger baking pan. Pour enough hot water into larger pan to reach one-third of way up sides of dish. Bake at 350 degrees for 1½ hours or until done. Paté will be slightly firm; do not overcook.

Remove dish from water. Set another dish, slightly smaller, on top of paté and fill dish with pastry weights or cans to pack paté as it cools. Drain off drippings as it cools. When cool, remove top dish and weights; wrap paté securely and refrigerate at least 8 hours. Unmold paté onto serving dish. Peel away bacon, smoothing surface of paté with back of spoon, if necesary.

Serve with assorted crackers and mustard sauce.

Track Talk
Churchill Downs adds $200,000 to the Derby purse and
guarantees the winner at least $100,000. The 1974 winner,
Cannonade, took home over $274,000.

Veal Pesto With Orzo

serves 8

Pesto Sauce:

1	garlic clove, minced
½	cup pine nuts or walnuts
1	cup fresh basil
½	cup parsley
¼	cup Parmesan cheese
½	cup olive oil

To make pesto in the food processor, drop garlic through feed tube of running processor. Add pine nuts and chop. Add basil, parsley and Parmesan; process well. Add olive oil through feed tube of running processor. Reserve 3 tablespoon pesto for orzo.

4-5	lb. veal shoulder roast, boned
1	T. olive oil
	salt and pepper
2	carrots, chopped
2	onions, chopped
2	T. butter
¼	lb. salt pork, sliced
½	cup white wine
½	cup chicken broth
1	large can Italian tomatoes, diced
½	cup white wine
½	cup chicken stock
	parsley
	Parmesan cheese
½	lb. orzo, cooked al dente and drained

Set oven on broil. Spread pesto on flat side of veal; place other piece on top and roll up lengthwise. Tie every two inches with string. Coat with oil, salt and pepper. Brown under broiler on all sides. Remove from oven and turn oven to 325 degrees.

On top of stove in an ovenproof casserole, sauté carrots and onions in butter until tender. Put meat in casserole and arrange vegetables on top of meat. Cover meat with salt pork. Pour in ½ cup white wine and ½ cup chicken stock. Place covered casserole in 325 degree oven, and bake for two hours. Remove from oven and place meat on a warm platter lightly covered with foil. In same casserole, add tomatoes, wine and stock; bring to boil. Turn down to a simmer and reduce sauce by one third. Take out 1 cup of sauce and add to drained orzo with the 3 tablespoons of reserved pesto; mix well. Carve veal in ½-inch slices. Spoon orzo around veal and sprinkle with parsley. Pass extra sauce and Parmesan cheese.

Wine: serve with a light Italian red

131

Country Ham Cooked Mike Best's Way

To prepare your ham for cooking, you should scrub the ham with a stiff brush and cool water to remove any excess mold. Mold is natural on Country hams, so don't be surprised to see it. Then, immerse the ham in water, fat side up. If possible cover the ham completely with water. Bring to a rolling boil, then reduce heat to a slow simmer for three to four hours, or until the bones protrude from the hock 2½ to 3 inches and the hip bone looks like it's ready to fall out. Remove the ham from the water and let it cool for 30-40 minutes. Then remove the hip bone and trim the excess fat and dark surfaces. If you can't remove the hip bone easily by hand, then the ham needs more cooking. Return to the cooker for another hour.

Note: Larger hams take longer to cook, so don't be surprised if it takes 5-6 hours to cook a large ham.

Handling Hint: A rack with handles makes it easier to lift the ham from the water to see how it's coming along. If a rack isn't available, two pieces of string, tied crosswise, with loops on top, will also work nicely. Use HEAVY STRING.

For appearances' sake, some people prefer to glaze the ham after it is cooked. Use your favorite glaze recipe or try mine, It's easy!

See page 118 for Glaze.

Spiced Round of Beef

serves 40-60

20	lb. round of beef
½	cup salt
½	lb. light brown sugar
1	T. nutmeg
1	T. ground cloves
1	T. powdered mace
1	T. pepper
1	T. basil
1	T. marjoram

Bone beef and tie tightly with string. Combine salt, sugar, spices and herbs; and rub well into meat, poking the mixture into any pockets between fat and meat. Wrap meat in clean cheese cloth. Place in a large glass or ceramic container and cover tightly with plastic wrap and foil. Refrigerate 7 days. Turn meat and baste with pan juices every day.

To bake, place in roasting pan and bake at 325 degrees for 12 minutes per pound. This will be quite rare.

Serve hot with horseradish sauce or serve cold on yeast rolls. Slice very thin.

Wine: serve with a Syroh, a California "Burgundy" or a Spanish full-bodied red.

EIGHTH RACE

SEAFOOD

COMMITTEE'S HANDICAP

1	DISHWASHER SALMON	SERVES 12
2	LA PECHE SHRIMP	SERVES 1-12
3	RAVIOLI DOMINIC	SERVES 16
4	SHAD ROE 	SERVES 2
5	BILL'S SUNDAY SUPPER	SERVES 4-6
6	CAJUN BLACKENED REDFISH	SERVES 6
7	ELIZABETHTOWN, KENTUCKY TROUT	SERVES 10
8	AMBROSIA FROM THE SEA (MICROWAVE)	SERVES 4

Committee Selections   1-6-3

Kentucky bred entry 4, 7

Elizabethtown, Kentucky Trout

(Sixth Avenue)   serves 10

5	fresh Rainbow Trout
½	lb. lump crabmeat, picked over
1	red Delicious apple, chopped
8	oz. Kentucky country ham, finely chopped
3	oz. black walnuts, finely chopped
3	eggs
	pepper to taste
20	bacon strips
1	small bag of sassafras or mesquite wood
	watercress for garnish

Skin trout from the back of the tail to the head, leave filets connected at the dorsal fin. Remove head and tail, then slice off dorsal fin. Cut trout in half. In a bowl, mix the crabmeat, apple, ham, walnuts and eggs. Season with pepper. (these ingredients may be chopped and mixed in a food processor.) Stuff trout and wrap tightly with bacon.

Grill trout on medium heat until bacon is brown and crisp and bake in 325 degree oven until done. Serve with Bourbon Apple Sauce underneath. Garnish with sautéed watercress.

Wine: Serve with a Riesling, a Ziinfandel or a Blanc de Noir

Bourbon Apple Sauce

3	red Delicious apples, diced
1	onion, diced
3	oz. Kentucky Bourbon
2	cups veal stock or veal bercy sauce (or 1 cup chicken broth and 1 cup beef broth)
3	oz. cream
2	oz. pinenut butter (made from a few crushed pinenuts and softened butter)

Sauté apples and onions for five minutes until soft. Add bourbon and flambe, being careful not to have bourbon near flame when pouring. Add chicken and beef broth to other ingredients and bring to a simmer for 5 minutes. Then add cream and reduce sauce until it begins to thicken. Finish sauce by adding pinenut butter and then strain.

Dishwasher Salmon   serves 20

Believe it or not! Salmon cooked in the dishwasher is delicious, moist and a wonderful source of conversation.

Have a salmon cleaned and deheaded. Scale the fish. Wrap in a double layer of heavy aluminum foil, securing the seams to make tight. Lay packet on top rack of dishwasher and turn the dishwasher on, using the regular cycle. When the cycle ends, Voila! There you have it. A very easy, elegant fish. Serve it cold with a dill sauce. Garnish with fresh dill and cucumber crescents and halved cocktail tomatoes.

Wine: Serve with a no-oak style Chardonnay, a Chablis or a white Bordeaux

SEAFOOD

Flounder Dijon

serves 3-6

6   flounder filets
3   T. butter or margarine, melted
2   T. Dijon mustard
      paprika (optional)
      lemon and lime slices (optional)

Place fish filets in a lightly greased 9x13 inch baking dish; brush with melted butter. Spread 1 teaspoon mustard over each filet. Bake, uncovered, at 375 degrees for 5 minutes or until flounder flakes easily. Garnish with paprika, lemon and lime slices, if desired.

Wine: Serve with a Chardonnay or a Chablis

Steamed Fish

serves 4

4   green onions
1   whole fish (1½-2 lbs.) scrod, white
      fish, cod, perch, sea bass or
      flounder
3   T. peanut oil
2   garlic cloves, minced
3   slices fresh ginger root, finely
      shredded
2   T. light soy sacue

Cut 2 green onions in half and place on a plate. Place fish on top of onions. Fill wok with enough water to be close to the steamer rack but not touching it. Bring to a boil. Place plate on steamer rack and cover the wok. Steam 15 minutes.

When almost cooked, shred 2 inch lengths of 2 green onions and set aside. Heat 3 tablespoons oil in saucepan and sauté garlic and ginger until golden; do not let burn. Add soy sauce. Remove fish and plate from wok. Pour off juices. Sprinkle shredded onion over fish. Top with hot garlic, ginger, oil and soy sauce. Serve immediately.

Wine: Serve with a Chablis, a Fumé Blanc, or a Loire Valley White

Cajun Blackened Redfish

serves 6

6   8-oz. redfish filets
¾   lb. butter, melted in heavy skillet
1   T. sweet paprika
2½   tsp. salt
1   tsp. onion-garlic powders and
      cayenne
¾   tsp. white pepper
¾   tsp. black pepper
½   tsp. dried thyme and oregano
      leaves

Coat fish, on both sides, with melted butter. Combine the seasonings of paprika, salt, onion-garlic powders and cayenne, white pepper, black papper, thyme and oregano leaves. Sprinkle the fish with this seasoning mix. Transfer to hot skillet. Sauté for 2 minutes on each side and serve.

*Red snapper can be used in place of redfish. It is much thinner.

Wine: Serve with a Fumé Blanc or a white Zinfandel

Paupiettes en Papillotes
(Flounder)

serves 4

5	T. butter
12	oz. jar mushrooms, chopped fine, or ¾ lb. fresh
1	medium onion, chopped fine
2	T. Madeira wine
3	T. heavy cream
¼	cup parsley, minced
1	tsp. tarragon, dried
1	clove garlic, minced
¾	tsp. salt
½	tsp. cracked pepper
4	filets of flounder (or non-oily, mild fish)
4	large romaine leaves
4	T. Madeira, warm

Preheat oven 350 degrees. Melt 3 tablespoons butter in heavy skillet; when it foams, add mushrooms and onions and cook until they are transparent (15-20 minutes). Add wine and cook over medium heat, stirring often until all liquid evaporates. (You will have a creamy, semi-solid mixture.) Add cream and cook until it dissappears also. Stir in parsley, tarragon, garlic, salt and pepper. Cool.

Grease center of 4 large squares of heavy aluminum foil with 2 tablespoons of butter (keep edges of foil clean). Lay filets out flat and spread with filling on each. Roll up jelly roll fashioned and set each roll seam side down in a lettuce leaf that has been ribbed. Fold lettuce around fish roll, place each bundle in foil square, fold in edges to encase completely and keep edges of foil on top.

Set paupiettes in a shallow pan and bake for 20 minutes. Unwrap. Pour 1 tablespoon warm Madeira over each filet, and serve at once.

Wine: Serve a oaky Chardonnay or a Mâcon Blanc

Bonnie and Lucy's Salmon Scallops

serves 12-16

1	salmon, about 4 lb., fileted
1	cup chopped shallots
3	T. butter
2	cups dry Vermouth
6	T. lemon juice
2	cups chicken or fish stock
¼	cup drained, preserved ginger, finely chopped
2	cups whipping cream
¼	cup chopped fresh dill
6	T butter
	salt and pepper

Slice salmon diagonally across the grain into thin "scallops". Each scallop should weigh 3 to 4 ounces. Line a cookie sheet with parchment paper. Place salmon scallops on top.

Prepare sauce: Cook shallots in butter over medium heat until softened. Add Vermouth and lemon juice. Reduce until syrupy. Add stock and ginger; reduce again.

Blend in whipping cream and dill. Continue reducing until sauce coats a spoon. Swirl in butter. Taste and adjust seasoning, adding salt and pepper if needed. Broil salmon scallops until opaque. Remove to serving platter and top with sauce. Garnish with sprigs of fish dill or lemon slices.

Wine: Serve with a white Bordeaux or a Chardonnay

SEAFOOD

Grilled Salmon Stuffed With Rice

serves 12

1	8 lb. salmon, boned
⅓	cup butter
1	lb. fresh sliced mushrooms or 2 cups drained canned mushrooms
1	medium onion, chopped
1	cup chopped celery
¼	tsp. thyme
¼	tsp. salt
¼	tsp. pepper
	grated peel of one lemon
¼	cup lemon juice
1⅓	cups water
1¾	cups Minute Rice
2	grapefruit, cut in thin slices
	heavy duty foil, cut in double thickness, oiled
⅓	cup melted butter
1	tsp. lemon juice

Heat butter and sauté mushrooms; add celery, onion, thyme, salt, pepper, lemon peel, lemon juice and water. Bring to a boil; then add rice, cover, remove from heat. Let stand for 5 minutes.

Pat fish dry and stuff with the rice mixture. Any remaining rice can be heated in a microwave just before serving. Using a double thread, sew the fish closed. Oil the heavy duty foil well and line the foil with thin slices of grapefruit and put a layer all around fish. Seal foil and cook on covered grill at low heat for 2 hours. Baste often with lemon butter. Serve with dill sauce.

Note: 7 lb. fish should be baked 1 ½ hours
6 lb fish should be baked 1 hour

Dill Sauce:

2	T. Dijon mustard
2	T. wine vinegar
½	cup olive oil
¼	cup fresh dill or 1 ½ T. dried dill
	salt and pepper to taste

Put mustard and vinegar in blender and beat well. Add olive oil in slow stream while beating until sauce is thick and glossy.

Fold in dill and season to taste with salt and pepper. Serve sparingly. Makes ¾ cup.

Wine: Serve with a Pinot Blanc, a Semillon, or a Chablis

Tasty Trivia
To keep tulips fresh longer, puncture a small hole in tulip stem right below the base of the flower.

Daily Double Shrimp and Scallops

serves 6

¾	lb. sea scallops, cut in quarters
¾	lb. shrimp, cut in half
⅔	cup Vermouth, dry
½	tsp. salt
½	tsp. white pepper
1	onion, chopped
½	lb. sliced fresh mushrooms
4	oz. freshly grated Parmesan cheese
¼	cup dry grated Parmesan cheese
½	stick butter
2	T. flour
¼	cup cream
	fine bread crumbs

Combine scallops, shrimp, Vermouth, salt and pepper. Cook until tender, about 5 minutes. Drain and reserve liquid. Sauté onion and mushrooms until tender. Set aside. Blend reserved liquid with flour and then add cream. Add cheese and stir over low heat until thick. Butter 6 scallop shells or individual ramekins. Mix scallops, shrimp, onions and mushrooms into sauce. Spoon into shells or ramekins. Sprinkle with freshly grated cheese and bread crumbs. Bake in a 350 degree oven until mixture bubbles.

Wine: Serve a Chardonnay, a Mâcon Blanc or a Guvi

Sole Stuffed with Shrimp and Ginger

serves 4

8	small skinless filets of sole, about 1 ½ pounds
¼	lb. fresh shrimp, shelled and deveined
3	T. butter
¼	cup finely chopped onion
¾	cup finely chopped mushrooms
½	cup finely chopped celery
	salt and freshly ground pepper
1	T. finely minced fresh ginger
½	cup fine fresh bread crumbs.(made from 2 slices of 2 day old bread)
1	T. fresh, finely chopped coriander leaves
¼	cup heavy cream
1	T. soy sauce
½	cup chopped scallions

Preheat oven to 425 degrees. Chop the shrimp finely and set aside.

Melt one tablespoon butter in a saucepan and add the onion. Cook until softened and add the mushrooms and celery. Cook about one minute, add salt and pepper to taste, and stir in ginger. Remove from the heat and transfer to a mixing bowl. Add the shrimp, breadcrumbs, salt, pepper, and coriander to the mixture and blend well.

Rub the bottom of a shallow baking dish with one tablespoon of the butter. Place four of the fish filets, skinned side down, in one layer in the dish, and sprinkle with salt and pepper. Spoon equal amounts of the filling on top of each of the filets. Cover each filet with another filet, skinned side down again.
Sprinkle the tops with salt and pepper, and brush with the last tablespoon of butter. Place the dish on the stove burner and heat over medium-high heat until the butter on the baking dish starts to bubble. Put the dish in the oven and bake 10 minutes.

Combine the cream, soy sauce and scallions. Spoon evenly over the stuffed fish. Return to the oven and bake 5-10 minutes, basting occasionally, or until the fish flakes in the middle.

Wine: Serve a Riesling or a Sauvignon Blanc

SEAFOOD

Adlai Stevenson's Dish

serves 6

Once when Adlai Stevenson entertained the John Kennedy's at luncheon he served this dish. It was cooked in a casserole, but there is no reason to do this unless to heat it.

6	T. butter
½	lb. mushrooms, sliced in thirds
¼	tsp. seasoning salt
2	rounded T. flour
1½	cups milk
½	cup grated Parmesan
1	T. Worcestershire
¼	tsp. paprika
	salt, pepper to taste
¼	tsp. soy sauce or Maggi sauce
2	cups cooked shrimp
1	small can crab meat (drained)
2	hard boiled eggs (sliced)
½	cup sm. can artichoke hearts (optional)
¼	cup Sherry, Madeira (or more to taste)
½	tsp. sugar if wine is dry

In a dutch oven or deep skillet melt butter. Add mushrooms and seasoning salt. Stir and let simmer 3-4 minutes covered. Add flour and stir to make a paste. Slowly add milk, stirring until it forms a cream sauce. Cook over low heat 5 minutes. Add Parmesan cheese and stir again until smooth, turning heat very low. Add seasonings and stir in all other ingredients except wine. If using artichokes, cut in half or quarter if large; do not use them if herbs have been added. Let mixture heat and add wine to taste, adding sugar if needed. Turn off heat and cover. Pass rice with this, spooning the mixture over it and making this the main dish. If made ahead put in a casserole and cover. Heat in a 375 degree oven until mixture is hot and this takes 30-35 minutes. This mixture is also good in patty shells or toast boxes.

Wine: Serve with a Chardonnay, an Italian white or a good table white

Barbecue Shrimp

serves 12-14

8-10 lbs. jumbo shrimp, unpeeled (20 shrimp to a pound)

Sauce:

1	lb. butter
1	lb. margarine
8	oz. Worcestershire sauce
4	T. ground black pepper
1	tsp. ground rosemary
5	lemons, sliced
1	tsp. Tabasco
5	tsp. salt
4	cloves garlic, crushed

Preheat oven to 400 degrees. Melt butter and margarine in saucepan. Add Worcestershire sauce, pepper, rosemary, lemon slices, Tabasco, salt and garlic. Mix. Divide shrimp in two 9x13 pyrex dishes and pour sauce over. Stir well.

Cook 400 degrees for 15-20 minutes, turning once. Serve immediately.

Great cold the next day to make shrimp salad.

139

Creamed Shrimp with Artichoke Bottoms

serves 6

5	T. butter
5	T. flour
⅔	cup half anf half
¾	cup whipping cream
	season salt and fresh cracked pepper to taste
⅓	cup dry Vermouth
1½	T. Worcestershire
¼	cup fresh Parmesan cheese, grated
¼	lb. Gruyere, grated
	garlic powder
	cayenne
2	lbs. large shrimp, cooked, peeled, deveined
2	cans artichoke bottoms, drained, sliced in half
½	pound fresh mushrooms, sliced in half and cooked in butter

Melt the butter in a skillet, remove from the heat and stir in the flour; mix well. Add the half and half a bit at a time, stirring after each addition. Slowly add the cream and return to low heat, stirring constantly. Add salt, pepper, Vermouth, Worcestershire, Parmesan and Gruyere cheese, garlic powder and cayenne. Keep cooking and stirring until the mixture thickens. Taste it and adjust seasonings. At the end, add shrimp, artichokes and mushrooms. When the last three ingredients are heated through, garnish with chopped parsley. Serve over rice.

Wine: Serve a Chardonnay, a white Mâcon, or an Italian white

Grecian Shrimp

serves 4-6

2	cups onion, coarsely chopped
2	T. oil
2	cloves garlic
½	tsp. thyme
½	cup parsley, chopped
1-2	T. fresh dill, chopped, or 1-2 tsp. dried dill weed
⅛	tsp. dry mustard
½	tsp. sugar
2	cups canned tomatoes, chopped
1	cup fresh tomatoes, peeled, seeded, chopped
1	cup tomato sauce
2	lbs. shrimp, peeled and deveined
¾	lb. Feta cheese, drained

Cook onion in oil until it begins to brown. Add garlic, thyme ¼ cup parsley, dill, mustard, sugar, tomatoes and sauce. Simmer 30 minutes.
Place the shrimp in a 9 x 13 baking dish and pour the hot sauce over them. The dish may be refrigerated at this point or may be baked now. If refrigerated, bring to room temperature before baking.

Before baking, sprinkle the Feta cheese over the top. Bake in a preheated 425 degree oven 10-20 minutes, or until the shrimp are cooked. Do not overcook, or the shrimp will be tough. They should just lose their translucent look. Sprinkle with the remaining ¼ cup chopped parsley. Serve with a rice pilaf.

Wine: Serve an Italian white

SEAFOOD

Casserole of Shrimp in a Cream Sauce

serves 4

Cream Sauce:
2   T. butter
1½ T. flour
1   cup cream, heavy
1   clove garlic, minced
     salt and freshly ground pepper
¼   cup dry white wine
     juice of ½ lemon
1   small tomato, seeded and finely
      diced

Rice:
2   T. butter
½   cup finely chopped onion
¾   cup long grain rice
1   cup water
½   tsp. salt
     freshly ground pepper

Shrimp:
2   T. butter
1½ lbs. small raw shrimp, peeled
      (med. shrimp cut in half)
¼   cup freshly grated Parmesan
      cheese

Preheat oven to 425 degrees. For the cream sauce, melt butter in a heavy saucepan. Remove it from the heat and stir in the flour; mix well. Add the cream a little at a time, slowly at first. Return pan to the heat, cooking slowly and stirring constantly. Add garlic, salt, pepper, wine and lemon juice. Keep cooking and stirring until mixture thickens. Taste to adjust seasonings. Set aside.

In another heavy oven-proof saucepan, melt 2 table-spoons of butter. Add chopped onions and cook slowly until soft but not brown. Add rice and sauté, stirring until the butter is absorbed and the grains look transparent. Heat water and salt but do not let it boil. Add the water to the rice.Cover rice with a circle of buttered aluminum foil (cut the size of the pan) and cover saucepan with its lid. Bring the rice to a boil and place in a 425 degree oven for 17 minutes, then remove the pan from the oven and let it stand, covered.

Heat 2 tablespoons of butter in a skillet and sauté the peeled shrimp approximately 1½ minutes on each side, being careful not to overcook. Set aside.

Taste rice for seasonings and add salt and pepper. Divide rice among four individual buttered casseroles. Then divide shrimp and place on the rice. Add diced tomato to sauce and cover shrimp with sauce. Sprinkle the top of each casserole with Parmesan cheese and brown under the broiler.

Serve with a fresh green salad and French bread.

Wine: Serve a Chardonnay, a white Macon or an Italian white

Shad Roe

serves 2

1   pair fresh shad roe
4   slices bacon
½   lemon, divided

Fry the bacon, drain off all but 2 tablespoons of the grease. Fry the roe in the hot pan for about 10 minutes on each side. Reduce heat, cover, and cook 10 more minutes. Drain on paper towels and serve immediately with bacon and lemon wedge.

Wine: Serve with a white Rhone or a Verdicchio

La Pêche Shrimp

serves 10-12

1	lb. butter
3	bunches scallions, chopped
16	garlic cloves, chopped
½	cup chopped parsley
2	tsp. salt
½	tsp. pepper
1 ½	cups dry Sherry
60	shrimp, peeled
3	red peppers, julienned
	chopped parsley, garnish

To make Sherry-butter:
Melt butter in a saucepan. Add the scallions and garlic: cook 3 minutes. Add parsley, salt, pepper and Sherry; simmer 2 minutes and set aside.

Pour a bit of the Sherry-butter into a sauté pan. Sauté the shrimp in batches, adding more Sherry-butter as needed. Put the sautéed shrimp on a serving platter (shrimp is cooked when it turns pink). Sauté the red peppers in the pan; add the rest of the butter mixture and pour over shrimp. Garnish with parsley.

Wine: Serve a Muscadet, a Soave or an Orvieto

Louisiana Shrimp

serves 6-8

2	lbs. shrimp
½	large lemon
1	small pod red pepper
5	whole cloves
5	whole allspice
1	small bay leaf
4	T. butter
1	medium onion, finely chopped
1	green pepper, finely chopped
1	red bell pepper, diced (or 1 canned pimiento)
¼	lb. fresh mushrooms, halved (or 1 small can mushroom halves)
1	small clove garlic, minced
2	medium tomatoes, peeled and chopped
1	small can tomato paste
	salt and cayenne pepper to taste
2	T. butter
⅓	cup Sherry

Rinse shrimp in cold water. Put in a pot and cover with cold water to which the juice and rind of ½ lemon have been added, along with the red pepper, cloves, allspice and bay leaf. Bring almost to a boil, remove from heat and cool in the liquid. Reserve 1 cup shrimp liquor. Shell and devein shrimp. In a large skillet, melt butter. Sauté onion, bell pepper, (or pimiento) mushrooms and garlic. Add tomatoes and cook uncovered until thoroughly blended. Add tomato paste and reserved cup of shrimp liquor, salt and cayenne. Boil all together for 10 minutes. Taste for seasoning. While this is cooking, stir the shrimp around in a little butter until hot. Then add to sauce. Heat thoroughly and just before serving add ⅓ cup good Sherry. Serve over fluffy rice.

Crabmeat Blanche

serves 4

7½	T. butter
7½	T. flour
2½	cups milk
	salt and papper
2	T. butter
1	lb. fresh mushrooms, chopped
1	lb. fresh backfin crabmeat
4	English muffins
	anchovy paste
1	cup fresh bread crumbs

In a saucepan, melt 7½ tablespoons butter; add flour and let cook until bubbly. Add milk slowly, stirring with a whisk. Cook over low heat until thick. Season with salt and pepper to taste. Set aside. Sauté mushrooms in 2 tablespoons of butter, about 5 minutes. Add the crabmeat and mushrooms to the cream sauce. Split English muffins; toast lightly and butter. Spread the anchovy paste on the split muffins and divide crabmeat mixture on top. Sprinkle muffins with bread crumbs; dot with butter and bake 15 minutes at 350 degrees. Serves 8 as a first course and 4 as a main dish.

Maryland Crab Cakes

serves 2

1	lb. backfin lump crabmeat
2	T. mayonnaise
1	egg, beaten
⅛	tsp. cayenne
2	T. chopped parsley
½	cup bread crumbs
½	stick butter

Carefully check lump crabmeat for pieces of shell and remove. In a large bowl, add crab, mayonnaise, egg, cayenne, and parsley. Very gently mix with a fork. Divide crab mixture in four parts to make 4 crab cakes and coat cakes with bread crumbs. Refrigerate for at least one hour. Remove from refrigerator and sauté in butter in a large skillet over medium heat until golden brown. Serve at once.

Suggested accompaniments: coleslaw and Elkridge tomatoes (See recipe in vegetable section)

Wine: Serve with a Muscadet, a Sancerre or a Sauvignon Blanc

Fish Creole

(Microwave)

serves 4

1	lb. sole or haddock filets, defrosted
1	can 8-oz. tomato sauce
1	can 2-oz. sliced mushrooms, drained
½	green pepper, diced
1	stalk celery, diagonally sliced
3	T. water
1½	T. instant minced onion
1	tsp. chicken bouillon granules

Rinse fish and pat dry with paper towels. In 12 x 8 x 2 inch dish arrange fish with thickest pieces to outside edges of dish.
In 1 quart glass measure stir together tomato sauce, mushrooms, green pepper, celery, water, minced onion and bouillon. Pour evenly over fish. Cover tightly with plastic wrap, turning back one corner to vent. Microwave at High 8-10 minutes, rotating dish ½ turn after 4 minutes, until fish flakes easily with fork. Let stand about 5 minutes before serving to blend flavors.

This recipe has the advantage of being low in calories.

Fried Oysters Country Style

serves 4

1	pint oysters, well drained
1	cup plain white cornmeal
¾	tsp. salt
½	tsp. pepper
1	cup cooking oil
	lemon wedges

Mix cornmeal, salt and pepper. Dip oysters in corn-mixture. Heat oil and fry oysters until golden brown. Serve with lemon wedges.

Wine: Serve a good table white or an Italian white with a slight frizzante

Pasta Primavera with Seafood and Basil Cream

serves 20-24

Pasta:
(Prepare 1-3 days ahead)
1	lb. Italian fettucine, broken into 2 in. pieces
	salt
3	T. light olive oil
1	T. white wine vinegar
½	T. Spanish Sherry wine vinegar
	freshly ground pepper, and salt

Pasta: Drop pasta into about 8 quarts of boiling, salted water. Boil rapidly until pasta is tender but still firm to the bite. Drain in colander, rinse with cold water and drain again. Transfer to large bowl. Add oil and vinegars and toss lightly. Season to taste with salt and pepper; toss again. Cover and refrigerate.

Vegetables (Prepare 1-2 days ahead)
16	very thin asparagus spears, trimmed of tough ends, cut into 1½ in. lengths
2-3	cups broccoli florets, cut in bite-size pieces
2-3	cups fresh peas, or frozen tiny peas, defrosted
8	green onions
1	pint small cherry tomatoes
1	lb. fresh young spinach leaves

Vegetables: Separately steam asparagus and broccoli just until crisp-tender; DO NOT OVERCOOK. Rinse in cold water to stop the cooking process. Steam fresh peas in the same manner; rinse in cold water. Store in plastic bags in the refrigerator. Mince 8 green onions and halve cherry tomatoes. Transfer to small bowl and refrigerate. Rinse spinach leaves, and wrap in plastic and chill.

Seafood (Prepare no more than 1 day ahead)
2	lb. bay or sea scallops
2	lb. uncooked large shrimp
3	T. olive oil
1	T. white wine vinegar
½	T. Spanish Sherry wine vinegar
1	clove garlic, minced
2	green onions, minced
	salt and freshly ground pepper

Seafood: If using sea scallops, cut in half. Gently poach scallops in water that is just below a boil until barely firm, about 2 minutes. Drain and rinse with cold water. Poach shrimp in their shells in the same manner just until they turn pink and are firm but not rubbery. Rinse with cold water. Shell and devein; cut shrimp in half. Transfer seafood to another large bowl. Add oil, vinegars and garlic; toss gently. Refrigerate fish. Reserve green onions.

SEAFOOD

Track Talk
The youngest jockey to win the Triple Crown is native
Kentuckian Steve Cauthen on Affirmed in 1978.

Basil Cream: (prepare 1 or 2 days ahead)
⅓   cup white wine vinegar
2   T. Dijon mustard
½   cup tightly packed fresh basil
       leaves, or 3-4 T. dried basil
1-2   large garlic cloves
⅓   cup vegetable oil
½   cup sour cream
½   cup whipping cream
3   T. minced fresh parsley or double
       if no fresh basil

Combine vinegar, mustard, basil and garlic in processor and mix until almost smooth. With machine running, drizzle in oil. Add sour cream, whipping cream, and parsley and purée until smooth. Season to taste with salt and pepper. Refrigerate until shortly before serving. Stir through several times before pouring into serving bowl. If thickening is needed, add more sour cream.

Assembly: About 30 minutes before serving, arrange spinach leaves around outer edge of a large serving platter. Gently toss pasta with vegetables and reserved green onion-tomato mixture. Arrange in center of platter with spinach leaves as border. Make well in center of pasta. Drain seafood. Toss with remaining green onion and season to taste with salt and pepper. Mound in center of pasta. Drizzle all with some basil cream and serve basil cream in a pitcher on the side.

Wine: Serve with a Soave, an Orvietto, a Verdiccio or a Chablis

New Orleans Seafood Gumbo

serves 12

3   cups shrimp (cut in 3 parts if
       jumbo shrimp)
3   cups red snapper
2   cups cooking oil
1   cup chopped onions
1   cup chopped green peppers
1   cup chopped celery
4   garlic cloves, chopped fine
3   bay leaves
1   pinch ground thyme
3   T. gumbo filé
½   cup flour
3   cups chopped, peeled tomatoes
1½   pts. select oysters, uncooked

Cook raw shrimp in enough water to cover. Cook until they reach the boiling point and remove when opaque (if shrimp in the shell is used, use the same cooking method as above, let cool in shell, peel off shell and devein.) In the same stock cook 1 or 2 pounds of red snapper to the same point as the shrimp. Remove fish and save stock. Strain liquid and set aside. Remove all bones from fish.

In a saucepan or skillet pour 1 cup oil and let heat to a medium temperature; add onions, green peppers, celery, garlic, bay leaves and thyme. Sauté until tender. Set aside. Into another skillet pour the rest of the oil and heat to a medium temperature. Add flour, stirring regularly to keep from burning. Stir until light brown in color and remove from heat. In same skillet add tomatoes and cook 5 minutes; stirring to keep from sticking. In a large container add all ingredients from both skillets plus 4 cups of fish-shrimp stock and cook to boiling point, stirring to keep from sticking. Boil 10 minutes. Add filé powder, shrimp, fish and oysters and simmer until oysters are cooked. If sauce is too thick add more fish stock.

Serve over rice.

Wine: Serve a Muscadet or a Sauvignon Blanc

Scallop Kebobs

serves 4

Marinade:
1	cup white wine
2	T. oil
1	T. tarragon
2	tsp. chopped mixed herbs (fresh, if possible - thyme, oregano basil, parsley (use ½ the amount if dried)
1½	lbs. sea scallops
6	T. butter, melted for brushing freshly ground black pepper paprika

Combine the wine, oil, tarragon and mixed herbs; pour over the scallops and mix well. Marinate in the refrigerator for 2-8 hours. (I use a Ziploc.)

Light the grill. Drain the scallops and thread them onto kebob skewers. Brush them generously with melted butter, sprinkle with pepper and paprika and broil or grill them about 3-inches from the heat, approximately 4-5 minutes, or longer if very large. Turn them once to baste, and brush often with melted butter.

Serve on a bed of rice, garnish with lemon wedges. Pass Béarnaise sauce, if desired, separately.

Wine: Serve with a Chardonnay or an Italian white

Ambrosia from the Sea
Microwave

serves 4

3	T. butter
2	T. minced green onion
1	lb. sole or flounder filets, cut into serving pieces*
1½	cups sliced fresh mushrooms
¾	cup dry white wine
2	T. flour
¼	cup heavy cream
1	tsp. salt
⅛	tsp. pepper
½	tsp. lemon juice
¾	cup shredded Swiss cheese

Place butter in 12 x 8 x 2-inch dish. Melt in microwave oven 1½ minutes. Spread butter over bottom of dish and sprinkle with onions. Arrange filets over onions and cover with mushrooms. Pour wine over top. Cook 7-9 minutes or until fish flakes with a fork. Cook at High.

Combine flour, cream, salt and pepper in 1 quart casserole until smooth. Carefully drain hot liquid from fish into cream mixture and stir well. Cover fish to keep warm while cooking sauce. Cook sauce mixture in microwave oven 2 to 3 minutes, stirring every minute.

Stir lemon juice into sauce. Pour sauce over fish and sprinkle cheese on top. Continue to cook in oven 3-5 minutes until cheese has melted. Garnished with parsley sprigs.

* A 1 pound package of frozen fish filets may be thawed in your microwave if package is made of all paper. Place unopened package in oven and cook on High for 3 minutes, turning every minute. Thawed fish should be still cold and slightly icy.

SEAFOOD

Poached Fish with Vegetables

serves 2-3

⅔ cup dry white wine or rosé
⅓ cup lemon juice
¼ tsp. salt
½ tsp. dried dill weed
12 whole peppercorns
3 medium carrots, scraped and sliced
2 large celery stalks, sliced
1 small onion, sliced
1 lb. orange roughy or flounder filets

In 8-inch square microwave dish, place wine, lemon juice, salt, dill and peppercorns. Stir to dissolve salt. Add vegetables and stir again. Cover with plastic wrap and microwave at High for 8-10 minutes, until carrots are still slightly firm when pierced with a fork.

Add fish filets, thickest area to edges of dish, and spoon vegetables over top. Recover and continue microwaving at High for 1 to 3 minutes, until fish turns opaque and thin areas flake easily.
Let stand several minutes, covered, to finish cooking the thick areas, and so the fish can absorb the flavors.

With microwaving, fish does not need to be completely covered with liquid to keep it moist. The acid in the wine and lemon juice helps reduce the odor of fish.

Bill's Sunday Supper

serves 4-6

4 T. oil
1 large garlic clove, slivered
1 medium white onion, diced
1 turnip, diced
1 carrot, diced
2 stalks celery, diced
1 red pepper, diced
1 cup green beans (fresh)
1½ qts. fish stock
1 cup dry Sherry or white wine
1 tsp. crushed green peppercorns
2 tomatoes, peeled, seeded and diced
1 lb. peeled shrimp
1 cup peas (fresh)

Heat large pot (Dutch oven-type), add oil, then garlic and onion. Cook until slightly brown on edges. Add turnip, carrot, celery, red pepper and beans. Cook for 15 minutes. Add fish stock, Sherry and peppercorns. Simmer for 15 minutes. Add shrimp, tomatoes and peas and cook for 10 minutes more.

Serve with a Sauvignon Blanc or a white Zinfandel

Ravioli Dominic
Seafood Stuffing:
Prepare ahead and chill

Thanks to Dominic Serratore
Chef Proprietor of Dittos Food & Drink
Louisville, Kentucky

1/4	oz. Olive Oil
1	oz. shallots (fine dice)
5	oz. small shrimp, peeled and cleaned
5	oz. scallops, chopped
1 1/2	oz. mild white fish
5	oz. crabmeat, flaked (can sub imitation crab)
1/2	oz. dry white wine
3/4	oz. cream sauce, chilled
3/4	oz. clam juice (thickened with corn starch)
	pinch basil, thyme, oregano
	pinch white pepper, salt
3/4	oz. Italian seasoned bread crumbs
	pinch chopped parsley
3/4	oz. grated Parmesan cheese

Stuffing: In large saute pan over moderate heat, cook shallots in olive oil. Add shrimp, scallops and fish. Stir often 3 - 5 minutes. Do not brown. When seafood has attained a whitish color, push to one side and reduce remaining liquid to a glaze.

Add crab, wine, cream sauce, clam juice and seasonings to liquid in pan. Cook until thoroughly heated and liquid is reduced.

Cool slightly before adding remaining ingredients. If too moist add more bread crumbs. Form into 1 oz. balls and move to refrigerator while making pasta.

Ravioli

1	cup unbleached all-purpose flour
	pinch salt
1	egg
	A little water, if necessary
	*Eggwash consists of water and egg in equal amounts.

Mix good quality flour and salt. Make a well and add beaten egg. Working with fingertips, blend flour and egg from center out, gathering flour from the sides. Add a few drops of water to bring it together as a mass.

Turn out on table and knead several minutes to a very firm, smooth and strong dough. If more flour is needed add early in the process. Knead 10-15 minutes then cover to prevent dry skin from forming and let it rest 45 minutes before rolling and cutting.

Use small amounts of dough to prevent drying out. Roll as thin as possible. After rolling, lightly flour and cut into 12" to 18" sheets. Brush with eggwash* and place 1 oz. balls 1 1/2" apart. Lay piece of ravioli sheet over top and depress air with hand by forming (a half heart) around stuffing balls. Cut with 3" round ravioli cutter. Crimp with small fork tines. Do not puncture into filling. Refrigerate on floured baking sheet until ready to use. Cook stuffed pastas, made with very thin dough, for 3 minutes in gently boiling salted water.

Sauce for Ravioli

2	shallots (finely diced)
1	oz. clarified butter
1 1/2	cups sweet shellfish stock (or clam juice lightly thickened)
1 1/2	cups heavy cream
	Salt, white pepper, to taste

In 10" saucepan saute shallots in butter over medium heat. Do not brown shallots. Add thickened stock or clam juice and cream. Bring to vigorous boil and adjust seasonings. Yield 2 cups or 1 oz. of sauce per ravioli. Place 4 ozs. of hot sauce per plate. Top with four cooked ravioli per person.

Wine: Serve with a Chardonnay

Optional garnishes of steamed clams, shrimp or scallops will enhance presentation.

NINTH RACE

VEGETABLES

COMMITTEE'S HANDICAP

1	ADELINE'S AND JANE'S CORN PUDDING	SERVES 6
2	CUCUMBERS WITH SNOW PEAS	SERVES 6
3	CHESTNUTS AND POTATOES	SERVES 6
4	BOURBON YAMS	SERVES 4
5	ARTICHOKES, STUFFED SICILIAN	SERVES 4
6	STUFFED CARROTS	SERVES 4-6
7	POTATO-ZUCCHINI PANCAKES	SERVES 4
8	FRIED GREEN TOMATOES	SERVES 8

Committee Selections   6-3-1

Kentucky bred entry 1, 4, 8

VEGETABLES

Artichokes Au Gratin

serves 6-8

2   9-oz. pkgs. frozen artichoke
       hearts
¼   cup margarine
⅓   cup flour
¾   tsp. salt
¼   tsp. dry mustard
1½   cups milk
1   slightly beaten egg
½   cup grated Swiss cheese
½   cup crushed Pepperidge Farm
       stuffing
       paprika

Preheat oven to 450 degrees. Cook artichokes as directed on package; drain, reserving ½ cup liquid. Melt margerine in saucepan. Stir in flour, salt and mustard. Gradually stir in milk and ½ cup artichoke liquid, stirring until thickened over low heat. Remove from heat, and stir sauce gradually into egg and half of cheese; blend well. Put artichokes in single layer in 9x12x2 inch baking dish. Pour sauce over to cover. Sprinkle with rest of cheese, then stuffing and paprika. Bake 15 minutes.

Artichoke Hearts or Brussels Sprouts with Gorgonzola

serves 6

¼   cup minced shallots
2   large garlic cloves, minced
¼   cup olive oil
2   9-oz. pkgs. frozen artichoke
       hearts, cooked and drained (or
       2 lbs. brussels sprouts, cleaned,
       "x" in bottom, parboiled 4-9
       minutes to crisp-tender)
2   T. fresh lemon juice
⅓   cup finely crumbled Gorgonzola
       or other Blue cheese
1   T. minced fresh parsley
½   cup walnut halves, toasted

In large skillet cook the shallots and the garlic in the oil over moderate heat, stirring, for 5 minutes. Add the artichoke hearts, and cook the mixture over moderately high heat until it is heated through. Add the lemon juice, remove the skillet from the heat, and add the Gorgonzola. Toss the mixture until the Gorgonzola is melted; transfer to individual serving plates and garnish with the parsley and walnut halves.

Broccoli Bake

serves 6-8

2   10-oz. pkgs. frozen broccoli, thaw
       and drain
1   cup seasoned medium white
       sauce or 1 cup Cream of
       Mushroom Soup
½   cup fresh mushrooms, sliced
1   cup sour cream
       Parmesan cheese, grated
2   T. butter

Preheat oven to 350 degrees. Arrange broccoli in a 9 x 12 inch casserole. Combine sauce or soup, mushrooms and sour cream. Spread over broccoli and sprinkle generously with Parmesan cheese. Dot with butter. Bake 30-45 minutes until thoroughly heated and slightly brown on top.

Carciofi Imbottiti Alla Siciliana

(Stuffed Artichokes Sicilian)   serves 4

1	cup herbed bread crumbs
4	T. grated Romano or Parmesan cheese
3	T. chopped parsley
2	large cloves garlic, minced salt and pepper
½	cup olive oil, approx.
4	large artichokes, ends of leaves snipped off

Mix bread crumbs, cheese, parsley, garlic, salt and pepper. Divide stuffing into 4 portions. Distribute one portion between the leaves of each artichoke, using one portion per artichoke. Select large saucepan for placing artichokes upright, fitting snuggly. Pour 1 or 2 tablespoons of olive oil over each artichoke. Put 2 or 3 tablespoons olive oil in the bottom of the saucepan. Fill saucepan with ½ inch water.

Cook very slowly, at a simmer, in tightly covered saucepan until a leaf comes out easily when pulled. It should take approximately 40 minutes.

Asparagus Gratin

serves 6-8

3	lbs. fresh asparagus
1	cup sliced green onion, both green and white parts
1	cup butter
½	tsp. thyme
½	tsp. rosemary
2	T. chopped red peppers
½	tsp. salt
½	cup Chablis
2	T. freshly grated Parmesan cheese

Preheat oven to 350 degrees. Steam asparagus until tender yet crisp, 5-8 minutes, no more. Place in flat buttered casserole. Sauté onion in butter. Stir in thyme, rosemary, red peppers and salt. Pour the Chablis over the asparagus. Spoon the onion-herb mixture over all. Sprinkle cheese on top and bake 10 minutes.

Barley Pilaf

serves 6-8

½	cup butter
2	medium onions, coarsely chopped
½	cup chopped celery
½	cup fresh mushrooms, trimmed and sliced
1½	cups pearl barley
2	cups chicken broth (or beef)
1	tsp. salt
⅛	tsp. cayenne pepper
½	cup chopped fresh parsley

Melt butter in skillet: stir in onions and celery. After 5 minutes, add mushrooms sauté for 5 minutes more. Add barley and cook until light brown (5-10 minutes), stirring occasionally. Transfer to a greased 2 quart casserole. Add broth, salt, cayenne and parsley. Cover and bake for about 50 minutes at 350 degrees, or until barley is tender and liquid is absorbed.

Tasty Trivia
If a vegetable or cereal burns, plunge the pan containing the burned mass into cold water and allow it to remain for a few minutes before pouring the contents into another pan. This will do away almost entirely with the burned taste.

VEGETABLES

Broccoli With Sesame Dressing

serves 4-6

1	large bunch broccoli
1	T. sesame seeds
	salt, freshly ground pepper
½	cup Oriental sesame oil
¼	cup rice vinegar
1	T. soy sauce
½	tsp. sugar
	pinch red pepper flakes

Separate the broccoli into small florets. Cut off and peel the stalks and cut them on a slant into uniform pieces about ½ inch thick. Wash the broccoli, then steam over simmering water until crisp-tender. Rinse in cold water and drain.

Sprinkle sesame seeds in a heavy skillet and toast over medium heat, until golden. Set aside.

Season broccoli with salt and pepper. Combine oil, vinegar, soy sauce, sugar and pepper flakes and mix well. Just before serving, pour over broccoli and toss. Sprinkle with sesame seeds. May be served hot, cold or at room temperature.

Clubhouse Carrot Casserole

serves 6

1	lb. fresh carrots
½	cup chopped onions
1	tsp. prepared mustard
1	tsp. sugar
½	tsp. salt
¾	cup grated cheese
½	cup mayonnaise
½	cup cracker crumbs

Peel carrots and slice at an angle. Place in a pan, cover with water, add onions and cook until fork tender. Drain, add mustard, sugar, salt, cheese and mayonnaise; mix well and place in a buttered casserole. Sprinkle crumbs on top and bake at 350 degrees until it bubbles, about 15 to 20 minutes. May be frozen.

Green Beans With Persillade

serves 4

1	lb. green beans
3	T. butter
2	lg. garlic cloves, minced
¼	cup finely minced parsley
¼	cup toasted pine nuts - optional
1	tomato, peeled, seeded and chopped - optional

String and take off the ends of the green beans. Leave whole if small and fresh or else cut in 1½ inch lengths on the diagonal. Add green beans to a large pot of boiling water and blanch 4-7 minutes, or until crisp-tender. Pour contents through a strainer and refresh under cold water. Set beans aside.

Melt the butter in a skillet and when the foam dies down, add the garlic. Sauté for a minute, and add the parsley. Stir well and add the beans. Continue to toss the beans in the persillade until they are well warmed up and serve immediately. Garnish with pine nuts, or a chopped tomato, if desired.

Track Talk
*Pensive, winner of the 1944 Derby, sired Ponder 1949 Derby
winner who sired Needles, the 1956 winner.*

Gingered Red Carrots

serves 6-8

1	lb. carrots, scraped
1	lb. beets, scrubbed, leaves removed
1	T. butter
3	T. orange juice
1	tsp. finely chopped fresh ginger
½	tsp. finely grated orange peel
	salt and pepper to taste

Slice the carrots on the diagonal (cut thick carrots in half lengthwise first) in ¼ inch thick slices. Steam 5 to 7 minutes, or until crisp-tender. Run under cold water; drain and set aside.

Place beets in covered saucepan; cover with water and bring to a boil. Cook 20-30 minutes, or until a fork, inserted into beet, goes in easily. Peel and slice in ¼ inch thick slices, about the same size as the carrot slices; halve slices when necessary.

Melt the butter in a saucepan. Add the orange juice, ginger and orange peel. Add the carrots and beets, toss in the juice, and taste for salt and pepper. Reheat and serve.

Variations: Substitute 2 tablespoons Raspberry Vinegar and 1 tablespoon beet juice for the 3 tablespoons orange juice.

Carrots And Celery With Pecans

serves 4

4	medium-sized carrots
6	stalks celery
1	cup water
¼	tsp. salt
¼	cup butter
1	cup pecans
½	tsp. dried dill weed
	pepper to taste

Cut carrots and celery diagonally. Place carrots, celery and salt in a saucepan with water and bring to a boil. Cook approximately 5 minutes until crisp-tender; drain. Sauté nuts in butter, add dill weed and pepper. Add nut mixture to hot carrots and celery; toss lightly.

Stuffed Carrots

serves 6

12	carrots, scraped
¼	small onion, chopped
3	T. grated sharp Cheddar cheese
	salt and pepper to taste
	cayenne pepper
2-3	soda crackers crumbled
1	T. milk
1	T. chopped parsley
	paprika
1	T. or more water

After scraping carrots, cut ends off to make uniform in length. Cook in water until barely tender. Carefully scrape out center, making a boat. Mash the removed part of the carrots. Add onion, cheese, salt, pepper, cayenne and cracker crumbs. Add milk if mixture is too dry. Mix in chopped parsley. Put mixture into each carrot boat and sprinkle with paprika. Bake in pyrex dish with a tablespoon or more of water at 350 degrees for 20 minutes.

VEGETABLES

Timbales Of Carrot Mousse

serves 8

2	lbs. carrots
2	cups water
1	tsp. salt
1¾	cups cream
5	egg yolks (extra large eggs)
¼	cup butter
8	slices firm bread (Pepperidge Farm Toasting)
⅓	cup oil
	parsley

Peel and slice carrots. Put carrots, water and salt in a saucepan. Bring to a boil and let simmer until carrots are tender. Drain. Reserve 24 small uniform cooked carrot slices for garnish. Add cream to the remaining carrots and bring to a boil. Cool mixture enough to handle safely, then blend until smooth in a blender or food processor. When mixture is cool, blend in egg yolks, one at a time. Taste for seasoning.

Preheat oven to 350 degrees. Butter eight 3 inch ramekins and divide mixture among them. About 25 minutes before serving time, put ramekins in a pan that is safe to use on the stove top or in the oven. Add boiling water to pan until depth reaches ½ way up ramekin side. Cover the pan with aluminum foil and bake for approximately 20 minutes. The center of the carrot mixture will be firm when done. While carrots are cooking, cut 8 pieces of bread the same size as the ramekins and fry in the hot oil until lightly browned. Unmold ramekins onto fried rounds. Garnish each timbale with 3 carrot slices and a small sprig of parsley.

Cauliflower with Poppy Seeds

server 8-10

2	heads cauliflower, cut into florets
1	cup olive oil
⅓	cup red wine vinegar
2	tsp. anchovy paste
2	tsp. lime juice
	salt and freshly ground pepper
3	T. poppy seeds

Steam the cauliflower 6 - 8 minutes, or until crisp-tender. Run under cold water to stop the cooking process.

Whisk the oil, vinegar and remaining ingredients. Toss the vinaigrette with the cauliflower and serve.

Baked Cherries

serves 4-6

1	large can sour pitted cherries (drain juice and save)
½	box graham crackers, crushed
⅔	cup brown sugar
6	T. butter

Butter a small casserole and put in a layer of cherries, follow with graham crackers, brown sugar, dot with butter, and repeat. Pour ½ cup juice over top just before baking.
Bake in 350 degree oven until hot, approximately 30 minutes.

Excellent with ham and fowl.

Track Talk
*The Derby has been run only twice in months other than May;
April 29, 1901 and due to wartime conditions, June 9, 1945.*

Walnut Carrots

serves 8

5	cups carrot sticks (about 40 3-inch julienne)
1½	cups water
½	tsp. salt
½	cup melted butter
2	tsp. honey
1	tsp. salt
½	tsp. coarsely ground pepper
2	T. lemon juice
¼	tsp. lemon rind
½	cup coarsely chopped walnuts

Cook carrots in water with salt until tender, but still crisp. Drain thoroughly. Heat remaining ingredients, except walnuts, in a small saucepan and pour this mixture over hot carrots. Toss in walnuts.

Cauliflower Medley

serves 6

1	cup white wine
1	cup chicken broth
1	T. butter
1	medium head cauliflower, cut into 1 inch florets
4	stalks celery, cut into ½ inch pieces
1	medium red bell pepper, cut into ¼ inch x 2 inch julienne
1	medium onion, cut into ½ inch dice
	salt and freshly ground pepper
¼	cup coarsley chopped pecans, toasted (optional)

Place the wine, broth and butter in a large sauce pan; add the cauliflower. Cook, covered, 10-15 minutes or until crisp-tender. Remove from saucepan, leaving cooking liquid. Add celery to pot, cover and cook 2 minutes, add onions and cook 1 minute, add red pepper and cook 2 more minutes. Remove cover and boil until liquid is reduced to ¼ - ½ cup. Return cauliflower to pot, reheat and taste for seasoning. Serve, garnished with pecans, if desired.

Celery Casserole

serves 4-6

4	cups celery, sliced in 1 inch pieces
1	5-oz. can water chestnuts, drained and sliced
1	can cream of chicken soup
¼	cup diced pimento
¼	cup toasted almond slivers
1	cup soft bread crumbs
4	T. butter, melted

Preheat oven 350 degrees. Cook celery in water to cover until just tender; drain. Mix celery, water chestnuts, soup and pimento. Place in a greased 13 x 9 x 2-inch pyrex dish. Toss the nuts, bread crumbs and butter together. Sprinkle on top of casserole. Bake until bubbly hot and crisp on top, approximately 20 minutes.

Bill's Chestnuts And Potatoes

serves 4-6

15-18	chestnuts, peeled (1½ cups measured after peeling)
3	cups chicken broth
5	large boiling potatoes
6	T. butter
½	cup cream, room temperature

Simmer chestnuts in chicken broth until tender (about 25 minutes). Boil potatoes until tender (about 30 minutes); peel then mash. In another bowl, mash chestnuts with 4 tablespoons butter; add to potatoes, plus the remaining 2 tablespoons butter. Incorporate well. Fold in cream. Serve hot as a side dish with meat or game.

Green Beans With Oranges

serves 6-8

2	lbs. green beans (french cut)
1	11-oz. can mandarin oranges, drained
4	T. butter
	salt and pepper to taste

Cook beans in salted water until crisp. Drain. Add orange sections and butter. Heat thoroughly, but do not cook. Season with salt and pepper.

Corn on the Cob with Mint Butter

serves 6

6	ears corn, with husks
12	mint sprigs
6	T. butter

Soak the corn, with husks and silk, in salted water for 1-2 hours. Remove the silk carefully, preserving the husks attached to base of ear of corn. Place a mint sprig on each side of the corn and dot with a tablespoon of butter. Replace the husks so the ear is entirely wrapped again. Place over the glowing coals of a fire and roast until tender, 10-20 minutes, depending upon the heat of the fire. Turn with long tongs every 5 minutes.

Cucumbers With Snow Peas

serves 6

3	cucumbers, peeled, split, seeded, sliced ¼ inch thick
2	T. butter
1	lb. snow peas, trimmed, string removed
	salt and freshly ground pepper
1	T. fresh tarragon, mint, basil or coriander or 1 tsp. dried.

Bring a large pot of water to a boil. Immerse cucumber pieces in the water to blanch for 2 minutes. Drain and refresh under cold water; drain well again. Blanch the snow peas 1 minute, drain and refresh under cold water; drain again.

Melt butter in a large skillet, add snow peas and sauté for 1 minute. Add cucumbers and toss constantly until both vegetables are warm. Sprinkle with the fresh herbs of your choice and serve immediately.

VEGETABLES

Track Talk
EXACTA: To win in Exacta wagering, you must pick the two horses finishing first and second in exact order.
DAILY DOUBLE: To win in a Daily Double bet, you must pick the winners in the first and second races. Wagers must be placed before the running of the first race.

Fried Corn

serves 4

6	tender ears of corn
½	cup hot water
	salt and pepper to taste
3	T. bacon fat
3	T. butter
¼	cup whole milk

Cut off corn and scrape cob with the back of a knife to get all the pulp and milk. Stir in hot water, salt and lots of pepper. In a heavy iron skillet, heat the bacon fat until hot. Pour in the corn mixture. Cook 10 or 15 minutes or until water begins to evaporate. Add a lump of butter and milk. Set over low heat to form crust on bottom, stirring occasionally to keep from burning.

Kentucky Corn Fritters

serves 4

1-2	ears corn
⅓	cup flour
½	tsp. baking powder
½	tsp. salt
2	eggs, separated
¼	cup oil

Cut corn off cob, scraping to remove juice. Place corn and juices in a bowl, mix with flour, baking powder and salt. Add beaten egg yolks and mix well. Fold in stiffly beaten egg whites.

In a heavy skillet add oil and heat until very hot (approximately 350 degrees). Drop batter by tablespoons into oil and turn fritters over when they are brown. Drain on paper towel.

Adeline and Jane's Corn Pudding

serves 4

1	10-oz. box frozen corn or 3 ears scraped corn (2 cups)
3	eggs
¼	cup sugar
1	cup whipping cream
1	tsp. salt
	butter for dotting on top

Preheat oven to 350 degrees. If using frozen corn, whiz in processor or blender until coarsely chopped. Mix corn, eggs, sugar, cream and salt. Put in casserole and dot with butter. Cook for 40-50 minutes. If recipe is doubled or tripled, cooking must be extended. May mix ahead and store in refrigerator. Stir before baking.

Mother Dunlap's Corn Pudding

serves 8

12	ears yellow corn
1	can cream of yellow corn
5	thoroughly beaten eggs
1	T. sugar (taste for sweetness)
¾	pint cream
½	stick melted butter

Preheat oven 300 degrees. Scrape kernels from ears of corn into a large bowl. Add cream corn, eggs, sugar, cream, and melted butter. Mix and pour into a 2 quart casserole. Bake for an hour, or until set.

157

Eggplant Pie
serves 8

1	eggplant, about 1 lb., peeled and cut into 1-inch slices
¾	tsp. salt
⅛	tsp. pepper
2	medium tomatoes, sliced
1	green pepper, seeded and cut into rings
1	onion, sliced
1	tsp. minced garlic
2	T. olive oil
½	tsp. oregano
½	tsp. basil
	salt
4	oz. Mozzarella cheese
½	cup Parmesan cheese

Sprinkle salt on eggplant; let sit 15 minutes, then blot with paper towels. Preheat broiler. Arrange eggplant on baking sheet 6 inches from heat. Season with salt and pepper. Brown under the broiler on one side. Arrange eggplant slices (overlapping and brown side down) in a 10-inch round pan. Put tomato, pepper, onion and garlic on top. Drizzle with oil, and sprinkle with herbs and salt. Bake for 25 minutes at 350 degrees. Remove from oven and cover with Mozzarella and Parmesan cheese. Bake 15 minutes longer.

Hot Fruit Compote
serves 8

12	dry macaroons, crumbled
4	cups canned fruit (peaches, pears, apricots, pineapple, cherries, well drained (do not use fruit cocktail)
½	cup toasted almonds
¼	cup brown sugar
½	cup dry Sherry
¼	cup melted butter

Preheat oven to 350 degrees. Butter 2½-quart casserole. Alternate layers of macaroons and fruit with crumbs on the top and bottom. Sprinkle with almonds, sugar and Sherry. Drizzle butter over top.

Bake for 30 minutes.

Winner's Circle Mushrooms
serves 6

2	T. butter
4	T. flour
1	cup milk, heated
¼	tsp. salt
	pepper to taste
1	lb. fresh mushrooms, sliced
2	T. butter
1	tsp. onion juice
1	cup melba toast crumbs, buttered
1	cup heavy cream

Preheat oven to 350 degrees. To make cream sauce: melt butter in a saucepan; add flour and stir until well blended. Pour in hot milk gradually, stirring constantly. Season with salt and pepper. Bring to a boil and stir for 2 minutes. Set aside.

In a large skillet, sauté mushrooms in 2 tablespoons butter for 3 minutes. Add onion juice; mix well. Place mushrooms, cream sauce and bread crumbs in layers in a small baking dish as follows: ¼ cup of mushrooms, ¼ of sauce and ¼ of crumbs. Continue this way with 3 more layers of mushrooms, sauce and crumbs. Pour cream over top. Bake for 20 minutes.

VEGETABLES

Marinated Green Beans

serves 6

4	cups green beans, cooked (or 2 16-oz. cans french style, well drained)
1	medium onion, thinly sliced
1	clove garlic

Place beans in large bowl and add onion (red onion is nice) and garlic which has been put through a press.

Marinade

2	T. sugar
1	tsp. paprika
¼	tsp. salt
⅛	tsp. pepper
1	tsp. oregano
½	tsp. dry mustard
5	T. vinegar
4	T. oil

Mix together the dry marinade ingredients. Add vinegar then add 1 tablespoon oil at a time, until well mixed. Pour over the beans and onions and toss gently. Refrigerate 2 hours or overnight.
Heat to serve as a vegetable, or use cold as a relish. Drain off excess liquid before serving.

Hubbard Squash

serves 4

1	Hubbard squash, peeled
3-4	T. butter
1	tsp. salt
1	tsp. freshly grated nutmeg.

Preheat oven to 350 degrees. Cut the squash into ¾ inch dice. Put in an oven-proof casserole. Dot with butter, then sprinkle with salt and nutmeg.

Bake 1 hour. Stir often. If you put a pan of hot water on the shelf below, the squash will be more moist.

Vegetable Lasagna
(Microwave)

serves 6-8

1	10-oz. pkg. frozen chopped spinach
2	8-oz. cans tomato sauce
1	6-oz. can tomato paste
1	4-oz. can sliced mushrooms
¼	cup onion, finely chopped
2	tsp. leaf oregano
1	tsp. basil
1	tsp. salt
¼	tsp. garlic powder
½	pkg, (16-oz.) lasagna noodles, cooked
2	cups (1 pint) small curd cottage cheese
1	6-oz. grated Mozzarella cheese

In 12 x 8 x 2-inch glass dish place unwrapped frozen blocks of spinach. Microwave at Low (30% power) 12 to 14 minutes, breaking apart after 10 minutes until thawed. Drain.

In small bowl mix together tomato sauce, tomato paste, mushrooms, onion, oregano, basil, salt and garlic powder. Spread ½ cup sauce over bottom of 12 x 8 x 2-inch dish. Over the sauce layer half lasagna noodles laid lengthwise, with spinach, half of cottage cheese, half of Mozzarella cheese, half of tomato sauce in dish. Repeat layers, with noodles laid horizontally. Microwave at Medium-High (70% power) 19-21 minutes.

Tasty Trivia
While cooking vegetables that give off unpleasant odors,
simmer a small pan of vinegar on top of the stove.

VEGETABLES

Pretty Party Peas

serves 6-8

2   pkgs. Tender Tiny Peas
1   pkg. Chinese Pea Pods or ¼ lb.
     fresh, cleaned and unstrung
pinch of sugar
Seasonings - salt and pepper,
     butter, Lawry's Seasoned Salt,
     favorite herb (pinch of rosemary
     or Herbes de Provence) or
     chopped parsley, or all!

Cook peas according to package directions in Microwave or regular way. Undercook pea pods. Mix together and season well. Pods should be slightly crunchy.

Pretend Pimientos

When sweet red peppers are at their summertime peak, freeze some and beat the cost of canned pimientos.

Boil whole peppers for 10-20 minutes or until the skin peels off easily. Time will vary. Drain and cover with cold water until cool enough to handle. Cut in half, remove seeds and ribs and skin them. It does not matter if they tear. Pack separately in small plastic bags, adding about a teaspoon of olive oil to each pepper. Freeze and use in place of canned pimiento.

Creamed Potatoes

serves 8

3   lbs. baking potatoes
3   cups milk
2   T. butter
1   clove garlic
     salt and freshly ground pepper
1   pint heavy cream

Peel and slice potatoes thinly. Put potatoes and milk in a large saucepan. Bring to a boil and simmer for about 15 minutes.

Grease a large au gratin dish with butter. Put garlic through press or chop finely and sprinkle it over the bottom of the dish. Drain the potatoes and reserve the milk. Place a thin layer of potatoes in au gratin dish. Season them with salt and pepper. Continue with additional layers until all the potatoes are used.
Add cream to milk and bring to a boil. Pour mixture over potatoes. The potatoes should be completely covered. An hour before serving time; bake at 400 degrees for one hour.

Peas Creole

serves 6-8

2	cups diced celery
2	medium bell peppers, diced
2	medium onions, chopped
1-2	T. butter, melted
1	6-oz. can tomato paste
1	10¾-oz. can tomato soup (undiluted)
2	T. flour, browned in oven
1	T. Worcestershire sauce
2	medium cans small English peas, drained
½	lb. sharp Cheddar cheese, grated

Preheat oven to 350 degrees. Sauté celery, peppers and onions in small amount of butter until soft. Add tomato paste, soup, flour and Worcestershire sauce. Carefully mix peas into mixture. Put a layer of pea mixture into casserole, follow with a layer of grated cheese, repeat layers, ending with a layer of cheese on top. Bake for 20 minutes or until bubbling.

Potato Pancakes

2	eggs
1	small onion, diced
6	medium potatoes, unpeeled and grated
	salt and pepper to taste
2	T. flour
1	T. soft butter
¼	tsp. sugar

In blender place onion and eggs for 15 seconds. Continue blending. Add grated raw potatoes, flour, butter, and seasonings. Blend until smooth. Bake by spoonfuls on hot griddle as regular pancakes.

Potato-Zucchini Pancake

serves 4

2	potatoes, unpeeled (1 lb. total)
1	medium zucchini, unpeeled and grated
1	egg, lightly beaten
2	T. flour
½	tsp. salt
½	tsp. freshly grated nutmeg
	fresh pepper
1	T. butter
1	T. oil

Grate potatoes and submerge in bowl of cold water. Drain and dry on cloth towel, removing as much water as possible. Toss with zucchini, egg, flour, salt, nutmeg, and pepper, using the hands to toss.

Heat 1 tablespoon butter and 1 tablespoon oil over medium-high heat. While sizzling hot, spoon 3 tablespoons of mixture into skillet and shape into 3-inch circle; cook until golden; turn over. Repeat with butter and oil, cooking all pancakes. Drain on paper-lined pan. Keep warm. Can be made ahead and reheated in 350 degree oven. (Do not preheat oven). Allow 10 minutes to reheat pancakes.

Tasty Trivia
To restore a fresh flavor to frozen vegetables, pour boiling hot water over them, rinsing away all traces of the frozen water.

Swiss Potatoes

serves 4 to 6

6   medium red potatoes, sliced ¼ in. thick
1½   cups Swiss cheese, grated
      salt and pepper
      butter
½   pint whipping cream

Peel and slice potatoes. Layer the following in 2 quart pyrex casserole: potatoes, cheese, salt and pepper then dot with butter, repeating layers as needed. Pour cream over layers. Cook at 300 degrees for 1 ½ hours.

Baked Rice

serves 4

1   onion minced
½   green pepper minced
2   T. butter
1   cup long grain rice
2-3   chicken bouillon cubes dissolved in 2 cups water
½   box thawed chopped spinach
      sour cream
      chives

Brown onion and green pepper in butter. Add rice and stir. Transfer to a casserole, add half the liquid and cover. Bake 300 degrees for 1 hour adding liquid as needed. Add spinach to heat through and top with sour cream and chives.

Feathered Rice

makes 3 cups

1   cup rice
2½   cups boiling water
1   tsp. salt
2   T. butter
4   T. minced parsley
2   T. minced chives
¼   cup coarsely chopped almonds, toasted

Spread rice in shallow pan and toast in a 425 degree oven, stirring, now and then, until golden brown. Put in a casserole, add water, salt, butter, cover tightly and bake 20 minutes at 400 degrees or 30 minutes at 350 degrees. When ready to serve, stir in herbs and almonds.

Tasty Wild Rice

serves 6

1   cup wild rice
1   onion, chopped
¼   lb. mushrooms - fresh
3   celery stalks
½   green pepper
½   red pepper - used for color
1   stick butter
½   cup almonds, sliced
3   cups chicken broth

Wash wild rice in cold water and drain. Sauté lightly the onion, mushrooms, celery, green and red peppers and wild rice in some of butter. Meanwhile, brown almonds in remainder of butter. Put into greased 3 quart casserole and stir in broth that has been heated. Add almonds and mix well. Bake 325 for 1½ hours or till liquid is absorbed and rice grains are puffed open. Serves 6.

162

California Rice

serves 6 to 8

3	T. butter or margarine
3	T. flour
1½	cups milk
1	cup shredded sharp Cheddar cheese
24	stuffed olives, sliced
1	small onion, grated
½	tsp. salt
⅛	tsp pepper
	few grains cayenne
3	cups cooked rice

Make white sauce by heating butter in pan until bubbling subsides. Stir in flour and cook 1-2 minutes. Gradually add milk, mixing until smooth after each addition. Add cheese, olives, grated onion and seasonings. Put rice in a greased 2-quart casserole. Pour cheese sauce over rice and bake one-half hour at 375 degrees.

Uptown Rice

serves 6-8

1½	cups raw rice
½	cup slivered almonds
½	lb. mushrooms, sliced (or 1 can, drained)
2	T. chopped onions
¼	lb. butter
3	cups chicken stock (from 3 cups hot water and 5 bouillon cubes)*
½	tsp. salt

Cook rice, almonds, mushrooms, and onions for 10-15 minutes on medium heat, stirring constantly. When almonds look barely toasted and rice has a yellow cast, remove from heat. Add stock and salt. Pour contents into a 2 quart casserole, cover tightly and bake for 1 hour at 325 degrees.

*Homemade stock is preferable.

Special Spinach Casserole

serves 10-12

4	10-oz. pkgs. frozen chopped spinach
½	lb. fresh mushrooms, washed and sliced
¾	cup butter
½	cup Hellman's mayonnaise
1	cup sour cream
1	cup Romano cheese, freshly grated
1	8½ oz. can artichokes, drained and quartered
2	tomatoes, sliced thin
⅔	cup fresh bread crumbs

Cook spinach according to package directions and drain. Sauté mushrooms in ¼ cup of butter. Combine mayonnaise, sour cream, and ⅔ cup of the Romano cheese; stir in spinach, mushrooms and artichokes. Turn into buttered 13 by 9-inch pan. Arrange tomatoes on the top. Melt remaining ½ cup butter stir in crumbs and remaining cheese, then sprinkle over top of casserole. Bake in a 350 degree oven for 30 minutes.

Note: This may be made a day ahead, refrigerated, then baked for approximately 40 minutes.

VEGETABLES

Julia's Spinach Casserole

serves 12-15

6	pkgs. frozen chopped spinach
	salt and pepper
1	stick butter
1	8-oz. pkg. cream cheese (allow to soften at room temperature)
	garlic powder
	onion powder

Cook spinach and press out water in a colander. Add salt and pepper to taste. Combine butter and cream cheese; melt carefully. (Easily done in a microwave on medium). Add pinch of garlic powder and onion powder. Toss with spinach and serve.

Also delicious cold on Bremner crackers.

Dilled Green Beans With Walnuts

serves 6-8

2	lbs. green beans
1	cup olive oil
⅓	cup red wine vinegar
2	T. lemon juice
	salt and pepper
3	chopped hard-boiled eggs
2	T. or more walnuts, chopped
3	T. fresh dill (or 1 T. dried)

Steam the green beans 6 minutes, until crisp-tender. Meanwhile, whisk oil, vinegar, lemon juice, salt and pepper. Stir in the eggs, walnuts and dill; toss with hot beans.

These are also good cold.

Creole Squash

serves 8-10

2	T. butter
½	cup diced green pepper
½	cup diced onion
3	cups diced tomatoes
	salt and pepper to taste
½	tsp. sugar
3	T. flour
6	cups sliced squash, cooked
1	cup grated Cheddar cheese
½	cup bread crumbs
1	T. butter

Preheat oven to 350 degrees. Melt butter. Add green pepper, onion and tomatoes; cook cbout 5 minutes. Add salt, pepper and sugar. Blend in flour. Place squash in a 2 quart casserole. Pour cooked mixture over top. Mix cheese with bread crumbs and 1 T. butter; sprinkle over top. Bake approximately 30 minutes.

Peas Italian

serves 6-8

2	T. butter
6	T. olive oil
2	cloves garlic, minced
2	10-oz. pkgs. frozen peas
6	strips bacon, fried crisp

Warm butter and olive oil in a pan on medium heat until butter has melted. Add garlic and sauté until transparent (do not brown). Remove pan from heat and place aside. Cook frozen peas until tender-crisp. Drain off excess water and toss peas with garlic butter mixture until well blended. Put peas in warm bowl. Crumble crisp bacon on top and serve. These tasty peas are even better the next day cold or tossed in a green salad.

Track Talk
*Derby attendance 1891…"The crowd was so great that
locomotion was almost impossible. The inner field presented
one mass of humanity from the head of the stretch…the
crowd was large enough that is was necessary to provide a
police escort to get the starter to his position…"*

Stuffed Squash
serves 6

6-8   yellow squash
10   oz. frozen peas, cooked and drained
2   T. butter
4   T. Parmesan cheese
2   T. cream
1   T. Worcestershire sauce
2   T. chopped parsley
¼   tsp. dill

Cook squash in large amount of boiling water until lightly resistant when pierced with a fork. Drain. Blend peas, butter, 2 tablespoons cheese, cream, Worcestershire, parsley and dill in blender or processor until smooth. Thin with cream, if necessary. Stuff squash with pea mixture. Top with 2 tablespoons cheese, and sprinkle with paprika. Bake at 350 degrees until brown, about 15 minutes.

Tomato Casserole
serves 6-8

8   whole cloves
8   whole peppercorns
1   bay leaf
2   2-lb. cans tomatoes
½   onion, chopped
  salt to taste
¾   cup brown sugar
3-4   slices white bread, torn into bite-size pieces
2   T. butter

Place cloves, peppercorns and bay leaf in cheesecloth, pulled together to form a bag. Cook undrained tomatoes, onions and cheesecloth bag for 30 minutes on simmer. Add salt to taste.
Pour tomato mixture into a 2-quart casserole, discarding cheesecloth bag. Add brown sugar and bread pieces; mix well. Dot top with butter. Bake at 325 degrees for 30 minutes.

Elkridge Tomatoes
serves 4

2   tomatoes, firm but ripe
  flour, salt and pepper
  butter
  brown sugar

Slice tomatoes. Mix flour, salt and pepper. Dip tomato slices in seasoned flour. Melt butter in heavy frying pan. Fry slices in butter until brown. Place slices in baking dish in one layer. Sprinkle with brown sugar, then place under broiler until sugar bubbles.

Serve with beef, also excellent with backfin crab cakes.

Fried Green Tomatoes
serves 8

6   medium tomatoes (green, but turning pink)
1   cup cornmeal
½   tsp. salt
¼   tsp. pepper
½   tsp. oregano
  bacon drippings

Cut tomatoes horizontally into ¼-inch thick slices, discarding the top and bottom slices. Mix cornmeal with seasonings. Coat the tomatoes well. In hot skillet containing bacon drippings, add tomato slices in one layer. Lower heat to medium and fry for about 6 more minutes, or until golden brown. Drain on paper towels. Repeat with remaining tomato slices.

VEGETABLES

Green Tomato Casserole

serves 6-8

8	medium green tomatoes, sliced
3	large onions, sliced
2-4	T. bacon grease
⅛	tsp. curry powder
	salt
	paprika
1½	cups sour cream
½	cup coarse rolled and buttered bread crumbs
2-3	T. Parmesan cheese, grated

In a large skillet, cook green tomatoes and onions in heated bacon grease until soft. Add curry, salt and paprika. Let cool, then stir in sour cream. Pour into a 2-quart casserole, and sprinkle with mixture of crumbs and cheese.

Cook at 350 degrees. Until bubbly and slightly browned on top.

Green Vegetables Medley

serves 6-8

1	10-oz. pkg. frozen peas
1	10-oz. pkg. frozen lima beans
1	9-oz. pkg. frozen French-style green beans
1	cup water
	salt
¼	cup finely chopped onion
2	T. butter or margarine, melted
1	T. all-purpose flour
½	cup sour cream
½	cup mayonnaise
½	tsp. basil leaves, crushed
¼	tsp. salt
⅛	tsp. pepper
¾	cup shredded sharp Cheddar cheese

Preheat oven to 325 degrees. Place frozen peas in a colander; pour hot water over peas to remove frost. Set peas aside. Combine lima beans, green beans, and 1 cup salted water in a saucepan. Bring to a boil; reduce heat and simmer 3 minutes. Drain; set aside. Sauté onion in butter in a large skillet until tender. Stir in flour; remove from heat. Add vegetables, sour cream, mayonnaise, and seasonings. Spoon mixture into a lightly greased 1½-quart casserole dish. Bake for 15 minutes. Sprinkle cheese on top and bake 5 minutes longer.

Zucchini Casserole

serves 4 to 6

4	medium zucchini, sliced (may be parboiled for 3 minutes, if desired)
3	tomatoes, sliced
1	large onion, sliced thin
½	cup grated Cheddar cheese
1	ear fresh corn, cut off cob
1	small green pepper (optional). diced
	salt and pepper to taste
¼	cup bread crumbs
1	T. butter

Preheat oven to 400 degrees. In a 2 quart baking dish, make layers of zucchini, sliced tomatoes, onion slices (separated into rings), Cheddar cheese, corn, green pepper, salt and pepper. Sprinkle with bread crumbs and dot with butter. Bake for 15-20 minutes, or until barely cooked. Do not overcook.

Zucchini A La Grecque

serves 3-4

3	cups young, tender zucchini, cut in ¼ inch slices
2	T. tarragon vinegar or wine
⅛	tsp. black pepper
1	bay leaf
⅔	cup chopped celery
2-3	sprigs parsley, chopped
2	sprigs thyme, minced
2	T. lemon juice
½	tsp. salt
1	clove garlic, slivered
¼	tsp. sugar
2	sprigs tarragon, minced
1	cup water
¼	cup olive oil (or ½ olive oil and ½ salad oil)

Prepare zucchini. Mix all ingredients (except zucchini) together, and simmer in a covered saucepan for 20 minutes. Add zucchini for the last 5 minutes of cooking. Cool. Store in refrigerator. Serve cold.

May be used as an appetizer or as a salad.

Zucchini Torta

serves 8-10

Pastry:

1¼	cups flour
½	tsp. salt
½	tsp. crushed anise seeds
½	cup butter
½	cup grated Cheddar cheese

In food processor bowl place butter, Cheddar cheese, flour, salt and anise seeds. Process until it forms a ball. Remove from bowl and pat dough evenly in layer over bottom and 1 inch sides of an 8-inch springform pan.

Torta:

8	slices bacon
2	T. bacon drippings
2	cups thinly sliced zucchini
½	cup finely chopped onion
2	tsp. minced garlic
6	eggs
1	cup sour cream
1	tsp. salt
2	cup cooked rice (¾ cup rice cooked in 1 cup water and 1 cup white wine)
1	cup grated cheese

Preheat oven to 350 degrees. Cook bacon in skillet until crisp; drain (reserving 2 tablespoons bacon fat). Crumble bacon and set aside. Heat reserved bacon dripping in skillet, add zucchini, onion and garlic; cook 10 minutes until soft, stirring occasionally.

In a large bowl, beat eggs; add sour cream, salt, cooked rice, cheese, cooked vegetable mixture and crumbled bacon. Turn filling into pastry shell and smooth top.

Bake about 55 minutes, or until golden brown and set. Let stand at least 5 minutes, then loosen the edges and remove sides of pan. Cut torta into wedges. Serve warm or cold.

This torta is very versatile and can be prepared ahead. It travels well for a picnic or party and can be reheated easily. It will not "fall".

Bourbon Yams
Heaven Hill Distilleries

serves 6

4	medium yams, unpeeled
1	stick butter
⅓	cup brown sugar
¼	cup Bourbon, Heaven Hill

In a large pot, place yams and cover with water. Boil gently until tender. Cool. Peel and slice lengthwise. Layer in a greased 2-quart casserole.

Melt butter in a saucepan. Add brown sugar and Bourbon. Heat this mixture until sugar is dissolved; pour over yams. Bake at 350 degrees about 20 minutes, or until bubbly. May be made a day ahead.

Carrots With Mustard And Dill
(Microwave)

serves 6-8

2	lbs. carrots, cleaned and cut into chunks (about 5 cups)
½	cup water

In 2 quart microwave casserole or bowl, place carrots and water. Cover with vented microwavable plastic wrap. Microwave at High for 10 to 14 minutes, until crisp-tender.

Sauce:

⅓	cup coarsely chopped onions
1	T. butter
½	cup mayonnaise
½	tsp. salt
¼	tsp. pepper
2	T. coarse brown mustard
1½	tsp. chopped fresh dill or ½ tsp. dry

For sauce: In a 2 cup measuring cup or bowl, place onions and butter. Microwave at High for 1-2 minutes, until onions are almost tender. Stir in mayonnaise, salt and pepper, mustard and dill. Pour over carrots and toss to mix well.

Ratatouille Supreme

serves 10-12

6	T. olive oil
1	medium eggplant, cubed
6	zucchini, sliced
1	green pepper, sliced
1	cup sliced yellow onions
1	large clove garlic, minced
4	large tomatoes, peeled and diced (or 1 large can Italian tomatoes, without juice)
1	bay leaf
¼	tsp. thyme
2	T. fresh chopped basil (or 1 tsp. dried)
2	T. chopped parsley
	salt and pepper to taste

In a large skillet on medium-hot heat, pour in 2 tablespoons of olive oil. Add eggplant and brown lightly; remove eggplant to a large casserole or dutch oven. Add zucchini to skillet and brown lightly; remove to casserole. Add remaining oil to skillet and cook onions, garlic and green peppers until tender, but do not brown. Place tomatoes on top of onion mixture, add all seasonings, cover and simmer over low heat for 20 minutes. Pour this mixture over eggplant and zucchini in casserole, cover and simmer over low heat for 30 minutes, or bake in 325 degree oven for 30 minutes. Stir carefully to keep mixture from sticking. If too much liquid, remove top and cook uncovered to evaporate juices.

May be served hot or cold.

TENTH RACE
SAUCES

1	LIBERTY HALL PUDDING SAUCE 	SERVES **12**
2	DERBY SABAYON	SERVES **4-6**
3	HOT BOURBON SAUCE	SERVES **8-10**
4	BILL'S THICK CARAMEL-PEAR SAUCE	SERVES **12**
5	TOMATO CREAM SAUCE	SERVES **8**
6	INVERNESS SAUCE	SERVES **4-6**
7	HENRY BAIN SAUCE #1	SERVES **10-15**
8	CRESTED BUTTE TERIYAKI	SERVES **40**

Committee Selections   3-7-5

Kentucky bred entry 1, 3, 6, 7

Barbecue Sauce

2 cups

½   cup ketchup
1   tsp. salt
1   tsp. celery seed
½   tsp. nutmeg
⅓   cup vinegar
1   bay leaf
    Tabasco to taste
1   cup water (if sauce is used with pork chops)
½   cup water (if sauce is used for ribs)

Mix all ingredients well; baste meat liberally and often with sauce. For pork chops, cook in a covered skillet 1½ hours. For ribs, bake 15 minutes, then grill.

Broccoli Sauce

makes 1½ cups

1   cup mayonnaise
½   stick butter, room temperature
1   T., or more, of Horseradish (prepared)
1   small onion, grated
½   tsp. prepared mustard
¼   tsp. cayenne
½   tsp. salt
¼   tsp. Tabasco

Place all ingredients in a double boiler and stir until well-blended. Do not over-cook, or it will curdle.

Serve over steamed broccoli.

Crested Butte Teriyaki

4 quarts

1   qt. Sherry (regular dry)
1   qt. soy sauce
1   pt. red wine vinegar
1½   cups sugar
2   T. Accent
3   T. garlic salt
46   oz. unsweetened pineapple juice

Mix all ingredients well and refrigerate. Use as a marinade for meat or chicken. It is very easy to slip meat & sauce into a zip lock bag and into the freezer. It will marinate as it thaws and be ready to cook.

SAUCES

Track Talk
*Elwood struck a blow for women's lib when he won the 1904
Derby. He was the first Derby winner owned by a woman, the
first starter owned by a woman and the first winner bred by a
woman.*

Flank Steak Marinade

Marinade   serves 4-6

¼   cup soy sauce
2-3 T. fresh lemon juice
2   T. honey
3   T. sake or dry Sherry
1   clove garlic, crushed
1   tsp. fresh ginger or ½ tsp. dry
2   T. vegetable oil
2   tsp. sesame seeds
2   chopped green onions
1½ lb. flank steak

Mix all the ingredients and pour over meat.
Let marinate at least 4 hours in the refrigerator, turning
over occasionally. Broil or grill for 7-10 minutes. Slice
very thinly across the grain of meat.

Mrs. Rodes's Green Tomato Catsup

makes 11 pints

Step 1

8   green peppers, chopped
2   quarts green tomatoes, measured
      after shredding in processor
2   quarts cabbage, measured after
      shredding
2   quarts onions, measured after
      shredding
¾   cup salt

Mix all step 1 ingredients and put in a cloth bag, let drip
overnight. Next morning put the mixture in a large pan
on top of stove and add the step 2 ingredients.

Step 2

3   lbs. sugar
1   cup brown sugar
1   qt. vinegar

Stir well and simmer for 15 minutes (stir, so it doesn't
stick)

Dressing:

1   cup flour
1½ oz. dry mustard
1   qt. cider vinegar

Cook in a double boiler until thick.

Step 3

2   T. celery seed
2   T. mustard seed
1   T. turmeric

Put combined step 1 and step 2 ingredients, dressing
and step 3 ingredients all together and cook 25 minutes,
stirring frequently. Pour into sterilized pint jars.

Fresh Tomato Sauce

2 ½ cups

5	medium tomatoes, peeled and seeded
½	cup chopped onion
2	T. butter
½	tsp. sugar (optional)
2	cloves garlic, minced
1	T. chopped parsley
½	tsp. salt
¼	tsp. thyme
⅛	tsp. black pepper
1	bay leaf

Chop tomatoes into small cubes. Sauté onion in butter. Add sugar. Stir tomatoes, garlic, parsley, salt, thyme, pepper and bay leaf into the onions. Cook 5 to 10 minutes. Purée mixture in blender or processor.

Galatoire's Remoulade Sauce

Remoulade Sauce for shrimp, scallops, etc. from Galatoire's in New Orleans.

serves 4-6

6	green onions
½	stalk celery
2	cloves garlic
	parsley
5	T. Dijon mustard
	salt and pepper to taste
2	T. paprika
⅔	cup olive oil
⅓	cup vinegar
1	lb. shrimp, scallops, etc., cooked, peeled and deveined

Chop onions, celery, garlic & parsley in processor. Add mustard, salt, pepper, paprika, oil and vinegar. Mix well. Marinate shrimp in the mixture overnight.

Serve over chilled, shredded lettuce. Nap with sauce. This sauce is excellent at Derby time because it can be prepared well ahead and will serve a crowd by doubling or tripling recipe.

Green Peppercorn Sauce

approx. ¼ cup

	pork drippings
½	cup chicken stock
¼	cup white wine
1-2	T. Dijon mustard
1	tsp. mashed green peppercorns
¼	cup heavy cream

Pour off fat from pan in which pork was cooked. Add about half a cup of chicken stock and about a fourth a cup of white wine. Cook over moderately high heat, scraping to loosen brown particles and glaze. Boil until reduced by half. Stir in one to two tablespoons of Dijon mustard and green peppercorns. Add heavy cream and let bubble up. (sour cream or yogurt may be substituted.)

This sauce is good served over pork chops or pork tenderloin.

Henry Bain Sauce I

makes 7 cups

1	(10 oz.) jar Raffetto Chut-Nut
2	(12 oz.) bottles chili sauce
1	(5 oz.) bottle A-1 sauce
1	(5 oz.) bottle Worcestershire sauce
1	(14 oz.) bottle tomato catsup Tabasco, to taste, or half of a 2 oz. bottle

Cut up or blend the Chut-Nut and add to all the other ingredients. Stir thoroughly. This sauce will hold indefinitely in the refrigerator. Serve with fish and meats.

Henry Bain Sauce II
Marion Flexner

makes 7 cups

1	cup Heinz tomato catsup
2	bottles Major Grey's East Indian Chutney (each: 2 lbs., 2 oz.)
2	cups Heinz chili sauce
½	cup Lea & Perrin's Worcestershire sauce
6	T. Crosse and Blackwell's walnut catsup or sauce
2	T. English or dry mustard
2 to 3	T. Tabasco

Whip all ingredients in a blender or processor until the consistency of thick catsup, or you may grind large pieces of chutney and add to other ingredients. This is hot. You may reduce the amount of tabasco to 1 tablespoon. Serve with meats and fish.

Idie and Herman's Marinade for Grilled Chicken

Enough marinade for 4 - 6 chickens

1	pt. vinegar
1	cup water
1	T. dry mustard
1	T. Worcestershire sauce
2	T. sugar
2	sticks butter, melted

Combine all ingredients and whisk together until the sugar is dissolved. Pour the mixture over the chicken pieces. Marinate in refrigerator for 1 - 6 hours, then grill.

Inverness Sauce

(Wedgewood Farm)
A marinade for steaks, pork or lamb on the grill.

makes 1 cup

2	cloves garlic, minced
½	cup oil (or olive oil)
3	T. soy sauce
2	T. catsup
1	T. vinegar
½	tsp. fresh ground pepper

Mix all ingredients well. Pour over meat. Cover and refrigerate overnight for best flavor. 2-3 hours of marinating will do in a pinch.

Jezebel Sauce

yields 5 cups

1	18-oz. jar pineapple preserves
1	18-oz. jar apple jelly
1	5-oz. jar horseradish, or to taste
1	1-oz. can dry mustard, or to taste
1	tsp. white pepper, or to taste

Thoroughly blend all ingredients. Let stand at least four hours. Keeps indefinitely in refrigerator.

Excellent with pork, beef, lamb, egg rolls or chicken.

Mighty Mustard

makes 3 cups

4	oz. best quality dry mustard
3	large eggs
1	cup granulated sugar
¼	cup white wine
1	cup white vinegar

In top of double boiler, blend mustard, eggs, sugar, wine and vinegar very well. Cook over simmering water, stirring frequently, until thick. Store in refrigerator. Keeps for several weeks.

Red Pepper Sauce

yields 1¼ cups

6	red peppers (large sweet ones)
3	green onions, slightly chopped
2	T. olive oil, optional
	salt, to your taste

Roast the red peppers or broil them until skin turns black all over. Put them in a brown sack to steam and cool for ten minutes. Peel, seed and remove pithy white part of peppers. Blend in blender or processor with onions, olive oil and salt; purée.

This is a beautiful, low calorie sauce to use on vegetables or with scallops.

Sauce for Game or Pork

yields 2 cups

1	cup apple cider
1	T. currant jelly
1	T. brown sugar
2	T. butter
½	cup orange juice
1	T. corn starch
3	T. Calvados or Apple Brandy

Place all ingredients in a double boiler; cook until thick. Add more cider if it is too thick, or thicken with more corn starch.

Tomato Cream Sauce

yields 2 cups

1	stick unsalted butter
3	T. green onion, minced
3	T. carrot, minced
3	T. celery, minced
2½	cups canned tomatoes, with juice, or fresh, peeled and seeded
½	cup cream (less, if lighter sauce desired)

Simmer butter, onion, carrot, celery and tomatoes in uncovered saucepan for one hour. Add cream. Serve immediately over any kind of pasta or a nice poached chicken.

Apple Chutney

makes 12-15 pints

10	lbs. York apples (Wolf River apples in Louisville are good)
1	qt. plus ⅔ pt. white vinegar
3	lbs. dark brown sugar
1¾	T. minced garlic
2	¾-oz. boxes of mustard seed
1½	T. red pepper
4¾	T. salt, or to your taste
3	16-oz. boxes seedless raisins, grind ½ the amount

Peel and core apples; slice thin, and put into a large covered pot. Cover with 1 quart vinegar to keep from sticking. Cook to mush, stirring often. Cover and let sit. Make syrup of brown sugar and remaining vinegar. Boil about 5 minutes and add syrup to apples. Cover pot and simmer, stirring frequently. Put in garlic, mustard seed, red pepper and salt. Stir. Add ground raisins; mix thoroughly. Let steam about 8 minutes, covered. Add remaining whole raisins. Mash any pieces of apple. Cook about 45 minutes on low heat. Stir often, as it burns easily. Put into sterilized jars (not hot, however). Use new sterilized lids and caps. Boil filled jars 5-10 minutes in a huge pot, with water covering lids by two inches. Remove from water bath and let lids "pop" to seal.

Peach Marmalade

makes 3 pints

6	**cups sugar**
6	**cups ground peaches**
1	**cup water, if peaches are not ripe**

In a heavy saucepan combine sugar and peaches, (and water if needed). Cook over medium heat until it becomes a heavy syrup. Skim off white foam during cooking. Pour the hot mixture into sterilized jars.

Pickled Oranges

makes 2 pints

6	**oranges**
1	**tsp. salt**
2½	**cups sugar**
¼	**cup white corn syrup**
½	**cup water**
1	**cup vinegar**
12	**cloves**
⅓	**stick cinnamon**

Wash oranges, cover with water and boil with salt for 25 minutes. Drain, cover with fresh boiling water and boil 20 minutes more. Cut each orange into quarters. Combine sugar, corn syrup, ½ cup water and vinegar. Cook, stirring constantly, until sugar is dissolved. Add cloves and cinnamon; boil 10 minutes. Arrange orange skins on baking dish. Pour syrup over slices. Cover and bake at 300 degrees for 1½ hours or until slices are transparent. Ladle into hot sterilized jars, seal and store in refrigerator.

Amaretto Sauce

serves 2

¼	**cup Amaretto (Almond liquer)**
1	**T. melted butter**
½	**tsp. dark brown sugar**
½	**tsp. sugar**
½	**tsp. cornstarch**

Combine ingredients over low heat, stirring constantly. Serve warm, when mixture is well blended. May be served over ice cream, pound cake, mousse, etc.

Bill's Thick Pear and Caramel Sauce

serves 4

½	**cup sugar**
½	**cup liquid from canned pears**
½	**cup cream**
1½	**canned pear halves, mashed well**

Melt sugar over medium heat in small, heavy skillet. Remove from heat and slowly add pear liquid. Reheat just enough to make a smooth sauce. Remove from heat and add cream and mashed pears. Serve over poached pears, ice cream, pound cake or whatever!

Note: Teflon coated pans, or something similar, work great for melting sugar.

Bourbon Sauce

makes 2 cups

2	cups sugar
2	sticks butter
1	cup half and half
½	tsp. cinnamon
¼	tsp. nutmeg
½	cup Bourbon or Amaretto

Caramelize sugar in a heavy saucepan over medium heat, stirring constantly, until the sugar melts into a golden brown syrup. Remove from heat, cool slightly; add butter, return to heat until butter is melted. Remove from heat and cool slightly. Whisk in half and half, cinnamon nutmeg and bourbon. Cook mixture until it thickens.

Serve with bread pudding, pound cake, ice cream, etc.

Bourbon Waffle Syrup

1	cup purchased syrup
2	T. butter
3	T. Makers Mark
	pecans

Heat syrup, butter and Makers Mark. Pour over waffles and sprinkle with pecans. (This is a very thin syrup).

Butterscotch Sauce

(Microwave)

makes 1½ cups

1	T. cornstarch
1¼	cups light brown sugar (packed)
½	cup half & half
2	T. light corn syrup
⅛	tsp. salt
¼	cup butter
1	tsp. vanilla extract

In 1½ quart casserole stir together cornstarch and brown sugar. Stir in half & half, corn syrup and salt. Add butter. Cover. Microwave at High 3½ to 4½ minutes, stirring after 2 minutes, until thickened and sugar is dissolved. Add vanilla and stir until smooth and well blended. Serve warm or cold.

Caramel Sauce

makes 1 cup

1	cup sugar
3	T. water
3	T. water
½	cup heavy cream

In a small, heavy saucepan combine the sugar with 3 tablespoons water. Cook the mixture over moderate heat, stirring and washing down the sides of the pan with a brush dipped in cold water, until the sugar is dissolved. Let it boil, undisturbed, until it is a pale, golden caramel (color) and remove from heat. Put the pan in the sink and add very carefully 3 tablespoons water. Cook the syrup over moderate heat, stirring, until the caramel is dissolved and add the heavy cream. Stir well and remove from heat. Serve over ice creams, puddings, plain cake, mousse, etc.

Derby Sabayon

makes 3 cups

6	eggs, separated
¾	cup sugar
¾	cup Kentucky Bourbon (good quality) or cream sherry
¾	cup heavy cream, whipped
1	tsp. vanilla

Beat egg yolks with sugar until creamy. Add Bourbon or sherry, stir and cook in double boiler until thick. Cool in refrigerator 10-15 minutes, or until cool. Add whipped cream and vanilla. Fold in stiffly beaten egg whites. Put in 12 small ramkins and chill 2-3 hours. Serve with a curl of bittersweet chocolate on top. It will begin to separate in 6-8 hours.

Variation: Slice fresh strawberries into a wine goblet or dish. Spoon Derby Sabayon generously over the berries. Other berries or fruit may substituted. Garnish with a sprig of mint.

Hot Bourbon Sauce
from the Willett family of Bardstown

makes 2½ cups

2	cups brown sugar, dark brown is best
1	T. butter
1	heaping T. flour
1	cup hot water
½	cup of Bourbon (Old Bardstown)

Put all ingredients, except Bourbon, in the top of a double boiler and heat over simmering water until mixture thickens slightly. Remove from heat and add Bourbon. Serve warm over almost anything! We love it best over Figi Pudding or Plum Pudding, but pound cake would also be good.

This sauce will keep for a year or more in the refrigerator. Just take out what you need and warm it before serving.

Crème Fraîche

makes 1 cup

Crème Fraîche I

1	cup whipping cream (do not use ultra-pasteurized cream)
1	T. buttermilk

Put ingredients in a mason jar and cover with lid and shake for at least a minute. Remove lid, cover with a paper towel and place in oven overnight. Do not turn on oven.

Shake with lid again and refrigerate. Will hold in refrigerator about 2 weeks.

Crème Fraîche II

1	cup heavy cream
½	cup sour cream

Follow the procedure as above.

Lemon Sauce

makes 1½ cup

½   cup sugar
1   rounded T. cornstarch
¼   tsp. salt
1   cup boiling water
1   tsp. grated lemon rind
3   T. lemon juice
2   T. butter

Mix together sugar, cornstarch and salt. Gradually stir in boiling water. Bring to a boil over low heat for 15 minutes, stirring until smooth, thickened and clear. Remove from heat. Stir in lemon rind, juice and butter.

Liberty Hall Pudding Sauce

serves 12

1   cup butter
2   cups sugar
4   eggs
½   cup good sherry
2   T. brandy or Kentucky Bourbon
½   cup blanched almonds, slivered and toasted
1   tsp. nutmeg

Cream butter and sugar. Add eggs, one at a time and beat until light and fluffy. Add Sherry, and continue beating until well blended. Pour into the top of a double boiler and set over low heat. Stir until mixture just coats a spoon (like boiled custard). Remove from heat and add brandy or bourbon. Pour into a sauceboat and sprinkle with almonds and nutmeg.

Serve with fruit puddings or ice cream.

Rum Sauce

makes 2 cups

1   cup sugar
½   cup butter
½   cup coffee cream
2-3   tsp. rum

Combine sugar, butter and coffee cream; heat and stir. Add the rum.

Serve over cakes, puddings, custards and ice cream.

Seasoned Salt

6   T. salt
½   tsp. thyme leaves
½   tsp. marjoram
½   tsp. garlic salt
2¼   tsp. paprika
½   tsp. curry powder
1   tsp. dry mustard
¼   tsp. onion powder
⅛   tsp. dill seeds
½   tsp. celery salt

Combine all ingredients in a small jar. Cover and shake until well blended or whiz in blender until well mixed.

Use this salt to season salads, meats and vegetables.

Mustard Pickle

makes 14 pints

2 medium heads cauliflower, cut into florets
4 medium onions, chopped
1 bunch celery, cut in ½-inch pieces
4 green peppers, seeded and chopped
12 very small green tomatoes, cut in halves and quartered
3 large cucumbers, halved, seeded, cut in chunks
1 cup salt
1 cup cider vinegar
1 recipe MUSTARD SAUCE (below)
2 8-oz. jars cocktail onions
1 16-oz. jar gherkins or midget pickles, drained

Sprinkle cut-up vegetable with salt and let stand for several hours. Drain thoroughly. Heat vinegar in roasting pan. Add cauliflower, onions and celery, simmer for 10 minutes. Add tomatoes and peppers; cook 5 minutes. Add cucumbers, and cook 2 minutes. Thin the mustard sauce with enough of the hot vinegar, so that it can easily be mixed with the vegetables. Stir well, and add the little pickled cucumbers and onions. Continue cooking for 2-3 minutes, stirring constantly to keep it from sticking to the bottom of the pan. Fill sterilized jars and seal at once.

Mustard Sauce
6 oz. Coleman's dry mustard
1 oz. curry powder
¾ oz. tumeric
1½ T. celery seed
1½ oz. white mustard seed
4 cups sugar
½ cup flour
1 qt. cider vinegar

Combine dry ingredients in a heavy pan. Gradually add vinegar, mixing well until there are no lumps. Cook over moderate heat, stirring constantly, until quite thick.

Peach Chutney

makes 9 pints

4 lbs. peaches, peeled, seeded
1 cup crystalized ginger
1 T. salt
1 T. chili powder (new jar)
1½ lbs. sugar
½ cup onions, paper thin
½ lb. raisins
2 T. mustard seeds (new box)
3 cups cider vinegar

Cut onions paper thin and peaches thin; add other ingredients and put in a large kettle over high heat; bring to boil, reduce heat and simmer for 2-3 hours. Do not mush mixture but stir gently so mixture does not stick to bottom of pan. Pour into sterilized jars and seal. (If mixture is too thin, remove solids and cook fluid down and re-add solids).

Note: Mangos may be used instead of peaches.

Notes

Notes

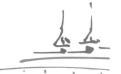

ELEVENTH RACE

BREAD

COMMITTEE'S HANDICAP

1	HOT SAUSAGE BREAD	SERVES 6-8
2	SPIRAL HERB BREAD	SERVES 8
3	BEATEN BISCUITS	SERVES 12
4	APRICOT BREAD	SERVES 8-10
5	PLAINVIEW SPOON BREAD	SERVES 6
6	MAKER'S MARK BOURBON BREAD	SERVES 8
7	KITTY'S OATMEAL BREAD	SERVES 6-8
8	QUICK BRIOCHE	SERVES 12

Committee Selections 3-6-8

Kentucky bred entry 3, 4, 5, 6

All Natural Wheat Bran Muffins

Makes 30 Muffins

2¾	cups flour
1	cup brown sugar
1½	cups wheat bran
1	cup all-bran
1½	T. baking soda
2	cups buttermilk
¾	cup vegetable oil
2	eggs
¼	cup molasses
1	cup raisins

Preheat oven to 350 degrees. Combine all dry ingredients except for baking soda. In a separate bowl combine buttermilk, oil, eggs, molasses and baking soda. Mix well. Make a well in the dry ingredients and add the liquid and mix well. Add raisins. Spoon into well-greased muffin pans and bake for 20 minutes.

Note: This recipe may be doubled. The batter will keep in the refrigerator for 2-4 weeks.

Blueberry Muffins

1½ dozen

½	cup oats, quick or regular
½	cup orange juice
1½	cups flour
¼	tsp. baking soda
½	tsp. salt
1¼	tsp. baking powder
½	cup oil
1	egg, lightly beaten
½	cup sugar
1	cup blueberries

Topping:
¼	tsp. cinnamon
1	T. sugar
1	T. brown sugar

Preheat oven to 400 degrees. Combine oats and orange juice; set aside. Sift the flour, soda, salt and baking powder three times. Add oil and egg to oatmeal-juice mixture and stir. Add sugar and finally the sifted dry ingredients; stir until just mixed. Add blueberries. In a separate bowl, combine topping ingredients. Pour batter into greased muffin tins or liners. Sprinkle on topping mixture. Bake for 18-22 minutes.

Gem Date Bran Muffins

42 miniature muffins or 18 regular muffins

1½	cups Kellogg's All-Bran
½	cup quick oats
1	cup boiling water
½	cup shortening
1¼	cups sugar
2	eggs
2½	cups unbleached flour
2½	tsp. baking soda
1	tsp. salt
2	cups buttermilk
1	cup Bran Buds
6	oz. dates, chopped
½	cup walnuts, chopped

Preheat oven to 425 degrees. Add boiling water to All-Bran and oats. Let sit after you have given it a few good stirs. Beat in shortening and sugar. Add eggs. Sift flour, soda and salt together. Add All-Bran mixture to shortening and sugar mixture and beat well. Add flour mixture alternately with buttermilk. Stir in by hand the Bran Buds, dates and nuts and mix lightly. Pour in greased muffin tins or paper liners. Bake 16-18 minutes for miniature muffins and 20 minutes for regular size muffins. These freeze well.

BREAD

Brown Sugar Muffins   14 muffins

1½	cups flour
¼	cup sugar
¼	tsp. salt
¼	tsp. cinnamon
3½	tsp. baking powder
¼	cup light brown sugar
1	egg, beaten lightly
½	cup oil
½	cup milk

Preheat oven to 350 degrees. Sift first 5 ingredients. Blend in brown sugar. Combine egg, oil and milk; stir into dry ingredients until moist. Fill oiled muffin tins ⅔ full. Bake at 350 degrees for 20 minutes.

Carrot Cake Muffins   12 muffins

1	cup grated carrots
1¼	cups whole wheat flour
2	T. white flour
1	egg
½	cup honey
½	cup butter, melted
½	tsp. cinnamon
1	tsp. baking soda
2	tsp. baking powder
¼	cup lemon juice

In a large bowl, combine all ingredients and mix well. Pour into greased muffin tins. Bake at 350 degrees for 20 minutes.

Pistachio Butter   ¾ cup

½	cup butter
2	T. honey
¼	tsp. ground cinnamon
¼	cup shelled natural Pistachios, finely chopped
	few drops of green coloring

Beat together butter, honey and cinnamon until smooth. Blend in pistachios and green coloring. Serve with biscuits, muffins, croissants, or waffles.

Maple Butter   1 cup

1	stick unsalted butter, room temperature
¼	tsp. maple flavoring
4	tsp. brown sugar
½	cup pure maple syrup

Use metal blade of processor to process butter, maple flavoring and sugar until creamy and smooth, about 1 minute. With machine running, pour syrup very slowly through feed tube. Process until mixture and syrup are thoroughly mixed. Transfer to a small crock or ramekin. Serve with biscuits, muffins, waffles or pancakes.

Tasty Trivia
Fresh ginger root may be peeled, sliced in ¼ inch pieces and stored in dry sherry in a jar in the refrigerator.

Pecan Muffins

36 muffins

2	cups all-purpose flour
4	tsp. baking powder
½	tsp. salt
1	egg, beaten
1	cup milk
2	T. butter, melted and cooled
½	cup sugar
1	cup pecans, chopped

Preheat oven to 350 degrees. Sift together the flour, baking powder and salt. To the beaten egg, add the milk, the melted butter and sugar. Gently stir in the flour mixture, until the flour is moistened. Add the pecans. Spoon batter into greased, small (1½ inch) muffin tins, filling half-full. Bake at 350 degrees for approximately 15 minutes or until firm to touch.

Apricot Bread

2 small loaves

1	cup dried apricots, chopped
1	cup cold water
½	lemon, juice only
½	cup shortening
1	cup sugar
2	eggs
2	cups flour, plus 2 tsp. for dredging nuts
2	tsp. baking powder
½	tsp. baking soda
1	cup broken pecans (optional)

Boil the apricots in cold water until tender. (Note: apricots may be chopped and soaked in cold water before cooking which will decrease the cooking time.) Add lemon juice to cooked apricots and let cool.

Creme shortening and sugar, then add eggs one at a time, beating after each addition. Sift and measure flour; add soda and baking powder and sift again. Stir flour into egg-sugar mixture. Fold in apricots after they have cooled. Fold in pecans which have been dredged in 1-2 teaspoons of flour. Pour into two 7 x 3-inch greased loaf pans. Bake 50-60 minutes at 325 degrees. Time and temperature will depend on size of pans.

Mini-Cinnamon Wheels

20 rolls

4	T. sugar
2	tsp. cinnamon
2	T. chopped nuts, optional
1	can crescent rolls
½	cup butter, softened

Preheat oven to 375 degrees. Mix sugar, cinnamon and nuts, if used; set aside. Separate rolls into 4 rectangles. Press perforations to seal. Spread with butter and sprinkle with cinnamon mixture. Roll, starting at short side. Cut each roll into 5 slices and place, cut side down, on ungreased baking pan with sides. Bake for 10-15 minutes. Watch carefully after 10 minutes.

Glaze:

1	cup powdered sugar
2	T. milk

Make a glaze of the powdered sugar and milk; stir until smooth. Drizzle over rolls while they are still warm.

Strawberry Muffins

From Sarah Fritschner's column in the *Courier Journal* and *Louisville Times*   12 Muffins

1¾	cups flour
¼	cup sugar
1½	tsp. baking powder
½	tsp. baking soda
2	T. butter, melted and cooled, room temperature
1	egg, beaten
½	cup strawberry preserves
1	cup sour cream
½	cup strawberries, (cut up the size of blueberries)

Preheat oven to 400 degrees. Sift flour, sugar, baking powder and baking soda onto waxed paper. In a medium bowl, beat butter, egg, preserves and sour cream. Add dry mixture and blend with a few swift strokes. Add strawberries and stir carefully. (The mixture will be lumpy and show spots of flour). Divide among 12 well-greased muffin tins and bake at 400 degrees for 20 minutes or until light brown.

Serve with strawberry butter.

Strawberry butter:

1	stick butter, room temperature
⅛	cup strawberry preserves

Whip together until well blended.

Whole Wheat Ginger Orange Muffins   10-12 Muffins

½	cup currants, soaked in 2 T. Triple Sec
1	cup all-purpose flour
½	cup whole wheat flour
½	cup granulated sugar
⅓	cup light brown sugar
2	tsp. ground ginger
2	tsp. baking powder
½	tsp. baking soda
¼	tsp. salt
2-3	T. minced crystallized ginger
1	T. grated orange peel
7	T. butter, melted and cooled
⅓	cup sour cream
⅓	cup orange juice
2	eggs, room temperature

Soak currants in the Triple Sec (or Grand Marnier) a few hours; stirring now and then. Preheat the oven to 400 degrees. Generously grease 2½ inch muffin cups or line them with paper baking cups.

Mix the flours with the sugars, ginger, baking powder, soda and salt; break up any lumps. Stir in the crystallized ginger and orange peel.

Whisk the butter, sour cream, orange juice and eggs in a bowl. Make a well in the middle of the dry ingredients and add the butter mixture and the currants to the well, stirring just until blended (some lumps may remain).

Spoon the batter into the prepared cups, filling each ¾ full. Bake until muffins are golden brown and tester inserted in center comes out clean, 18-20 minutes. Cool 5 minutes and turn out of pan. Serve warm.

Tasty Trivia
Beaten Biscuits were not noted in menus before 1900.
Before the invention of a beaten biscuit board (actually a
slab of marble with two rollers attached), the dough was
folded and beaten with a mallet until the dough popped. Now
motorized boards are operated with a sewing machine foot.
The late Hugh Wood of Hopkinsville gave this recipe to
Laurie Lussky in 1972. He was 89 years old.

BREAD

Beaten Biscuits

3½ dozen

4½ cups flour
½ tsp. salt
1½ tsp. baking powder
3 T. sugar
½ cup lard
½ cup milk
½ cup ice water

Sift dry ingredients. Cut in lard until it resembles meal. Add liquid quickly (as for pie crust). Knead for a few minutes, then beat with a rolling pin (or put through pasta rollers) until it pops and blisters. Divide dough into 3 parts and fold it over each time before passing it through the rollers. Cut with a small biscuit cutter. Pierce each biscuit several times with the tines of a fork, (to allow air to escape). Bake at 350 degrees for 30 minutes, or until the tops are a light golden color.

"Quick" Beaten Biscuits

72 halves

2 cups all-purpose flour
1 tsp. salt
½ cup unsalted butter, cut into pieces
½ cup ice water

Preheat oven to 350 degrees with rack in middle position. Place the flour and salt in work bowl of food processor. Turn processor on and off twice to aerate mixture. Add butter and process until mixture is consistency of cornmeal. With machine running, pour ice water through the feed tube in a steady stream. Process until mixture forms a ball, then process for an additional 2 minutes.

Roll dough out on a lightly floured surface to a rectangle ⅛" thick. Fold dough in half to form two layers. Cut through both layers of dough with a 1½" round cutter with a fluted edge. Place biscuits on ungreased cookie sheets and bake in oven for 25-30 minutes or until golden brown. Remove from oven and split biscuits immediately. If centers are soft, return split halves to oven for an additional 3-4 minutes to assure a crisp base for spreads.

Biscuits for a Party

300-500 biscuits

5 lbs. self-rising flour
3 lbs. can Snow Drift shortening (leave 1 inch of shortening in can.)
2 13 oz. cans Carnation evaporated milk
1-2 cans water (milk can)

Preheat oven to 400 degrees. Cut shortening into flour. Add milk and enough water to make dough of proper consistency to roll. Working with ¼ of the dough at a time, roll out and fold over until it reaches the proper thickness. Cut with biscuit cutter and place on cookie sheet. Freeze and place in Ziploc bag. Remove from freezer and bake at 400 degrees until brown. If completely thawed before baking, the baking time will be shorter.

186

Richard's Delicious Biscuits

Chef Richard, River Valley Club, Louisville, KY   10 to 12 biscuits

1	tsp. salt
2	cups all purpose flour
4	tsp. baking powder
1	tsp. baking soda
½	cup shortening
1	cup buttermilk

Preheat oven to 400 degrees. Mix salt, flour, baking powder and baking soda together. Cut in the shortening and blend this mixture until it is the texture of cornmeal. Pour in the buttermilk slowly, constantly stirring the batter. Knead this mixture with your hand in the bowl until all the dough comes clean from the sides. If the dough does not clean the sides of the bowl then the biscuits will not be right! This dough can be made up to a week in advance and stored in the refrigerator. Cover the dough with a damp cloth and then cover with plastic wrap. Roll out on a lightly floured surface ½-inch thick. Fold dough over into a half-circle and cut with biscuit cutter. Bake for 10-12 minutes at 400 degrees.

Whole Wheat Biscuits   2 dozen

2	cups whole wheat flour
5	tsp. baking powder
2	tsp. sugar
½	tsp. salt
½	tsp. soda
⅓	cup shortening
1	cup buttermilk

Preheat oven to 450 degrees. Sift together the dry ingredients. Cut in the shortening and add the buttermilk. Mix with fork and roll out ½-inch thick. Bake for 20 minutes.

Breakfast Puffs   12 muffins

⅓	cup shortening
½	cup sugar
1	egg, room temperature
1½	cups sifted flour
1½	tsp. baking powder
¼	tsp. nutmeg
½	tsp. salt
½	cup milk
½	stick butter, melted
½	cup sugar
1	tsp. cinnamon

Preheat oven to 350 degrees. Cream shortening and sugar; add egg and beat. Sift flour, baking powder, nutmeg and salt; add, alternating with milk. Fill greased muffin cups ½ to ⅔ full. Bake at 350 degrees for 20-25 minutes. May be baked in regular sized tins (makes 12) or small tins (makes 24). Mix the remaining sugar and cinnamon. After baking, dip muffins very quickly into melted butter and roll in cinnamon-sugar mixture.

BREAD

Caraway Cheese Bread

1 loaf (9 x 5) or 2 loaves (7 x 3)

2	cups sifted flour
½	tsp. baking soda
½	tsp. salt
2	tsp. baking powder
1	T. caraway seeds
1½	cups grated sharp cheese
1	cup evaporated milk
1	T. vinegar
1	egg, beaten slightly
1	T. melted butter

Sift dry ingredients together. Add caraway seeds and cheese. Combine remaining ingredients and add to dry ingredients, stirring until moistened. Bake in greased loaf pans at 350 degrees. One 9x5-inch pan takes about 50-60 minutes. Two 7x3-inch pans take about 35 minutes. Let cool on rack a few minutes. Turn out to finish cooling. Serve warm with butter. This bread can be frozen.

Broccoli Bread

12-16 squares

1	pkg. frozen chopped broccoli, thawed and drained well
1	large onion, chopped (or 2 T. dried onions)
6	oz. cottage cheese
1	stick butter, melted
4	eggs, beaten
1	tsp. salt (optional)
1	box Jiffy corn muffin mix

Preheat oven to 400 degrees. Mix broccoli, onion, cottage cheese, butter, eggs and salt; mix well. Stir in the corn bread mix. Pour into a greased casserole dish (9 x 13 or 9 ½ x 7-inches). Bake for 25 minutes, or until it tests done in the center.

Maker's Mark Bourbon Bread

2 loaves

⅓	cup Makers Mark Bourbon
¾	cup raisins
1¼	cups softened butter
1½	cups sugar
6	eggs, separated
2¼	cups flour
1½	tsp. vanilla
1	cup coarsely chopped pecans (or walnuts)

Soak raisins in Makers Mark for 2 hours. Drain, reserving Bourbon. (Should be ⅓ cup—if not, add more Bourbon to make ⅓ cup). Grease two 8 ½ x 4 ½ x 3-inch loaf pans and line bottoms of pans with waxed paper. Preheat oven to 350 degrees.

In bowl, cream butter and ½ cup sugar until fluffy. Add egg yolks, one at a time, beating well. Add flour in thirds, alternating with Bourbon, mixing until well blended. Stir in raisins, vanilla and pecans.

In a large bowl, with clean beaters, beat egg whites until soft peaks form. Gradually beat in remaining 1 cup sugar and beat until fluffy. Gently fold egg whites into batter. Turn batter into prepared pans and bake one hour or until it tests done.

Track Talk
Though Man O'War won the Preakness and Belmont, he did
not run in the 1920 Derby. In fact, he never raced in Kentucky.

Cheese Waffles

5 waffles

2	cups flour
½	tsp. salt
2	tsp. baking powder
1¼	cups milk
3	egg yolks, beaten
5	T. melted butter
1	cup grated sharp cheese
3	egg whites, stiffly beaten

Sift dry ingredients. Mix milk and egg yolks; add to flour. Beat until smooth. Add butter and cheese. Beat egg whites until stiff and fold in batter. Bake in a hot waffle iron. Can also be baked on a hot griddle.

These waffles are good alone, topped with butter and sprinkled with more cheese. They also may serve as a base for creamed chicken or turkey, or similar dishes.

Glenis' Egg Cornbread

6-8 wedges

1	cup cornmeal
1	cup flour
4	tsp. baking powder
3	T. sugar
1	tsp. salt
1½	cups milk
2	eggs
2	T. shortening (bacon grease is also good)

Preheat oven to 400 degrees. Melt shortening in a 9-inch cast iron skillet in the oven, while preparing batter. Mix and sift dry ingredients. Combine with milk, eggs and shortening. Beat well. Pour into hot skillet. Bake for about 20 minutes, or until brown on top. Serve hot.

Granola

approx. 12 cups

1	cup sunflower seeds or other nuts
1	cup bran
5	cups oats
1	cup wheat germ
1	cup powdered milk
1	can (8oz.) coconut
½	tsp. ground cloves
1	tsp. cinnamon
1	tsp. freshly grated nutmeg
1	cup safflower oil
1	cup honey
2	tsp. vanilla

Mix sunflower seeds, bran, oats, wheat germ, powdered milk, coconut, cloves, cinnamon and nutmeg in large bowl. Heat oil, honey and vanilla in a saucepan, stirring often. Pour over dry ingredients and mix well. Bake at 275 degrees for 30 minutes, stirring frequently.

Comments: This is a great "pick up" snack for house guests and a nice breakfast treat as well. The powdered milk gives it a very different and good taste.

Herbed French Bread

1 loaf

1	loaf unsliced French or Italian bread
¼	lb. melted butter
¼	tsp. paprika
½	tsp. thyme
¼	tsp. summer savory
¼	tsp. salt
1	clove garlic, finely minced dash cayenne

Cut the loaf of bread in diamonds by cutting diagonally in 2-inch thick slices in one direction and then again diagonally in 2-inch thick slices back in the opposite direction to create diamonds.

Mix the butter with the remaining ingredients and brush on all cut surfaces, in the diamonds of the bread, and on top. Wrap in foil and heat in a 425 degree oven for 15 minutes. Uncover the top and cook an additional 5 minutes. Serve while warm.

If fresh herbs are available, increase the thyme and summer savory to three times the amount of the dried herb.

Hot Sausage Bread

1 loaf

3	cups flour
1	tsp. ginger
1	tsp. pumpkin pie spice
1	tsp. baking powder
1	tsp baking soda
1	cup cold coffee
1	lb. hot sausage
1½	cups light brown sugar
1½	cups granulated sugar
2	eggs, room temperature
1	cup pecans, chopped
1	cup raisins, soaked in water to cover for 5 minutes and drained

Mix together flour, ginger, pumpkin pie spice and baking powder. Set aside. Mix baking soda and coffee and set aside. In a large bowl mix together sausage, brown sugar, granulated sugar and eggs. Add pecans, raisins and flour mixture; stir well. Add coffee mixture; stir well. Pour into greased and floured bundt pan and bake at 350 degrees for 1 hour and 15 minutes.

Keeps in refrigerator for 3-4 weeks

Hot Water Cornbread for Corn Cakes

Serves 2-4

2	cups white corn meal
1	tsp. salt
	boiling Water

Have griddle hot and well-greased. Pour enough boiling water over corn meal to make a medium-thick consistency. Put on hot skillet immediately, a spoonful at a time. Turn when brown on one side. Place on a warm platter and serve.

BREAD

Quick Brioche

3-4 dozen

1½	cups flour
1½	tsp. baking powder
½	tsp. salt
2	T. sugar
2	eggs
¾	cup cream
2	T. soft butter
1	egg yolk
1	tsp. water

Preheat oven to 300 degrees. Sift together flour, baking powder, salt and sugar. Beat eggs and cream until blended. Stir in the flour mixture, beating constantly. Add the soft butter and continue beating for 5 minutes. (May use mixer with a dough hook.) Drop heaping table-spoons of dough onto buttered baking sheets. Bake 10 minutes. Increase heat to 400 degrees and bake 8-10 minutes longer. Mix the egg yolk and water. Just before they are done, brush the brioches with the egg yolk glaze. Good hot or cold.

Pineapple-Apricot Nut Loaves

4 large loaves or 6 small loaves

2 ¾	cups all-purpose flour
1	T. baking powder
¼	tsp. baking soda
¼	tsp. salt
¾	cup sugar
⅓	cup butter or margarine, melted
1	egg
⅓	cup milk
1	(8 oz.) can crushed pineapple, undrained
⅓	cup dried apricots, chopped
¼	cup light raisins
1	T. candied green cherries or citron, chopped (optional)
1	cup nuts, chopped-pecans or walnuts

Preheat oven to 375 degrees. Grease and flour six (4 ½ x 2½ x 1-inch) or four (5 ¾ x 3 x 2⅓-inch) loaf pans.

Sift flour with baking powder, baking soda and salt. In large bowl, combine sugar, melted butter and egg; using wooden spoon, beat until ingredients are well blended. Add milk, pineapple, apricots, raisins and cherries; blend well. Add flour mixture; beat just until combined. Stir in nuts. Pour into prepared pans. Bake 20 to 25 min-utes, or until cake tester inserted in the middle comes out clean. Let cool in pan 10 minutes. Remove from pan and let cool on cake rack.

Plainview Farm Spoon Bread

Serves 4

2	cups milk
⅛	tsp. salt
2	T. sugar
⅓	cup cornmeal
1	T. butter
2	large eggs, separated

Preheat oven to 350 degrees

Bring the milk, salt and sugar to a boil and reduce to simmer. Stir in cornmeal and continue to stir until it thickens. Remove from the heat and add the butter. Cool 5 minutes. Beat in the egg yokes, slightly beaten. Cool slightly and fold in the whites, stiffly beaten. Bake in a buttered 1½ quart casserole or soufflé mold for 25 to 35 minutes. Serve immediately with sweet butter.

BREAD

Processor Bourbon Raisin Banana Bread

1 loaf

1	cup raisins
4	T. Bourbon
½	cup walnuts
1	medium-size Granny Smith apple, peeled and cut in eights
½	cup butter, cut in pieces
1	cup granulated sugar
2	large eggs, room temperature
3	medium-size ripe bananas, cut in pieces
1	tsp. vanilla
½	tsp. salt
1	tsp. baking soda
2	cups all-purpose flour

Soak the raisins in Bourbon overnight. Place walnuts in the bowl of the food processor and with the metal blade, chop with several quick pulses of the machine and set aside in a small bowl. Place the apple in the work bowl and chop into fine pieces with several quick pulses of the machine and set aside in a bowl.

Cream the butter and sugar in the work bowl with the metal blade until well mixed. Add the eggs and process until smooth and no longer grainy. Add the bananas and process until smooth. Add the vanilla, salt and baking soda; mix with 2 quick pulses. Add the flour in 3 equal additions with 2 quick pulses after each addition. Mix until flour is moistened. Add the raisins and bourbon, nuts and apples. Pulse 2 times just to mix. Pour into a well-greased 9 x 5 x 3 inch loaf pan or 2 7½ x 3½ x 2¼ inch pans. Bake at 350 degrees for 60 minutes or until tester comes out clean from the middle. Take out of pan and cool on wire rack.

Laurie's Buttermilk Bread

2 (9 x 5) loaves

2	cups buttermilk
1	stick butter
½	cup warm water
2	T. dry yeast
8	cups unbleached flour—maybe more
2	tsp. salt (optional)
¼	tsp. baking soda
3	T. sugar

Heat milk and butter in saucepan until butter is melted. Cool to lukewarm. Dissolve yeast in warm water in a small bowl. Let "proof" 10 minutes, until it swells. Add it to the milk mixture. Sift 2 cups flour with other dry ingredients, add to liquid mixture. Add small amounts of flour until dough is stiff and workable and smooth. Knead well. Cover bowl with plastic wrap; let rise for an hour, or until double in bulk. Punch down and let rise again.

Put dough on a floured surface and knead until smooth. Divide into 2 portions and let it rest for a few minutes, then shape into 2 loaves. Place in 2 well-greased 9 x 5-inch pans. Gently cover with a clean dish towel and let rise about 40 minutes, after placing in a cold oven (free of drafts), or until a dent remains in dough when you poke it with your finger. Remove towel. Turn on oven to 350 degrees and bake 35-40 minutes or until a nice brown top is achieved. Turn out of pans onto their sides on a wire rack to cool. If you want a soft top, wrap the loaves in dish towels while warm. When completely cool, store in plastic bags and seal with bag ties.

Cheese Carrot Bread

2 loaves (8 x 4)

1	**pkg. dry yeast**
1 ¾	**cup warm water (110°-120°)**
	pinch sugar
2	**T. sugar**
⅓	**cup non-fat dry milk**
2 ½	**cups sharp Cheddar cheese, grated before measuring**
½	**cup grated raw carrots**
3	**T. vegetable oil**
2	**tsp. salt**
5-6	**cups all-purpose flour**

Grease 2 medium loaf pans (8 ½ x 4 ½). In a large mixing bowl, sprinkle yeast over water. Stir and add pinch of sugar. Let rest 3-4 minutes until bubbles appear. Add 2 tablespoons sugar, milk, cheese, carrots, vegetable oil and salt. Stir with a wooden spoon or electric mixer for 30 seconds. Add 3 cups of flour and beat at medium speed for 3 minutes or 100 strokes with a wooden spoon. Add 2 cups more flour, mixing with the spoon and then by hand until dough pulls away from the sides of the bowl.

Turn dough onto a floured surface and knead, adding small portions of flour until dough is no longer sticky. Knead about 8 minutes until ball is smooth and satiny. Return dough to oiled bowl; cover tightly with plastic wrap and let double in bulk in a warm spot. Test dough by poking a finger into it. If a dent remains, it has risen properly.

Remove wrap, punch down with fist and turn out onto a floured surface. Cut into 2 equal pieces with sharp knife. Shape into 2 loaves and put into loaf pans.

Cover with plastic wrap and return to warm place to double in bulk.

Bake for 35-45 minutes at 350 degrees or until golden brown. When tapping the bottom of the bread, if there is a hard, hollow sound, the loaves are done.

Turn out onto racks to cool.

Squash Bread

2 loaves

½	**cup butter (or 1 cup oil)**
2½	**cups sugar**
4	**eggs, room temperature**
3½	**cups flour**
2	**tsp. baking soda**
1	**tsp. cinnamon**
1	**tsp. nutmeg**
1½	**tsp. salt**
⅔	**cup water**
2	**cups winter squash (Hubbards or butternut)**

Preheat oven to 350 degrees. Grease and flour two 3 x 11-inch pans, or two 9 x 5-inch pans. Mix butter and sugar well. Beat in eggs, one at a time. Sift together flour, soda, cinnamon, nutmeg and salt; add to butter and sugar mixture, alternating with water. Add squash and mix well. Pour into pans and bake for 50-60 minutes, or until cake tester inserted in middle, comes out clean.

193

Dee Cunningham's Kuchen

1 large or 2 small kuchen

½   cup milk
4   T. butter or margarine
¼   cup sugar
1   tsp. salt
1   package yeast
¼   cup warm water (110°-120°)
2   eggs
3 ½ cups all purpose flour

Scald milk. Add butter, sugar and salt; let milk cool to below 120 degrees. Dissolve yeast in warm water. Add yeast mixture to the milk mixture. Beat in the eggs, then beat in the flour. Cover and put in a warm place for 1-1½ hours, or until doubled in bulk. Turn out on a floured board and roll to fit a large greased cookie sheet, or two 9-inch greased cake pans. Pinch the edges to form sides. Put in a warm place again for 45 minutes to 1 hour. Meanwhile prepare either topping to be poured on before the kuchen is baked. Bake at 350 degrees for 25-30 minutes.

Cheese topping:
1   8-oz. cream cheese, softened
3   eggs
½   cup sugar
¼   tsp. cinnamon
1   small can crushed pineapple,
     drained (optional)

Mix ingredients well. Pour on crust after second rising. Bake.

Butter topping:
1   stick butter
1   cup sugar
3   eggs
½   tsp. vanilla
¼   cup chopped pecans (optional)

Mix all ingredients well. Pour on crust after second rising. Bake.

Homemade Crackers

18 huge crackers

1   T. dry yeast (1 pkg.)
5   cups unbleached flour
     salt to taste
¾   tsp. sugar
1¼   cups warm water (110°-120°)
1   stick unsalted butter, melted

Mix yeast, flour, salt and sugar in bowl. Add warm water to melted butter and pour over dry ingredients, making sure that the water is not too hot for the yeast. Add a little more water if needed. Mix thoroughly.
Cover bowl with a piece of plastic wrap and let dough rise for about an hour. Pinch off small balls of dough and roll as thin as possible. (You can use a pasta roller for this if you have one). Preheat oven to 350 degrees and bake crackers on ungreased cookie sheet for about 15 minutes, or until a medium brown color.

BREAD

194

Homemade Rolls

4 dozen

1	pkg. dry yeast
½	cup warm water
½	cup boiling water
½	cup solid vegetable shortening
½	cup sugar, or less, if preferred
¾	tsp. salt
1	egg, beaten
3	cups flour
½	cup butter, melted

Dissolve yeast in warm water (110-120 degrees). Pour boiling water over shortening, sugar and salt; and mix until well blended. Add beaten egg and yeast mixture; blend well. Add flour one cup at a time blending well after each addition. Refrigerate overnight, covered. Roll out on floured surface, cut in circles and dip in melted butter; fold over in half. Cover rolls with waxed paper and refrigerate until ready to use. Let rise at room temperature 3 hours, uncovered. Bake 7 minutes at 400 degrees, or until medium brown.

French Bread
processor

2 loaves

1	pkg. dry yeast
1½	T. sugar
1¼	cup water (10 oz.)
1	tsp. salt
3½	cups flour
1	T. oil
	white corn meal
1	egg white, optional

In a 2-cup measure put 1¼ cups water, 115 degrees (a temperature probe in a microwave is an easy way to heat it to proper temperature.) Add sugar and yeast and let "proof". In work bowl with metal blade, combine flour and salt; process for several seconds. Through feed tube add the yeast mixture along with oil. Process until dough "forms". Run 1 minute more to knead. Put into a greased bowl. Cover and allow to rise until triple in size. (at least 1 hour). Punch down. Let rise again for 20 minutes. Remove from bowl and divide in two parts. Roll each piece into a rectangle, then roll each up into a long loaf, smoothing ends. Place on baking sheet sprinkled with cornmeal, or bake in double baguette pans which have been sprinkled with cornmeal. Let rise again for about 40 minutes or until light. Cut slashes in tops, if desired, and brush with a little milk or some egg wash (1 egg white beaten with 1 tablespoon water), Bake at 400 degrees for about 20 minutes or 25 minutes in baguette pan.

Tasty Trivia
Kneading the dough for a half minute after mixing improves the texture of baking powder biscuits.

Grace Smith's Honey Wheat Bread

makes 2 (1¾ pound) loaves.

Breadmaking-In-Bag™

4	cups all purpose flour
3¾	cups whole wheat flour
2	pkgs. active dry yeast
2 ½	cups warm water (105°-115°)
¼	cup honey
¼	cup nonfat dry milk
2	T. vegetable oil
1	T. salt

Combine in plastic bag
(2 gallon heavy duty freezer bag):
   1 cup all purpose flour
   2 packages active dry yeast
   1 cup warm water (110-115 degrees F)
   2 tablespoons honey

Squeeze upper part of bag to force out air. Close top of bag tightly between thumb and index finger. Rest bag on table; mix by working bag with fingers about 20 seconds or until all ingredients are completely blended. Let rest in bag 15 minutes.

Add remaining ingredients:
   1½ cups warm water
   2 tablespoons honey
   ¼ cup non-fat milk
   2 tablespoons vegetable oil
   1 tablespoon salt

Mix by working bag with finger. Add whole wheat flour; mix thoroughly. Gradually add remaining all purpose flour until a stiff dough is formed, about 2½ cups or until dough pulls away from bag. Turn dough out onto floured surface. Divide dough in half. Knead each half 5 minutes or until dough is smooth and elastic. Add more flour if necessary. Cover with plastic bag. Let rest 10 minutes.

Flatten dough into a 12 x 7-inch rectangle. At narrow end fold corner to center to form a point. Beginning with point, roll dough tightly towards you. Pinch the edges to seal. Press dough at each end to seal and fold ends under. Place seam side down in a greased 8½ x 4½ x 2¼-inch loaf pan. Repeat with second loaf.

Cover loosely with plastic bag and let rise in warm place 45-60 minutes or until doubled. Uncover. Bake on lower rack in 400 degree oven 30-35 minutes or until deep golden brown. Remove from pan immediately. Cool on rack.

Variations: of Honey Wheat Bread:

Mountain Top Bread: Brush tops with melted butter or margarine. Sprinkle with all purpose flour. Repeat with second loaf. Let rise 45-60 minutes. Before baking, carefully make a shallow cut with sharp knife down center of each leaf. Bake as directed.

Track Talk
*The oldest jockey to win the Kentucky Derby is Bill
Shoemaker at age 54 on Ferdinand in 1986. He has ridden
four Derby winners and has the most Derby mounts.*

Variations of Honey Wheat Bread *continued*

Country Crust Bread: After greasing loaf pans, coat bottoms and sides of pans with wheat germ, wheat bran or whole wheat flour. Shape loaves; place seam side down in prepared pans. Brush tops of loaves with vegetable oil. Sprinkle tops of loaves with ¼ cup wheat germ, wheat bran or whole wheat flour. Let rise and bake as directed.

Iced Honey Raisin Bread: For two loaves, in small bowl, mix together 1 cup raisins, ½ cup packed brown sugar and 2 teaspoons cinnamon. Flatten each dough piece into 12 x 7-inch rectangle and brush each piece with softened butter or margarine. Sprinkle raisin mixture on dough. Press raisins in lightly. Shape into loaves, let rise and bake as directed. When cool, frost loaves with Easy Icing: Beat until smooth 1 cup powdered sugar and about 1 tablespoon water.

Party Bundt Bread: Shape loaves as directed *except* do not seal ends. Pinch loaves together to form ring. Place ring seam side up in greased 12-cup bundt pan. Let rise until dough reaches top of bundt pan, about 45-60 minutes. Bake in 375 degrees F oven 40-45 minutes. Invert immediately and cool on rack. When cool, drizzle with

Honey-Nut Glaze: Stirring constantly, bring to boil ¼ cup coarsely chopped nuts, ¼ packed brown sugar, ¼ cup honey and 2 tablespoons butter or margarine.

Soft 'N Salty Pretzels: Divide dough into 24 equal pieces. Roll each piece into 18-inch rope. Twist ropes into pretzel shape and place on greased baking sheets. Brush pretzels with vegetable oil and sprinkle with coarse salt. Cover: let rise until doubled, about ½ hour. Bake in 425 degree F oven 15 to 20 minutes or until golden brown. Cool on rack and store in container with loose fitting cover.

Substitutions: Molasses, brown sugar or granulated sugar may be used in place of honey.
1 cup lukewarm milk and 1½ cups warm water may be used in place of nonfat dry milk and water.
Softened butter or margarine may be used in place of vegetable oil.
All purpose flour may be used in place of whole wheat flour.
Two 9 x 5 x 3-inch pans may be used.

BREAD

Kitty's Oatmeal Bread

1 loaf

1¼	cups milk
1	T. margarine
1½	tsp. salt
¾	cup Quick Quaker Oats
⅜	cup dark brown sugar
1	pkg. yeast
¼	cup water, 110°-120°
4-4½	cups flour

Scald milk; add margarine, salt, oats and sugar. Cool. Proof yeast in warm water. Add yeast mixture and stir in flour. Knead 7-10 minutes. Grease top of dough and let rise in a warm spot until double in size. Punch down and let rise again. Knead 35 times. Form into a 9 x 5-inch loaf and put into a greased loaf pan. Let rise again. Bake at 400 degrees for 10 minutes; then bake at 350 degrees for 40 minutes.

Maple Oatmeal Bread

2 loaves

1	tsp. sugar
2	pkg.(¼ oz. each) active dry yeast
¼	cup warm water (110°-120°)
2	cups regular rolled oats
1	cup real maple syrup
1	cup hot strong decaffeinated coffee (2 ½ tsp. instant coffee to 1 cup water)
⅓	cup butter or margarine
2	tsp. salt
6	cups flour (approximately)
2	eggs, lightly beaten

Sprinkle sugar and yeast over warm water and mix gently. Set aside until bubbles form on surface. Combine and mix oats, maple syrup, hot coffee, butter (cut in pieces), salt, and 1 cup flour in a large mixing bowl. Cool to lukewarm (about 115 degrees); add yeast. Beat in eggs until mixture is smooth. Mix in remaining flour, cup by cup until the dough forms a ball. Knead on a smooth surface until dough is smooth and elastic (about 12-15 minutes). Place the dough in an oiled bowl. Cover with plastic wrap. Let rise 1-½ to 2 hours, until doubled in bulk.

Punch down dough and divide in half; form into 2 loaves and place in buttered 9 x 5 x 3-inch pans. Cover and let rise until doubled in bulk, about 1 hour. Slash the tops and glaze with a beaten egg white mixed with one teaspoon water.

Bake in a preheated 350 degree oven for 45 minutes or until bread sounds hollow when tapped on the bottom with knuckles. Cool on rack.

This bread is best toasted.

Raisin Bread

2 loaves

1 ½	cups milk
4	T. butter
⅓	cup sugar
1	tsp. salt
2	T. dry yeast
2	eggs, lightly beaten
4½-5	cups unbleached flour
2	T. melted butter
1	cup raisins (soaked ½ hour in Sherry, if desired)
	nutmeg to taste

Warm the milk, butter, sugar and salt until butter just melts. Cool to lukewarm (110-120 degrees) and sprinkle in the yeast. Cover with a clean dish towel and proof for 10 minutes. Beat in eggs and flour. Cover pan and let rise for one hour. Punch down. Divide into 2 balls. Roll out each ball into a rectangle. Brush with melted butter and sprinkle with raisins (drained) and nutmeg. Roll up jelly roll fashion. Put in greased 9 x 5-inch loaf pans and let rise about 45 minutes. Bake at 350 degrees for 35 minutes or until brown on top. This bread may be iced with powdered sugar mixed with a small amount of boiling water, or dusted with powdered sugar only.

Note: Raisins and nutmeg may be added to the dough at the beginning, shaped into loaves without rolling up jelly roll fashion.

Mother's Rolls

4 dozen

4	T. sugar
1	tsp. salt
6	T. butter
1	cup boiling water
1	T. dry yeast
3	T. warm water (110°-120°)
1	egg
4	cups flour

Mix sugar, salt, butter and boiling water; let cool until lukewarm. Dissolve yeast in the 3 tablespoons warm water; let proof. Whip egg and add to yeast mixture, then to first mixture. Add flour, beating after each cup. Stir and mix well. Roll out a scant inch thick and cut with a biscuit cutter. Let rise until double in size. Bake at 400 degrees about 15 minutes.

Variation: Mother's Coffee Cake

4	T. unsalted butter
2-3	T. cinnamon
½	cup sugar (brown or white)
	roll dough

After rolling out dough, brush with melted butter, sprinkle with sugar and cinnamon. Roll up as for jelly roll, beginning at wide side. Seal by pinching ends of dough together. Lay in a 10-12 inch round or square greased pan in a spiral (hole in center). Bake at 350 degrees for 45 minutes to one hour, or until a deep golden brown.

Horseshoe Derby Bread

1 loaf

1   recipe dough from Spiral Herb
     Bread
1   egg, beaten slightly with 1 tsp.
     water
     sesame seeds
     poppy seeds

Grease a cookie sheet After the bread has risen once, punch it down and pinch it off into 20 pieces. Form balls 1½ to 2 inches in diameter. The first 9 balls, brush with the beaten egg, dip the tops in sesame seeds and form in a horseshoe shape on the greased cookie sheet. The next 11 balls, brush with egg and dip in the poppy seeds. Place them in a second horseshoe around the first. Cover loosely with plastic wrap and let rise until almost double in size. Place in a preheated oven of 350 degrees for 30-40 minutes or until golden brown.

Spiral Herb Bread

1 loaf

Herb filling:
2   fresh shallots, minced
1   cup minced fresh parsley
1   clove garlic, peeled and minced
3   sprigs fresh thyme, minced or ¼
     tsp. dried thyme
15   basil leaves, minced or ½ tsp.
     dried basil
2   T. butter, softened
1   egg, slightly beaten
¼   tsp. salt
     pinch cayenne
     freshly ground pepper to taste
     few drops of Tabasco

Bread:
1   T. dry yeast
½   cup warm water (110°-120°)
½   cup warm milk (110°-120°)
1   T. sugar
1½   tsp. salt
4   T. butter or margarine
3-4 cups all-purpose flour
1   egg, slightly beaten

In a skillet, sauté the shallots and herbs in the butter over moderate heat for about 10 minutes. Set aside in a bowl. Stir in one egg, and other seasonings and let cool. Dissolve the yeast in the water and let proof 10 minutes in a large bowl. Add the milk, sugar, salt and butter. Stir well; then add flour, one cup at a time, mixing well. Let the dough stand for 10 minutes then knead on a floured work surface for 10-15 minutes. Put in an oiled bowl; turn the dough to coat with oil and let rise in a warm spot, cover with plastic wrap, until doubled in volume or about an hour. Punch the dough down, let stand another 15 minutes, then roll out the dough into a rectangle ¼ inch thick and about 10 inches long. Brush with half the beaten egg, then spread the herb mixture on it, almost to the edges. Roll up jelly roll fashion. Place in a greased loaf pan (11½ x 3½ x 3 or 9 x 5 x 2½ inch pan). Brush the top with the remaining beaten egg and let rise in a warm place for another hour, covered with plastic wrap.

Bake in a preheated 375 degree oven for 40-50 minutes or until the top is a deep brown. Cool on wire rack.

TWELFTH RACE

DESERTS

COMMITTEE'S HANDICAP

1	**MILDRED'S CHESS PIE**	SERVES **8**
2	**BISQUE ICE CREAM**	SERVES **6-8**
3	**HOT ORANGE SOUFFLÉ**	SERVES **8**
4	**CHARLOTTE RUSSE**	SERVES **10**
5	**CADIZ FUDGE CAKE**	SERVES **12-16**
6	**TRANSPARENT BOURBON PIE**	SERVES **8**
7	**AMARETTO ICE CREAM**	SERVES **6**
8	**MAMIE'S COCONUT PIE**	SERVES **8-10**

Committee Selections   5-1-3-7

Kentucky bred entry 1, 2, 4, 6

Apple Nut Cake

serves 16-20

3	eggs, beaten
2	cups sugar
1¼	cups oil
3	cups all-purpose flour
¾	tsp. salt
1	tsp. baking soda
1	tsp. cinnamon
2	tsp. vanilla
3	cups chopped apples
1	cup chopped English walnuts or pecans

Preheat oven to 350 degrees. Beat eggs. Add sugar and oil. Sift flour with salt, soda and cinnamon. Add to egg mixture. Stir until well mixed. Add vanilla. Stir in nuts and apples. Put into lightly greased and floured 9 x 13 pan. Bake for about 50 minutes. Cool and pour following topping over.

Topping:

1	stick butter
1	cup brown sugar
¼	cup cream (may substitute canned milk)
1	tsp. vanilla

In saucepan, bring to boil the butter, sugar and cream. Cook at a full boil for 4-5 minutes. Remove from heat and add vanilla. Beat for about 2 minutes. Pour over cake.

May be baked in two 8 x 8 inch pans for about 45 minutes or in three 7 x 3 inch pans for about 30 minutes.

Cadiz Fudge Cake

serves 12-16

2	cups sugar
1	cup flour
½	cup cocoa
⅛	tsp. salt
1	cup butter, melted and cooled
4	eggs, slightly beaten
1	tsp. vanilla
2	cups chopped pecans

Preheat oven to 350 degrees. Grease 9x13 inch pan.

Mix dry ingredients. Add butter and eggs alternately. Add vanilla. Mix for approximately 1 to 2 minutes at medium speed on electric mixer. Fold in pecans. Pour into pan and bake for 25-30 minutes. Cool in pan.

Icing:

1	lb. confectioners' powdered sugar
½	cup cocoa, dissolved in 6 T. very hot water
½	tsp. vanilla
1	cup melted butter

Mix all ingredients together until smooth. Spread on cake. If too thin, add more confectioners' sugar.

DESSERTS

Track Talk
WIN: When you bet a horse to win, you win if your horse finishes first.
PLACE: You win if your horse finishes first or second.
SHOW: You win if your horse finishes first, second or third.

Fresh Coconut-Carrot Cake

serves 8

1	cup light vegetable oil
2	cups brown sugar, firmly packed
4	eggs
1	tsp. vanilla
2	cups carrots, shredded in processor
1	whole coconut, brown rind removed, shredded or grated in processor
1	cup chopped pecans
1½	cups whole wheat flour
½	cup unbleached flour
1½	tsp. baking powder
1	tsp. baking soda
1	tsp. salt
2	tsp. ground cinnamon
2	tsp. freshly grated nutmeg
3	T. wheat germ

Preheat oven to 350 degress. By hand or with a mixer, mix oil and and sugar in large bowl. Add eggs, one at a time, beating well after each addition. Beat in by hand the vanilla, carrots, coconut and pecans. Stir in whole wheat flour by hand. Sift unbleached flour, baking powder, baking soda, salt, cinnamon and nutmeg together; stir into batter by hand. Add wheat germ. Grease two round or square 9-10 inch cake pans. Spoon batter into pans and bake for 35 minutes or until cake begins to shrink from sides of pan. Let rest 10 minutes. Remove from pans. When cool, frost with cream cheese frosting (recipe follows). Garnish with carrot curls and a little reserved coconut and pecans, if desired. Chill.

Cream Cheese Frosting

1	8-oz. package cream cheese, softened
½	cup unsalted butter, softened
1	16-oz. package powdered sugar, sifted
1	tsp. vanilla

In the processor, or with a beater, mix cream cheese and butter. Add powdered sugar and vanilla slowly. Spread over cakes. For a thinner icing, add 3-5 tablespoons whipping cream.

German Chocolate Cake With Orange Marmalade

serves 8

15	oz. German sweet chocolate
¾	cup plus 3 T. butter
1½	T. grated orange rind
5	T. flour
4	eggs, separated
¾	cup sugar
¾	cup orange marmalade pinch salt

Preheat oven to 375 degrees. Grease 8 inch round cake pan and line bottom with wax paper. Butter and flour paper. Melt 6 ounces chocolate with ¾ cup butter, orange rind and flour. Mix sugar and egg yolks. Add to chocolate mixture. Beat egg whites with salt until stiff. Fold into chocolate mixture. Bake for 30 minutes. Cool.

Heat orange marmalade and cover cake with marmalade. Then melt another bar of chocolate with 2 tablespoons water and 3 tablespoons butter and pour over cake.

Hummingbird Cake

Helen Wiser's recipe won Favorite Cake Award at the 1978 Kentucky State Fair.

serves 12

3	cups flour
2	cups sugar
½	tsp. salt
2	tsp. baking soda
1	tsp. ground cinnamon
3	eggs. well beaten
1¼	cups salad oil
1½	tsp. pure vanilla extract
1	8-oz. can crushed pineapple, drained
¾	cup chopped pecans
¼	cup black walnuts
2	cups chopped banana

Preheat oven to 350 degrees. Sift flour, sugar, salt, baking soda and cinnamon together several times. Put into mixing bowl. Add eggs and salad oil. Stir until dry ingredients are moistened. Do not beat with a mixer. Stir in vanilla, pineapple and both nuts. Finally add the bananas. Spoon the batter into 3 well greased and floured 9 inch round cake pans. Bake for 25-30 minutes or until cake tests done. Cool in pan for 10 minutes, then turn onto cooling rack. Cool completely before frosting.

Ice with the Cream Cheese Frosting that follows or Caramel Icing included in dessert section.

Cream Cheese Frosting:

2	8-oz. packages cream cheese, softened
1	cup butter at room temperature
2	16-oz. boxes powdered sugar
2	tsp. pure vanilla extract
1	cup chopped pecans

Combine cream cheese and butter; cream until smooth. Add powdered sugar, beating with an electric mixer until light and fluffy. Stir in vanilla.

Frost the tops of all 3 layers, stack and then frost edges. Carefully draw a circle on the layer with a toothpick and fill in that circle with the chopped pecans.

(Left over frosting keeps well in the refrigerator)

Kentucky Bourbon Cake

yield 10 inch cake

½	lb. butter
1	lb. confectioners sugar
6	eggs, separated
4	cups flour
2	tsp. baking soda
1	tsp. baking powder
1	T. nutmeg
1	cup Kentucky Bourbon
½	cup molasses
8	oz. raisins, plumped in hot water and drained well
8	oz. dates, chopped
1	lb. pecans, chopped

Preheat oven to 275 degrees. Cream butter and sugar. Add egg yolks and beat. Sift flour, soda, baking powder and nutmeg; add dry ingredients alternately with Bourbon and molasses. Mix in raisins, dates and pecans. Bake for 1 hour or more in a greased 10 inch tube pan or 2 to 3 loaf pans (depending on size). Do not overcook as it will lose the bourbon flavor; cool in the pan. Glaze with heated white corn syrup while warm.

This cake gets better as it sits.

Track Talk
*The Churchill Downs racing strip was labeled fast 65 of the
first 100 runnings of the Kentucky Derby. Twelve of the Runs
for the Roses were contested over good tracks, seven were
labeled slow, nine were heavy, five muddy and two sloppy.*

Crème Caramel

serves 6

1⅓   cups sugar
4   cups whole milk (or cream, if you
      really want it to be rich)
1   cups sugar
4   eggs, beaten
1   tsp. vanilla
      garnish: whipped cream

Caramelize ⅔ cup sugar by placing the sugar in a 1-quart heavy saucepan. Over medium heat, watch carefully for the sugar to start melting. Wash down the sides of the pan with a pastry brush dipped in water to get rid of any stray sugar crystals. Do not stir. The edges will start to turn brown first, and soon after, the rest will take on a golden color and then turn a deep amber. Immediately take off the heat and pour out onto an oiled cookie sheet. When it cools, put the caramelized sugar, or praline, into the food processor and puliverize it until finely chopped. This is to be used on top of the custards, so set aside.

Caramelize another ⅔ cup sugar and pour to evenly coat the bottoms of six 6-ounce custard cup molds or ramekins.

Heat milk and sugar slowly for 5 to 6 minutes; do not boil. Add ½ cup milk slowly to beaten eggs, then add eggs to milk, whisking to blend. Add vanilla. Strain into caramel-lined custard cups; remove any air bubbles. Place cups in a pan filled with 1-inch water. Bake at 300 degrees for about 1 hour. NEVER let the water in the pan come to a boil. Remove from oven and water. Let cool completely, then refrigerate. (They will keep for days, but the praline topping must be added just before serving.)

When ready to serve, unmold each one onto a pretty plate, garnish with whipped cream and some of the pulverized caramel.

Note: For extra special guests, make French Lace Cookie Baskets and unmold the crème caramel into these. Use same garnish.

Macerated Oranges

serves 4

6   oranges (navel are best)
1   lemon
4   T. sugar (or less)

Peel and slice 4 oranges. Put in a flat container and cover with juice of other 2 oranges. Grate peel of 1 lemon over oranges, and add its juice. Add sugar; toss. Leave overnight. Baste with juice. Garnish with mint leaves.

205

Lutece Chocolate Cake

serves 8

Cake:
¼   lb. sweet butter
4   oz. semi-sweet chocolate
1   oz. bitter chocolate
4   eggs
¼   cup sugar
¾   cup flour
1   tsp. baking powder
¼   tsp. salt
¾   cup coarsely chopped walnuts
1   tsp. vanilla

Filling:
¼   lb. sweet butter
1   cup confectioners sugar
1   T. reserved chocolate mixture

Icing:
½   cup unsweetened cocoa
4   T. sugar
2   T. cream
4   T. sweet butter
½   tsp. vanilla

Preheat oven to 350 degrees. Melt butter and both chocolates together and set aside. Reserve 1 tablespoon for filling. Beat eggs until light and add sugar, beating until pale color. Mix flour, baking powder and salt together. Add chocolate, vanilla and dry ingredients to egg-sugar mixture. Fold in nuts. Pour into two eight inch cake pans, which have been buttered and floured. Bake for 12-15 minutes. Invert and cool completely.

Mix filling ingredients without heating, fill cake and chill.

Combine icing ingredients and heat until melted and smooth. Pour at once over chilled cake.

Make one day before serving.

Pound Cake

serves 16

2   sticks butter, room temperature
3   cups sugar
6   eggs
1   tsp. vanilla
3   cups sifted cake flour
1   cup whipping cream

Cream butter and sugar until fluffy. Add eggs one at a time, beating well after each addition. Add vanilla. Fold in cake flour alternating with cream, starting with flour and ending with flour. Pour into a greased and floured bundt pan. DO NOT PREHEAT OVEN. Start in cold oven. Bake at 325 degrees for approximately 1 hour and 40 minutes.

This is the basic recipe. For variation, add chocolate chips and walnuts or pecans. It is best baked in a heavy bundt pan when using chocolate chips to prevent excessive sticking. The recipe is good with a package of frozen coconut added, and almond flavoring substituted for vanilla.

Mrs. Pollard's Sour Cream Cake

serves 12

3   cups flour, sifted
¼   tsp. baking soda
1   cup butter, softened
3   cups sugar
6   eggs, separated
1   cup sour cream

Preheat oven to 300 degrees. Sift and measure flour, then sift twice more with soda. Cream butter and sugar in mixer or by hand. When well-creamed, add egg yolks, one at a time, and beat well. Add sour cream, then flour sifted with soda. Beat egg whites until stiff; fold into cake batter. Bake in a bundt pan which has been greased and floured. Bake for 1½ hours. It should come out with a nice brown crust on top. It is important to turn cake out of pan immediately after taking it from oven.

13th Century Nun's Cake

serves 12

2⅔   cups all purpose flour or 3 cups cake flour
2½   tsp. baking powder
1   tsp. cinnamon (rounded)
½   tsp. powdered coriander seeds, rounded*
1   T. caraway seeds
¼   tsp. salt
1   cup butter (no substitutes)
1½   cups sugar (granulated or 2 cups powdered)
5   egg yolks
1½   tsp. rose water**
¾   cup milk
2   egg whites, stiffly beaten
   powdered sugar to dust on cake

If using all purpose flour (and that was the only sort used in the 13th century), sift before measuring. If using pastry flour or cake flour, sift after measuring. Sift three times, the last with baking powder and spices. Add caraway seeds and salt. Set aside.

Cream butter and sugar, using an electric mixer if handy, adding one egg yolk at a time and beat until it resembles cake batter and is light and lemon colored. Add rose water. Remove butter-sugar-egg mixture from the beaters and fold in the flour mixture by hand, alternating with the milk. Last of all fold in the stiffly beaten whites. Pour batter into a lightly buttered, floured loaf pan (3x12x2½ inches) if you do not own a 10 inch tube pan or Turk's Head pan. These are usually made of copper lined with tin and the cake bakes better in them than in the loaf pan although both will produce fine cake. Place in a preheated 350 degree oven and leave until cake tests done. This takes from 1 hour to an hour and ten minutes. Do not bake too long or cake will be dry. As soon as it tests done remove from stove. It should be moist, the consistency of fine butter cake. Let remain in pan 5 minutes before loosening edges with a dull knife, Turn upside down on a wire cake rack covered with waxed paper. Dust with powdered sugar. Let remain until it reaches room temperature before serving. Store in a tin box with a tight fitting lid.

Serve with stewed or fresh fruits, ice cream, custard or what have you.

*Coriander seeds (powdered) are sold by Spice Islands

**Rosewater can be purchased at most drug stores

207

Orange Date Cake

1	orange
1	cup dates
1	cup sugar
½	cup butter
2	cups flour
1	tsp. baking soda
1	tsp. baking powder
½	tsp. cinnamon
1	tsp. cloves
1	cup sour milk (see note)
1	tsp. vanilla or whiskey
2	egg whites

Filling:

½	cup brown sugar
2	egg yolks
4	T. butter

Icing: Use any good 7-minute icing

Preheat oven to 350 degrees. Grind the orange and dates together (may use food processor); do not purée. Cream sugar and butter; add orange-date mixture. Sift flour, baking soda, baking powder, cinnamon and cloves; add sifted dry ingredients to batter alternately with sour milk. Add vanilla. Beat egg whites until stiff and add to batter, carefully folding them in. Bake in two 9-inch round cake pans which have been greased and floured. Bake for 30-40 minutes; do not overbake.

When cool, put the layers together with filling. Cook and stir constantly the brown sugar, egg yolks and butter in top of double boiler until thick. Cool to room temperature. Spread between cake layers.

Ice the cake or serve with a good pudding sauce, such as a Bourbon sauce.

Note: To sour milk, add 1 tablespoon white vinegar or lemon juice to 1 cup milk and let stand 10-15 minutes, or substitute buttermilk.

Atlanta Cheese Cake

serves 12

1	pkg. zwieback crumbs, finely grated
1	cup finely grated walnuts or pecans
⅓	cup butter, melted
1	cup sugar
1¼	lbs. (20-oz) white cream cheese (Farmers' or Bakers' cheese)
¼	tsp. salt
1½	tsp. pure vanilla
1	tsp. freshly grated lemon rind
4	eggs, separated
1	cup heavy cream, whipped
½	cup sifted flour

Preheat oven to 325 degrees. Lightly grease bottom and sides of a 9-inch spring form pan. Combine zwieback crumbs, grated nuts, butter and 2 tablespoons sugar. Mix with fingers and firmly press down mixture on bottom of pan. Mix cream cheese with about ½ the remaining sugar, salt, vanilla and lemon rind. Beat in egg yolks. Beat egg whites until soft peaks form. Add remaining sugar to whites, a tablespoon at a time, beating after each addition; beat until very firm. Pour whipped cream on top of stiff whites, then add cream cheese mixture. Pour flour on top and fold all together very gently but completely. Pour into pan and bake 1½ hours. DO NOT OPEN OVEN DOOR FOR THE FIRST HOUR. When cake is a light golden brown, turn off oven, but do not remove cake until oven has cooled, approximately 4 hours. Do not open door while it is cooling.

Chocolate Amaretto Cheesecake

serves 12

2	cups chocolate wafers, crushed
2	cups finely chopped cashews
15	T. unsalted butter
1	cup heavy cream
3	tsp. vanilla
½	cup confectioner's sugar
5	oz. semi-sweet chocolate
1½	oz. unsweetened chocolate
2	8-oz. pkg. cream cheese
½	cup sugar
3	large eggs, separated
½	cup Amaretto
2	T. sugar

Topping:

2	cups sour cream
¾	cup sugar
2	T. Amaretto

Preheat oven to 350 degrees. Mix well the wafers, cashews and butter. Butter a 10-inch springform pan and press the above mixture into it, bottom and sides. Place in refrigerator.

Whip the cream. Add vanilla and confectioner's sugar; cover and refrigerate. Melt both chocolates, allow to cool. In a bowl, beat cream cheese and ½ cup sugar. Add egg yolks slowly, then Amaretto, and finally the cooled chocolate and chilled whipped cream. In another bowl, beat egg whites; and 2 tablespoons sugar and beat until stiff peaks form. Fold into egg mixture, gently but thoroughly. Pour into pan. Bake for 50 minutes. Turn off oven. Do not open oven door for 4 hours. Remove from oven. Preheat oven to 425°. Combine last three items for topping and spread over top of cheesecake. Bake 10 minutes. Remove from oven. Cool 4 hours. Cover and refrigerate overnight. Remove from pan and garnish with shaved chocolate.

Pumpkin Cheesecake
From Heaven Hill Distillery "Cooking with Bourbon"

⅓	cup butter, softened
⅓	cup sugar
1	egg
1¼	cups flour
2	8-oz. pkgs. cream cheese
¾	cup sugar
2	cups pumpkin, cooked
2	tsp. cinnamon
½	tsp. ginger
½	tsp. nutmeg
	dash of salt
2	eggs
1	T. bourbon

Cream butter and sugar and blend in egg. Add flour and spread dough on bottom and up the sides of 9 inch springform pan. Bake qt 400 degrees for 5 minutes and remove. Lower oven temperature to 350 degrees.

Combine cream cheese and ¾ cup sugar and beat until smooth. Bland in rest of ingredients and pour into crust. Bake 350 degrees for 50 minutes. Loosen from sides of pan and cool. Remove rim and chill. Serve with whipped cream.

209

Tasty Trivia
Do not use an electric mixer to blend in flour for cakes,
breads and pastries, stir in by hand with a wooden spoon.

Caramel Icing

¼	lb. butter
⅓	cup half and half
1½	cups brown sugar
1½	cups confectioners' sugar
1	tsp. vanilla

Heat butter, half and half and brown sugar, until butter is melted and sugar is dissolved. Beat in confectioners sugar and vanilla. This is enough icing for a 2-layer cake.(Icing will keep in refrigerator. To soften, add cream.)

Amaretto Ice Cream

½	gallon natural vanilla ice cream
2½	oz. sliced almonds, toasted
3	oz. Amaretto liqueur
1	cup small Amaretto cookies (opt.)

Layer ingredients in processor. Mix only. Return to carton and place in freezer for at least 5 hours before serving. Volume will decrease about one fifth.

Bisque Ice Cream
(Original recipe from Hertel's Parkway Confectionary, located on West Market Street in Louisville)

yield 1 quart

¼	tsp. ice cream powder, gelatin or cornstarch, or 1 Junket tablet for thickening
1	cup sugar
1	cup evaporated milk
2	cups cream
1	T. vanilla
18	almond macaroons, toasted and crushed by hand (or 12 Amaretti cookies, crushed)

Mix thickener with sugar. Add milk, cream, vanilla and macaroon crumbs. Chill. Freeze in hand or electric ice cream freezer according to the manufacturer's directions.

Peach Ice Cream

yield 3 quarts

1	quart ripe peaches, mashed
1½	cups sugar
	juice of ½ lemon
1	quart half and half
1	pint milk
1	can Eagle Brand Condensed Milk
½	pint heavy cream

Add sugar and lemon juice to mashed peaches. Add half and half, milk, condensed milk and heavy cream. Stir until well blended. Pour ingredients in ice cream freezer and freeze according to machine's instructions.

This is a delicious fresh peach ice cream that does not "ice up".

DESSERTS

Lemon Sherbet with Mint Sauce

Chef Ernest Brokos of the Hyatt

serves 4-6

Mint Sauce

1	cup granulated sugar
⅓	cup water
1	bunch fresh mint-1½ cups firmly packed with stems
	peel of ⅓ lemon
1½	inch piece of stick cinnamon
⅛	tsp. vanilla
2½	T. green Creme de Menthe

Boil the sugar and water in a heavy pot, stirring at first until the sugar dissolves and washing down the sugar from the sides of the pot with a wet pastry brush dipped in cold water. Let boil 3 minutes. Put the washed and dried mint in a heatproof bowl and pour the hot sugar syrup over it. Stir well. Add the lemon peel and cinnamon stick and let cool overnight in the refrigerator. Strain and add the vanilla and Creme de Menthe.

Lemon Sherbet

1	quart lemon sherbet
	grated peel of 1 lemon, boiled in water for 2 minutes.

Mix the grated lemon peel into the sherbet and return to freezer until ready to serve. Pour some mint syrup over sherbet when ready to serve. Garnish with mint sprig.

Six Threes Ice Cream

yield 1 gallon

3	cups milk
3	cups heavy cream
3	cups sugar
	juice of 3 lemons
	juice of 3 oranges
3	ripe bananas, mashed

Combine milk, cream and sugar. Stir until sugar dissolves. Freeze until mushy. Add fruit juices and bananas. Continue freezing until firm.

Note: This may be halved to fit into a counter-top ice cream freezer.

Vanilla Ice Cream

Hertel's Parkway Confectionary

yield 4 quarts

1¾	cups sugar
5	cups whipping cream
1	quart milk
3	T. vanilla

Mix all ingredients and pour into hand or electric ice cream freezer. Pack with crushed ice and ice cream salt according to manufacturer's instructions. Freeze.

Fresh fruit may be folded in if you like.

Cream Cheese Pastry

2 9-inch pie shells

2	3-oz. pkgs. cream cheese, chilled
2	sticks butter, chilled
2	cups flour

In food processor, blend softened butter and cream cheese. Gradually blend in flour ½ cup at a time. Stop when flour is just blended. Refrigerate, wrapped in waxed paper for at least 30 minutes.

211

Tasty Trivia
To prevent soggy pie crust in an unbaked pie shell, brush with a thin coating of egg white. Especially good for fruit pies.

Pie Crust with Lard, Southern Style

yields 4 single pie crusts

5	cups flour
1	T. salt
2	cups lard (1 lb.)
1	egg
	water

Combine flour, salt and lard; mix until crumbly with fork and knife, using cutting motions. Beat one egg in a one-cup measuring cup and fill with water to make one cup. Gradually add this to flour mixture using the fork to toss. Shape into 4 balls. Store in plastic wrap in refrigerator. It may be kept one month or more; can be frozen.

Rich Shortcrust Pastry

(conventional)

yield 2 shells

2	cups flour
	pinch of salt
6	oz. butter, very cold
2	tsp. sugar (if sweet pastry is needed)
1	egg yolk
2-3	T. cold water

Sift the flour with a pinch of salt into a mixing bowl. Drop in the butter and cut it into the flour until the small pieces are well coated. Then rub them in with the fingertips until the mixture looks like fine breadcrumbs. Stir in the sugar. Mix egg yolk with water; work into the butter and flour and mix quickly with a palette knife to a firm dough. Turn onto a floured board and knead lightly until smooth. If possible, chill in refrigerator (wrapped in wax paper, plastic bag or foil) for 30 minutes before using.

Rich Shortcrust Pastry
(Processor method)
Same ingredients as above

With metal blade in place, add flour, butter (which is cut into 1 tablespoon pieces) and salt to beaker of food processor. Process, turning on and off rapidly, until butter is cut into flour and very small granules are formed, about 10 seconds. Add egg and water. Continue processing until ball of dough forms on blades. If dough seems too soft, sprinkle with 1-2 tablespoons flour and process until combined, about 6 seconds. Refrigerate. Makes two 8- or 9-inch pastry shells.

Mamie's Coconut Pie

1	coconut, milk drained and reserved, brown skin removed, meat grated
¼	cup milk or cream
4	egg yolks
1½	cups sugar (or less, if you prefer)
1	tsp. vanilla
1	10-inch pie shell, partially baked
4	egg whites
½	cup sugar

Preheat oven to 350 degrees. Mix just until blended, the coconut milk, milk, egg yolks, sugar and vanilla. Add grated coconut and pour into partially baked pie shell. Bake until filling bubbles and pastry is almost brown, approximately 30 minutes. Remove from oven and cool completely, at least an hour. Beat egg whites until they hold their shape; gradually add sugar. Beat well until stiff and glossy. Spread over pie, and bake until meringue is brown, about 10-15 minutes.

Almond Cream Pie

(Camille Glenn)   serves 8

1	cup almond paste
2	cups milk
4	egg yolks
1	T. gelatin, softened in ¼ cup cold water
¼	tsp. vanilla extract
1	cup heavy cream
1	baked pie shell
	Chocolate curls for garnish

Dissolve almond paste in milk over a low flame. Stir until the milk is hot and smooth. Stir the almond milk into the egg yolks and cook over boiling water until the custard coats a spoon.

Stir in the gelatin and water. Add vanilla extract.

Stir the custard over a bowl of cracked ice until it is cool and barely begins to set.

Whip the cream and fold into custard. Pour into baked and browned 9-inch pie shell. Sprinkle with chocolate curls. Place in refrigerator to set.

Mother's Apple Cheese Crisp

serves 8

1	quart apples, sliced (4 cups)
½	T. lemon juice
6	T. water
1	cup sugar
½	T. cinnamon
½	cup dry non-fat milk
½	cup sifted flour
¼	tsp. salt
⅓	cup butter (5⅓ T.)
1	cup shredded cheese

Preheat oven to 350 degrees. Spread apples in bottom of a 10 inch buttered baking dish; add water and lemon juice.

Mix dry ingredients; cut in the butter. Work in shredded cheese. Spread over apples and bake for 30-35 minutes.

Serve warm with whipped cream.

Fresh Blueberry Tart

serves 8

Crust:

1	cup flour
2	T. powdered sugar
½	cup butter

Sift flour and sugar; cut in butter until consistency is like cornmeal. Chill 30 minutes. Turn into an 8-inch pan, press firmly onto bottom and sides. Bake 425 degrees 10-15 minutes or until golden brown. Cool.

Filling:

2	cups fresh blueberries
1	jar (10-oz.) red currant jelly
1	cup sour cream
2	T. chopped walnuts

Rinse berries and drain; dry well. Spread blueberries on crust. Melt jelly on low heat and pour over berries. Cool and refrigerate. Before serving, spread with sour cream and sprinkle walnuts on top.

Louisville Bourbon Pie

serves 6-8

2	**cups sugar**
¾	**cup butter**
4	**eggs**
1	**T. flour**
⅓	**cup cream**
3	**T. Bourbon**
	9-inch pie shell, partially baked

Cream butter and sugar. Beat in eggs, flour, cream and Bourbon. Pour into partially baked pie shell. Bake at 350 degrees for 50 minutes - 1 hour, or until set. Let cool 30 minutes before serving.

Pie Shell

1⅓	**cups flour**
½	**tsp. salt**
⅓	**cup vegetable oil**
3	**T. cold milk**

Preheat oven to 350 degrees. Combine flour and salt. Combine oil and milk. Add the liquid to the dry ingredients and toss lightly to moisten. Press the mixture into a 9-inch pie pan. Bake for 5 minutes.

Fabulous Spice Cake

serves 6

¾	**cup butter**
2	**cups brown sugar**
2	**egg yolks**
1	**tsp. ground cloves**
1	**tsp. cinnamon**
1	**tsp. baking powder**
¾	**tsp. salt**
2⅓	**cups flour**
1	**tsp. baking soda**
1¼	**cups sour milk (see note)**
1	**tsp. vanilla**

Preheat oven to 350 degrees. Cream butter and sugar well. Add egg yolks, mixing well. Sift together cloves, cinnamon, baking powder and salt with flour. Mix together baking soda and sour milk. Add to sugar mixture the dry ingredients, alternately with sour milk and soda. Add vanilla. Pour into well greased 8-inch square pan; bake for 30-40 minutes, or until firm yet moist. Let cake cool completely before adding meringue.

Meringue:

2	**egg whites**
1	**cup brown sugar, moist and lumps removed**
	chopped nuts

Meringue: Beat egg whites until stiff. Add brown sugar gradually; beat until smooth. Spread over entire cake. Sprinkle with chopped nuts. Bake at 325 degrees for 10-15 minutes.

Note: To make sour milk, add 1 tablespoon white vinegar or lemon juice to 1 cup milk; set aside 15 minutes.

DESSERTS

Mildred's Chess Pie

serves 6-8

1	whole egg, room temperature
3	egg yolks, room temperature
1	tsp. vinegar
3	T. water
2	T. flour
1	cup sugar
1	stick butter, melted and cooled
1	8-inch pie shell, pricked with fork

Preheat oven to 375 degrees. Place eggs and yolks in a bowl; mix until well blended but not foamy. Mix vinegar and water together and stir into eggs.

Mix flour and sugar together. Slowly add liquid mixture; mix well with wooden spoon. Add cooled, melted butter and stir until well mixed. Pour into pie shell and bake for 30 minutes.

Variation: Strawberry Chess Pie

½	cup currant jelly
1	pt. fresh strawberries, washed and stemmed

Bake then cool "Mildred's Chess Pie" for at least 30 minutes. Melt the currant jelly (in a microwave or over a pan of boiling water). Brush the top of the pie with the jelly. Place ¼ inch thick slices of strawberries on top and brush the strawberries with the currant jelly. Place in a 350 degree oven for 3 minutes. Let cool about 15 minutes before serving. An additional garnish could be mint leaves.

Lemon Chess Pie

serves 6-8

2	cup sugar
4	eggs
1	T. flour
1	T. cornmeal
¼	cup melted butter
¼	cup milk
¼	cup lemon juice
	9-inch pie shell, unbaked

Preheat oven to 350 degrees. Beat sugar and eggs. Add remaining five ingredients and mix well. Pour into 9-inch pie shell.

Bake 45 minutes until puffed and set in middle.

Chocolate Fudge Pie

serves 10

½	cup butter or margarine, melted
1	cup sugar
2	eggs
3	T. cocoa
1	tsp. vanilla (or ½ oz. rum)
½	cup flour
½	cup chopped pecans (optional)

Preheat oven to 325 degrees. Mix butter and sugar. Add eggs; mix well. Add cocoa, flavoring, flour and pecans. Pour into greased 9-inch pie plate. Cook for 25 minutes. Does not look done, but it is. Serve with a dollop of whipped cream or a small scoop of ice cream.

Tasty Trivia
Meringues should be cooked at 225 degrees for 45 minutes. Turn oven off and leave in for 1 hour. Reheat for 15 minutes. Crush center and lace with a drop of rum. Cold egg whites make better meringues because they do not break down.

Jam Caramel Pie

serves 6-8

1   **cup butter**
2   **cups light brown sugar**
5   **eggs, whole**
1   **cup blackberry jam (homemade is best)**
     9 in. unbaked pastry shell

Preheat oven to 350 degrees. Blend butter and sugar well. Add eggs, one at a time, until blended; do not beat the mixture. Add jam and mix well. Pour mixture into pastry shell. Bake for 45 minutes. Cool. Add a dab of whipped cream on top if you like; pie is so rich it is not necessary.

Gainsborough Tart

serves 6-8

4   **T. butter**
2   **eggs, well beaten**
4   **oz. sugar**
8   **oz. coconut, freshly shredded**
¼   **tsp. baking powder**
     pastry-lined 7″ flan ring or tart mold
     raspberry jam

Preheat oven to 350 degrees. Melt butter; stir in the well-beaten eggs. Add sugar, coconut and baking powder; mix well. Pour into the pastry shell that has been generously coated with the raspery jam. Bake 40 minutes, or until golden brown. Serve cold.

Museum Winner's Pie

serves 6-8

1   **stick butter**
1   **cup sugar**
2   **eggs, beaten**
½   **cup flour**
     pinch of salt
2   **T. Kentucky Bourbon or 1 tsp. vanilla**
1   **cup chocolate chips**
1   **cup chopped pecans**
1   **9-inch pie shell, partially baked**

Preheat oven to 350 degrees. Cream butter and sugar. Add beaten eggs, flour, salt and Kentucky Bourbon (or vanilla). Add chocolate chips, and nuts. Stir well. Pour into partially baked pie shell and bake for 30 minutes, or until center is set. Serve with whipped cream or vanilla ice cream.

Peach Praline Pie

serves 8

½   **cup sifted flour**
¼   **cup brown sugar**
½   **cup pecans,chopped**
4   **T. butter**
1   **9-inch pie shell, unbaked**
4   **cups peaches, sliced (6-7 medium peaches)**
½   **cup sugar**
2   **T. quick cooking tapioca**
1   **tsp. lemon juice**

Combine flour, sugar, pecans and butter. Place ⅓ of it in pie shell. Combine peaches, sugar, tapioca and lemon juice. Pour over crumb mixture. Top with rest of mixture. Bake at 450 degrees for 10 minutes. Turn to 350 degrees for 20 minutes. Top with whipped cream.

DESSERTS

Poached Pears

(Microwave)   serves 2

2	fresh pears, firm but ripe
1	6-oz. can pineapple juice
1	T. sugar
1	(2 inch piece) stick cinnamon
3	packets Equal sugar substitute

Halve pears, peel and remove core with a melon baller. Place in a one quart casserole with cover, the pineapple juice, sugar and cinnamon. Cook on High for 1 minute. Stir.

Add pears to juice, cover and cook for 2 minutes at High, covered, cut side down. Check for doneness, and if too firm, cook another 30 seconds to one minute.

Remove from oven, turn cut side up, and sprinkle Equal over pears. Refrigerate when cool.

This is a low calorie recipe.

Butter Crunch Lemon Chiffon Pie

serves 6-8

Crust:

½	cup butter
¼	cup brown sugar, packed
1	cup flour
½	cup chopped pecans, walnuts, or coconut

Preheat oven to 400 degrees. Mix the butter, brown sugar, flour, and nuts by hand. Spread into a large baking pan with sides, and bake for 9-10 minutes until an even golden brown but not yet darkened at the edges. Take the mixture out of the oven and stir with a spoon. Save ¾ cup for the topping. Immediately press the rest of the mixture against the bottom and sides of a 9-inch pie pan; let it cool.

Lemon Chiffon Filling:

½	cup sugar
1	envelope unflavored gelatin
⅔	cup water
⅓	cup lemon juice, freshly squeezed
4	egg yolks
1	T. grated lemon rind
4	egg whites
½	tsp. cream of tartar
½	cup sugar

Blend the first ½ cup sugar, gelatin, water, lemon juice and the slightly beaten egg yolks thoroughly in a saucepan. Cook the mixture over low heat, stirring constantly until it comes to a boil. Stir in grated lemon rind. Place the pan in cold water with ice cubes and cool, stirring constantly, until the mixture mounds slightly when dropped from a spoon, about 10-15 minutes.

Beat the egg whites with the cream of tartar until frothy. Gradually beat in the ½ cup sugar, a little at a time, and beat until very stiff and glossy. Fold this meringue mixture into the gelatin mixture. Pour the filling into the cooled crust. Sprinkle the reserved crumbs over the the top and chill for an hour.

Peanut Butter Pie

serves 6-8

Crust:

1	cup graham cracker crumbs (4 double)
¼	cup light brown sugar
¼	cup butter, melted
½	cup chopped peanuts

Mix together in a processor or by hand. Press into an 8-inch springform pan on bottom and sides.

Filling:

12	ozs. chocolate chips
8	T. coffee
2	cups crunchy peanut butter
2	cups sugar
2	tsp. vanilla
3	small pkgs. cream cheese
2	T. melted butter
1½	cups whipped cream

Melt 6 ounces semi-sweet chocolate chips with 4 tablespoons coffee. Spread this mixture on top of crust. Mix next five filling ingredients well. Fold in whipped cream. Pour filling over crust. Melt another 6 ounces chocolate chips with 4 tablespoons coffee and pour over filling. Chill 6 hours and serve.

Sugar Cream Pie

serves 6-8

1	cup brown sugar, packed
6	T. flour
½	tsp. salt
1	tsp. vanilla
	cinnamon
2½	cups whipping cream
	9-inch unbaked pie shell

Mix sugar, flour, and salt together. Add whipping cream and vanilla. Mix until mixture is a smooth consistency. Pour into unbaked pie shell and sprinkle top with cinnamon.

Bake for 10 minutes at 400 degrees. Lower oven to 350 degrees and continue baking for 30 minutes.

Note: You can substitute Half and Half Cream for the whipping cream for a less rich dessert.

Amaretto Soufflé

serves 6-8

3	whole eggs
5	egg yolks
½	cup superfine sugar
½	cup Amaretto
1½	cups crushed almond macaroons
2	cups heavy cream, whipped

In a mixer bowl, beat whole eggs, egg yolks, and sugar for 12 minutes on highest speed. Reduce speed and add Amaretto. Fold in crushed macaroons and whipped cream.

Pour into 2 quart soufflé dish. Chill.

DESSERTS

Track Talk
*The twin spires atop the grandstand have become the
trademark of Churchill Downs and are synonymous with the
Kentucky Derby.*

Lemon Or Chocolate Pie

serves 6-8

½	cup flour
2	T. cornstarch
⅛	tsp. salt
1½	cups sugar
2	cups boiling water
3	egg yolks
	butter the size of an egg
6	T. lemon juice or 3 oz. squares bitter chocolate
1	tsp. vanilla
1	9-inch pie shell, baked
1	cup whipping cream, whipped

Sift flour, cornstarch, salt and sugar together into the top of a double boiler. Add 2 cups boiling water and stir over boiling water until the custard leaves the sides of the pan. Add 3 egg yolks and cook 5 minutes. Turn off heat and stir in butter the size of an egg. This is the moment of decision. If you are foolhardy and a traitor to the cause, add 6 tablespoons lemon juice and content yourself with lemon pie. However, if you can throw discretion to the winds and be oblivious to calories, ignore the lemon juice and save it for iced tea. In its place, add 3 squares of bitter chocolate and stir until melted. Finally, add vanilla. Pour into baked pie shell. When cool, cover pie with whipped cream. Restrain yourself until meal time.

Chocolate Sabayon Pie

serves 8

Chocolate Crust:

1	tsp. unsalted butter, room temperature, for greasing pie plate.
1⅓	cup chocolate wafer crumbs
1	tsp. granulated sugar
⅓	cup lightly salted butter, melted

Butter a 9 inch pyrex pie dish. Press the mixture of chocolate wafer crumbs, sugar and melted butter firmly into dish.

Chocolate Filling:

1½	pkgs. unflavored gelatin
1½	T. cold water
4	oz. semi-sweet chocolate, broken into pieces
3	large egg yolks
2	T. granulated sugar
6	T. dry sherry
¾	cup whipping cream
4	oz. semi-sweet chocolate, soft , but not melted

Dissolve gelatin in cold water. Melt 4 ounces chocolate in a double boiler. Heat the chocolate until smooth, then remove from heat. In a separate bowl, blend egg yolks, sugar and sherry. Add to this mixture the dissolved gelatin. Now blend this 'sabayon' mixture into the melted chocolate in the double boiler, over medium heat. Stir this mixture until it begins to thicken. Remove from heat and allow this chocolate mixture to cool to room temperature.

Meanwhile, in a separate bowl, whip the cream until it forms soft peaks. Slowly fold the whipped cream into the cooled chocolate filling. Pour this filling into the pie crust. Refrigerate until it is completely set. Scrape the remaining 4 ounces of soft chocolate into curls and decorate the top of the pie with these curls, made with a potato scraper.

Hasenour's Raspberry Soufflé

serves 6

1   cup sugar
4   oz. frozen raspberries or 1 cup fresh
4   tsp. Chambord
1   tsp. lemon juice
3   egg yolks
2   tsp. cornstarch, dissolved in cold water
2   tsp. cold water
6   egg whites, beaten stiff
     pinch of salt

Combine sugar and raspberries in a saucepan and cook over medium heat, stirring constantly until sugar dissolves. Add Chambord and lemon juice to raspberry mixture. Temper egg yolks into raspberry mixture, by adding a little of the latter to the yolks first, then adding the remaining yolks to the raspberry mixture; continue stirring. Dissolve cornstarch in cold water and add to mixture. Bring to a boil; turn down to a simmer, and stir until thickened and glossy. Cool to room temperature. Gently fold the stiffly beaten egg whites into the raspberry mixture. Coat 6 individual serving cups with a thin layer of butter and granulated sugar. Gently fill them with the soufflé; cook 350 degrees for 15 minutes, or until risen, avoiding any excessive movement to prevent falling of soufflé. Sprinkle with powdered sugar and serve either as is, or with Hasenour's Vanilla Sauce.

Vanilla Sauce
1⅓   cups milk
⅔   cup plus 2 T. sugar
2   egg yolks
2   tsp. heavy cream
2   tsp. butter
½   tsp. vanilla
1   T. cornstarch
4   tsp. cold water

Combine milk and sugar in sauté pan and cook over medium heat, stirring constantly. Mix egg yolks with heavy cream; stir in a few tablespoons of the hot milk-sugar mixture, then slowly stir this mixture into the milk and sugar mixture, continually stirring. Stir butter into sauce. Add vanilla to flavor sauce. Dissolve cornstarch in water; add to the sauce, bring to a boil and continue stirring until thickened and glossy.

Serve with raspberry soufflé.

Ice Cream Soufflé

serves 6

1   quart vanilla ice cream
8   macaroons, crumbled
3   T. Grand Marnier
1   cup cream, whipped
¼   cup chopped toasted almonds
1   T. powdered sugar

Add macaroons to soft ice cream; stir in Grand Marnier. Gently fold in cream and pour into 1 quart soufflé dish. Cover with Saran Wrap and freeze until firm. Let stand at room temperature for 5-10 minutes before serving. Sprinkle with almonds and powdered sugar. Serve with a strawberry or raspberry sauce.

Berry Sauce
2   pints fresh strawberries or raspberries, washed and cut in half
⅓   cup sugar
3   T. Grand marnier

Simmer 2 pints fresh strawberries or raspberries, with ⅓ cup sugar. Cook until soft but not mushy. Remove from stove and stir in 3 tablespoons Grand Marnier. Spoon over soufflé or serve in a side dish.

DESSERTS

Chilled Chocolate Raspberry Soufflé

serves 4-6

6	oz. bittersweet or semi-sweet chocolate
2	oz. unsweetened chocolate
4	large egg yolks
10	oz. pkg. frozen raspberries, thawed and drained (reserving ½ cup syrup)
6	large egg whites, room temperature
¼	tsp. cream of tartar
¼	cup sugar
1¼	cups heavy cream, chilled
1	recipe Raspberry coulis

Lightly oil a 1 quart soufflé dish. Form a foil collar that extends about 3 inches above the rim by folding in half a piece of aluminum foil long enough to go around dish; lightly oil the foil and paper clip in place. Melt the broken up chocolates in a heat-proof bowl set over barely simmering water; stir occasionally until smooth, and set aside to cool to room temperature.

In a bowl with an electric mixer beat the egg yolks until they are thick and pale; meanwhile heat the reserved raspberry syrup to a simmer. Add the syrup in a thin stream to the beaten egg yolks, beating constantly. Beat the mixture for 1 minute more. Add the yolk mixture in a stream to the chocolate mixture, beating constantly and gently stir in the raspberries.

In a large bowl, with the electric mixer, beat the egg whites with the cream of tartar until they are frothy and beginning to thicken. Add the sugar, a little at a time, and beat the whites until they hold soft, glossy peaks.

In a chilled bowl, beat the cream until it just holds soft peaks. Stir ¼ of the whites into the chocolate mixture; fold in the remaining whites; just before they are incorporated completely, fold in the cream gently but thoroughly. Spoon the mixture into the soufflé dish; smooth the top. Chill, covered loosely with plastic wrap for at least 3 hours, or until it is set.

This soufflé may be made a day in advance.

To serve, remove the foil collar, garnish with fresh raspberries or shaved chocolate. Serve individual servings in a pool of raspberry coulis.

Raspberry Coulis: One 10-ounce package frozen raspberries and 2 tablespoons Eau de Framboise-optional. Defrost raspberries and pureé in processor or blender. Pour into a strainer set over bowl. Push through the pureé to eliminate the raspberry seeds. Stir in the Framboise. Chill.

Hot Orange Soufflé

serves 6

4   T. butter
½   cup sugar
½   cup orange juice
     grated zest of 1 orange
4   egg yolks
5   egg whites
     powdered sugar to sprinkle

Butter a 1-quart soufflé dish and refrigerate. When cold, butter it again. Do not sugar it.

In a heavy pan, (not aluminum) heat the butter with ¼ cup of the sugar and the orange juice, until melted. Take off the heat, let cool 5 minutes, and beat in the egg yolks, one at a time. Add the orange zest. Heat very gently, stirring constantly until the mixture thickens to the texture of heavy cream. Let cool. (This can be done 3-4 hours ahead of time. Keep covered, at room temperature.)

20-30 minutes before serving, preheat oven to 425 degrees. Beat egg whites until stiff, add ¼ cup sugar and beat until glossy (just 20 seconds or more). Gently heat the orange mixture until warm, but not hot, and stir in ¼ of the egg whites. Fold in all the egg whites very gently. Pour into soufflé dish and bake 12-15 minutes. Sprinkle with powdered sugar and serve immediately.

Frozen Lemon Soufflé

serves 6

8   eggs
1   cup sugar
2   pkgs. unflavored gelatin,
     dissolved in juice of 1 lemon
½   cup fresh lemon juice
1   T. grated lemon rind
2   cups heavy cream, whipped to
     soft peaks

Take a piece of waxed paper or aluminum foil long enough to fit, with a little overlap, around a 2 quart soufflé dish; fold in half, and butter on one side heavily. Tie the waxed paper or foil around the soufflé dish, buttered side inward, so it is 3-4 inches above the rim.

Beat the eggs and sugar in a mixer bowl for 15-20 minutes, until light and creamy; mixture should spin a ribbon. Add the dissolved gelatin to the egg mixture on high speed then lower the speed and add the rest of the lemon juice and rind, mixing just enough to blend. Fold in the whipped cream and pour into prepared soufflé dish. Put in freezer for 3 hours. Remove the paper collar and decorate with whipped cream, lemon slices and mint.

You may store the soufflé for two days in the freezer and move it to the refrigerator two hours prior to serving time so it will thaw properly.

DESSERTS

Track Talk
*The first tunnel from the grandstand area to the infield was
under construction in 1936. The second tunnel, leading from
the third turn, was completed in 1966 and first used in 1967.*

Almond Bavarian Cream With Raspberry Coulis and Caramel Sauce

serves 10-12

Almond Bavarian Cream:

1	quart milk
¾	cup sugar
⅓	cup (3-oz.) almond paste
½	cup (2-oz.) finely ground almonds
½	cup cold water
3	envelopes unflavored gelatin
2	cups heavy cream, cold
2	T. yellow Chartreuse-optional

Lightly oil a 12-cup mold or 2 6-cup molds; set aside. In
a heavy saucepan, bring milk, sugar, almond paste and
ground almonds just to a boil, stirring occasionally. Remove from heat and pour into a metal bowl. Let cool to
room temperature.

Place the cold water in a heat-proof cup or bowl; sprinkle the gelatin over the top and leave 2-5 minutes until
softened. Place the bowl in a shallow pan of hot water
on the stove; heat and stir until the gelatin is dissolved.
Stir the gelatin into the cooled almond mixture. Set the
metal bowl over a larger bowl filled with ice and stir the
mixture constantly until it begins to thicken slightly. remove from the ice.

In a separate bowl, whip cream until soft peaks appear
and fold into the thickened mixture. (If the almond mixture has thickened to a jello-state, reheat slightly and
then chill slightly again.) Fold in the Chartreuse. Pour the
mixture into the oiled mold. Tap to settle. Chill in the refrigerator until completely set(about 4 hours).

When ready to serve, unmold onto a serving platter and
garnish with fresh raspberries and/or fresh mint leaves.
To serve, cut wedges of the bavaroise and place on a
serving plate. Spoon 1-2 tablespoons raspberry coulis
around ½ of the plate and caramel sauce around the
other half of the plate. (Caramel Sauce recipe under
"Sauces")

Raspberry Coulis: 1 10-ounce package frozen raspberries and 2 tablespoons Eau de Framboise-optional.
Defrost raspberries and purée in processor or blender.
Pour into a strainer set over a bowl. Push through the
purée to eliminate seeds. Stir in the Framboise. Chill.

Chad Mitchell's Bread Pudding
(Graduate of La Varenne)

serves 4-6

3	eggs
3	eggs, separated
1	sugar
3	cups whole milk
3	tsp. vanilla
4-5	thick slices of day-old French bread (approx. 3 cups)
½	cup raisins, soaked in Kentucky Bourbon to cover, drained
3	tsp. cinnamon
1	tsp. nutmeg

Place whole eggs and yolks from separated eggs into a large bowl; reserve the whites for meringue. Add about ¾ cup of the sugar to the eggs and whisk until the mixture is light and bubbly. Add milk and vanilla. Break the bread into very small pieces and add to mixture. Add the raisins, plain or soaked half an hour. Add the cinnamon and nutmeg to taste. Pour the mixture into a well-greased 1½ quart heat-proof casserole. Bake in a water bath by placing casserole in oblong pan with 1 inch of boiling water, in a 350 degree oven for about an hour, or until a knife inserted in the center comes out clean. Remove pudding and turn oven up to 425 degrees. Let pudding cool.

Make meringue with the reserved egg whites and remaining sugar. Beat egg whites until stiff and gradually add sugar. Immediately spread meringue over pudding and sprinkle with nutmeg. Return to oven and bake until meringue is evenly browned; 5-10 minutes. Serve warm or at room temperature.

Alternate method: Bake pudding in oblong pan, omitting meringue. Cut in squares and surround pudding with hard sauce, made with Kentucky Bourbon, and top with a dollop of whipped cream.

Pavé A Lite
(Pave=paving stone   Lite=summer)

serves 6-8

1½	cups sifted powdered sugar
4	egg yolks
⅓	cup cream (heavy, or half and half)
4	oz. butter
1	tsp. vanilla
24	lady fingers
⅓	cup Kirsch
1	quart strawberries
½	cup powdered sugar
2	tsp. Kirsch
1	T. milk or crème fraîche

Over low heat, combine sugar and egg yolks. Add cream. Remove from heat and beat in butter, a pat at a time. Add vanilla. Beat and chill.

Sprinkle lady fingers with Kirsch. Arrange half of lady fingers in serving bowl. Pour in chilled cream. Arrange layer of strawberries. Put rest of lady fingers on top and chill. For icing, combine ½ cup sugar, Kirsch and milk or crème fraîche.

Near serving time, spread icing over lady fingers. Garnish with strawberries and crème fraîche or whipped cream.

DESSERTS

Apple Graham Pie
(Microwave)   1 (9-inch) pie

½	cup butter
¼	cup sugar
2	cups graham cracker crumbs
5	cups thinly sliced appples (4-6 medium)
½	cup sugar
1	tsp. cinnamon

In large glass mixing bowl place butter. Cook at High 1 minute until melted. Add sugar and crumbs. Mix well. Press half of mixture firmly and evenly into 9-inch pie plate.

In large mixing bowl place apple slices; they should be ⅛ to ¼-inch thick. Add sugar and cinnamon, mixing well. Mound and press down into crumb crust.

Cover apples with remaining crumbs to make top crust. Press crumbs down firmly, especially at edges, to prevent boilover.

Insert temperature probe so tip is in center of pie. Cover with waxed paper. Attach cable end at receptacle. Cook at High with temperature setting at 199 degrees. Let stand 10 minutes, then remove paper so topping can crisp.

For ovens without a probe, cook until apples are almost tender (8-10 minutes) then let stand as stated above.

White Charlotte Russe and Hot Butterscotch Sauce
serves 8-10

3	cups milk
½	cup sugar
3	T. unflavored gelatin
1	pint whipping cream, whipped
1¼	tsp. vanilla
½	cup freshly grated coconut
	ladyfingers-optional

Put 2 cups milk and ½ cup sugar in a heavy saucepan; bring just to the boiling point and remove from heat immediately. Sprinkle the gelatin over 1 cup milk and let sit aside to soften. Add hot milk and sugar to the gelatin mixture, stir well. Cool by setting the pan over a bowl of ice cubes; stir occasionally. When it starts to gel, fold in the whipped cream and vanilla. Pour into 1½-quart mold or soufflé dish.

Optional: You may line the mold with ladyfingers. Unmold and cover with fresh grated coconut. Serve with hot butterscotch sauce.

Hot Butterscotch Sauce

½	cup butter
2	cups sugar
1	cup half and half

Melt the butter in a skillet until brown. Watch carefully when the butter starts to brown around the edges; it will turn from browning to burning very quickly. Add sugar to cream in a saucepan, bring to a boil and cook about one or two minutes. Add to butter in skillet and boil about one minute. Keep warm in double boiler until ready to serve.

Lil's Irish Trifle

serves 80-100

1   **4-gallon glass bowl**
5   **recipes plain Jelly Roll from Joy Of Cooking, spread with:**
5   **10-ounce jars red currant jelly**
3   **quarts "boiled" custard**
6   **cups heavy cream, whipped and drained**
½   **flat (6 quarts) fresh strawberries, not large ones**
1   **quart Old Bushmill's Irish Whiskey**

Boiled Custard:
1   **dozen eggs**
1⅓   **cups sugar**
⅓   **cup flour**
2½   **quarts milk**
1   **T. vanilla**

A double recipe of jelly roll is just right for 11 x 16 inch pan. Make 2 this size; bake remaining single cake in standard 9 inch x 13 inch pan. Roll the cakes filled with (beaten to soften) jelly, starting from SHORT end. May be made days ahead, wrapped well, and frozen whole.

Make custard a day or two ahead; no reason not to, as it should be cold. Place the egg yolks in a large saucepan and with a whisk, gradually beat in the sugar. Continue beating for a minutes or two until mixture is thick, pale yellow and forms the ribbon. Beat in the flour, then beat in the hot milk in a thin stream. Set over moderately high heat and stir slowly and continuously with a wire whip, reaching all over bottom and sides of pan until mixture thickens. As it turns lumpy, beat vigorously to smooth it out. Lower heat and continue stirring for several minutes to cook the flour and thicken the cream. Add vanilla. The consistency should be halfway between poured custard and pie filling.

Whip the cream to a good peak a day ahead: Drain, (optional, but it will keep it from separating, and the whiskey supplies all the liquid this creation needs): Line a bowl large enough to contain the cream with linen tea towel. Raise towel an inch from bottom of bowl and secure it well with heavy rubber band. Place the whipped cream on towel; cover and refrigerate until needed. Whey will collect on bottom of bowl; simply take cream off with rubber spatula as needed. Note: the cream is left unflavored.

Prepare berries: Wash, hull, and drain on a bath towel. Turn the bowl to be used upside down on counter; draw pencil mark around it to make a pattern. Select the most perfect berries and arrange them, wall to wall, in the penciled circle; these are used to pave the top of the finished trifle. Slice remaining berries...food processor good here.

Get ready: Slice jelly rolls (preferably still frozen) about ⅔ inch thick. Pour 2 jiggers whiskey into a cut-glass tumbler. Pour remaining whiskey into a shallow bowl. Drop a couple of ice cubes into the cut-glass tumbler and make sure the whiskey is fit to use in the trifle. Quickly dip slices of cake into bowl of whiskey and line bottom and sides of bowl, making sure of the perfection of the pinwheel effect as seen from the outside of the bowl. Some slices will be left for the middle layer of the trifle.

Now spread half the custard over jelly roll. Add ⅔ of the sliced berries, half the whipped cream, and remaining slices of jelly roll. Repeat, (using remaining ⅓ sliced berries). Carefully transfer berries (from the pattern you made on the counter) to top the cream. Refrigerate until serving time. Garnish with a bouquet of fresh mint. Serve with an enormous spoon; use a restaurant model if necessary. Remember there are two layers of everything; you have only to dig halfway down for the first half of the servings.

Do not, unless there is a real emergency, serve the trifle on paperware, even if the preceding dinner has been done so. That would be a tacky way to treat such a sumptuous dessert. While the recipe is designed, sort of , for about 80 more than respectable servings, it will serve 100. Do not trust anyone but yourself to serve it; if left to themselves, about 20 guests would devour it and have to be hospitalized, probably resulting in lawsuits.

Bourbon Dates

Pit dates and soak in Kentucky Bourbon overnight. Remove from Bourbon, put pecan in center of each date; roll in granulated sugar. Store in an airtight tin. These will keep for several weeks.

Bluegrass Peaches

serves 4

4	peeled peach halves (substitute drained, canned cling peaches if desired)
4	T. brown sugar
4	slices butter (about ½ T. each)
4	T. Makers Mark Bourbon
	vanilla ice cream

In each peach-half cavity, divide the butter, sugar and Makers Mark, Bake at 325 degrees until sauce is hot and bubbly. Serve peaches with vanilla ice cream.

Pears A La Bomhard

(Named for Moritz von Bomhard, founder of the Kentucky Opera)

serves 4

2	hard pears very thinly sliced
½	pint heavy cream
3	cups sugar
¼	cup pure vanilla or almond liqueur

Core and slice pears. Combine pears, 2 cups of sugar, enough water to cover pears and ⅛ cup of vanilla or liqueur and poach until pears are transparent.

Remove pears from liquid with slotted spoon. Add remaining sugar and the heavy cream to liquid and reduce until just before soft ball stage.

Return pears to mixture, add remaining vanilla or liqueur and simmer to reduce a bit more. Serve in patty shell, sweet crepe, or phyllo.

Optional topping of ½ pint heavy cream, ¼ cup sugar and 2 tablespoons vanilla whipped.

Note: Since pears have a very mild and delicate flavor, it is wise not to substitute other flavorings or add other fruit to this recipe.

Snowball

serves 10-12

13	oz. semi-sweet chocolate
1	cup coffee
10	oz. sugar (1 ½ cups plus 1 T.)
13	oz. unsalted butter (3 ¼ sticks)
6	eggs, room temperature
1¼	cups cream, whipped with 3 T. superfine sugar

Preheat oven to 300 degrees. Melt the chocolate in the coffee. Add the sugar and heat until dissolved. Add the butter in pieces, whisking, over the heat. Remove from the heat; add the eggs, one at a time, whisking well after each one. Immediately strain into a 3-quart foil-lined stainless bowl. (To line the bowl, use extra wide foil. Turn the bowl upside down and form the foil over the outside of the bowl. Transfer the foil to the inside, pushing the foiling evenly around the interior.)

Bake until the mixture rises, cracks and almost burns around the edges, approximately 1 hour 10 minutes. It will not set up solid until it cools. Let cool at least one day. Remove from bowl, trim edges to make a nice dome shape and invert on a serving plate. Pipe rosettes of sweetened whipped cream all over with a pastry bag and a star tip. Chill.

DESSERTS

Fresh Strawberries in Port

serves 6

2	pints fresh strawberries
½	cup sugar, or to taste
1	cup red Port
	whipped cream
	fresh mint sprigs

Gently wash the berries, drain on paper towels and hull. Toss the berries with the sugar and add Port. Chill at least 2 hours, stirring occasionally. To serve, top with a dollop of sweetened whipped cream and a sprig of mint. Serve with ladyfingers or shortbread.

Variation: Substitute for the Port ¼ cup Brandy and ¾ cup Marsala wine.

Meringue Dessert Shells

serves 12

½	cup egg whites, cold (warm ones give more volume, but also break down in cooking)
¾	cup sugar
1	tsp. vanilla
	parchment paper

Preheat oven to 200 degrees. Beat egg whites until stiff, about 3 minutes. Slowly add granulated sugar; don't beat more than 2 or 3 minutes. Fold in vanilla. Line a heavy sheet pan with parchment paper. Shape meringue into 3 or 4 inch circles with a spoon or pastry bag, making sides on the circles to hold a filling. Bake for about 2½ hours. Let cool in oven. Store in tighly covered tin box. Fill with custard, ice cream or whipped cream, flavored with rum, and topped with fresh berries.

Idie's Schaum Torte

serves 6

6	egg whites-room temperature
1	tsp. cream of tartar
1	tsp. vanilla
1	tsp. vinegar
2	cups sugar
1	tsp. baking powder
	fresh fruit, sprinkled with sugar
¾	cup heavy cream, whipped

Preheat oven to 325 degrees. Beat egg whites until foamy with cream of tartar. Add vanilla and vinegar, beat a little more. Add sugar, a little at a time. Beat until stiff. Beat in baking powder and spread in a 9 inch spring mold. Bake for approximately 1 hour.

After it cools, the top will fall in; pick out the pieces carefully and set aside. Fill the torte with sugared fruit and sweetened whipped cream. Carefully place the top on (it will be very cracked). Garnish with fresh fruit slices. Serve at the table.

Poached Pears with Crème Anglaise

¼ cup lemon juice
6 firm, ripe, unblemished pears
2 cups dry white wine
¾ cup sugar
1 stick (or ½ tsp.) cinnamon
½ cup ground pecans or toasted almonds
½ cup confectioners sugar
2 T. brandy
Crème anglaise (recipe follows)
Chocolate sauce (recipe follows)
Whipped cream (optional)

Fill a large bowl ¾ full with water and add 2 tablespoons of lemon juice. Peel pears, leaving the stems attached. Using the rounded end of a potato peeler, dig into the core from the bottom of the pear, removing the seed area as well as possible. (Do not worry about this too much, the core area of the pear is small and unobtrusive.) Place pears in lemon water.

In a saucepan, combine wine, remaining lemon juice, sugar and cinnamon. Bring to a boil. Drain pears and drop them into this boiling syrup. Simmer 8 to 10 minutes, until pears are barely tender. They should hold their shape. Remove from syrup and drain.

Combine nuts, powdered sugar and brandy to make a stiff paste. Set aside.

Make crème anglaise and chocolate sauce. (These may be made in advance—the custard should be refrigerated until ready to use.) When pears are cool enough to handle, stuff the hollowed core with the nut-sugar mixture. (The pears can be refrigerated several hours at this point.)

Creme anglaise:
1¾ cups hot milk
½ cup sugar
1 tsp. cornstarch
4 egg yolks
1 tsp. vanilla

Heat milk in a heavy saucepan over medium flame. Mix sugar and cornstarch. Beat sugar and egg yolks until they are fluffy. Continue to beat as you add hot milk in a thin stream. Pour the mixture back into the saucepan (or into a double boiler). Stir constantly until the sauce thickens just enough to coat the back of a spoon with a light, creamy layer (170 degrees). Do not let the custard simmer, or it will curdle. Remove from heat and continue stirring for a minute or two. Strain through a fine sieve and stir in vanilla. Chill before serving.

Chocolate Sauce:
4 oz. semi-sweet chocolate
2 oz. unsweetened chocolate
½ cup cream

Melt semisweet chocolate with unsweetened chocolate. Slowly whisk in cream and mix until blended. This will become very firm on standing. Reheat gently in a bath of simmering water or in a microwave—if it looks curdled, beat very briskly and often. As it begins to cool it should return to normal.

To serve, divide crème anglaise among 6 serving plates. Top with a pear standing upright. Drizzle with a little chocolate sauce and garnish, if desired, with whipped cream.

THIRTEENTH RACE
COOKIES/CANDIES
COMMITTEE'S HANDICAP

1	**CHOCOLATE MACAROONS**	SERVES **10**
2	**MRS. FIELDS FAUX CHOCOLATE CHIP COOKIES**	SERVES **10-20**
3	**MINT JULEP KISSES**	SERVES **12**
4	**MODJESKAS**	SERVES **12**
5	**FRENCH LACE COOKIE BASKETS**	SERVES **24**
6	**KENTUCKY BOURBON BALLS**	SERVES **10-20**

Committee Selections   1-6-4

Kentucky bred entry 3

Tasty Trivia
If cookies brown too quickly on the bottoms, don't use a cookie sheet, instead place the cookies on top of a baking pan that's turned upside down. The problem is solved when only the pan edges touch the hot oven rack.

Apricot Bars

yield 2 dozen

1	cup butter, room temperature
½	cup sugar
2	cups flour
½	tsp. vanilla
2	egg whites
1	cup confectioner's sugar
½	tsp. almond extract
1	12-oz. jar apricot preserves
½	cup sliced almonds

Cream butter and sugar. Add the flour and blend. Add vanilla. Press into 9 x 13 pan. Bake at 350 degrees for 15 minutes. Cool.

Make meringue by beating egg whites and gradually adding the confectioners sugar. Add almond extract with the last addition of the sugar. Do not overbeat.

Spread the preserves over the cooled crust; spread meringue over the preserves. Sprinkle nuts on top. Bake at 400 degrees for 20 minutes. Cool and cut.

Ginger Snaps

yield 3-4 dozen

1	cup sugar
¾	cup shortening
1	egg
1	cup molasses
2	cups sifted flour
¼	tsp. cloves
½	tsp. ginger
2	tsp. baking soda
½	tsp. cinnamon
⅛	tsp. salt
	granulated sugar

Cream sugar and shortening. Blend in egg and molasses. Sift together flour, cloves, ginger, baking soda, cinnamon and salt; mix in gently but thoroughly. Chill overnight in refrigerator.

Preheat oven to 350 degrees.
Shape the dough into balls, roll in granulated sugar and place on a greased cookie sheet. Bake for 10 minutes.

German Chocolate "Pig-Out"

yield 2 dozen

1	box German Chocolate cake mix
¾	cup butter, melted
1	cup walnuts or pecans, chopped
14	oz. caramels
½	cup evaporated milk
12	oz. semi-sweet chocolate chips

Preheat oven to 350 degrees. Mix cake mix, butter and nuts. Press ½-¾ into bottom of 9 x 13-inch greased and floured pan. Bake for 6 minutes.

Melt caramels in the evaporated milk in a double boiler (or microwave for 5 minutes at Medium Power). Spread the chocolate chips evenly over the baked first layer, then pour the caramel-milk mixture over chocolate. Top with the remaining cake mixture. Bake 13-18 minutes. Cool in the refrigerator for 30 minutes before cutting. Freezes well.

Bitter Chocolate Biscuits

yield 4-5 dozen

½ cup butter
1 cup sugar
few grains of salt
1 egg
4 (1 oz.) squares unsweetened chocolate
1 tsp. vanilla
1½ cups flour

Preheat oven to 375 degrees. Cream butter and sugar. Add salt and egg; beat until well-blended and fluffy. Meanwhile, melt chocolate in the top of a double boiler. Remove from heat and add to butter-egg mixture; add vanilla, and stir well to mix. Pour this mixture into the flour and stir again.

Chill dough until stiff enough to handle. Roll small amounts about ¼-inch thick on a floured board with a floured rolling pin. Use just as little flour as possible. Cut out dough with a small biscuit cutter and place an inch apart on an ungreased cookie sheet. Bake until cookies are firm but not browned at edges.

These superb cookies contain no baking powder and the "biscuits", when done, are on the soft side, almost the consistency of brownies. However, if you like your cookies crisp, chill the dough well and roll thin between sheets of floured waxed paper. Cut out and transfer to a cookie sheet and bake until cookies are done inside. (Break one open to test.) The thin cookies will become crisp when cool.

An unusual dessert—perfect for ice creams, fruits or a tea biscuit in winter.

Hill's Chocolate-Coconut Squares

yield 5-6 dozen

½ lb. butter (2 sticks), room temperature
2 cups sugar
6 eggs
1 lb. chocolate wafer cookies
½ cup milk
1 7 oz. bag of coconut
2 cups butterscotch chips

Preheat oven to 300 degrees. Grease a 9x13 pan. Mix all ingredients in a food processor in 2 batches and spread in pan. Set the pan in a larger pan with lukewarm water halfway up the sides. Bake 1 hour and 15 minutes. Cool and cut into squares.

Chocolate Cookies

yield 3 dozen

¼ stick butter (2 T.)
1 pkg. (12 oz.) chocolate bits
1 can Eagle Brand milk
1 cup cake flour
1 tsp. vanilla

Melt butter and chocolate in double boiler. Add Eagle Brand milk, flour, and mix. Fold in vanilla. Drop from teaspoon onto an aluminum foil-covered cookie sheet. Bake for 12 minutes at 300 degrees. Check carefully; don't overcook.

Tasty Trivia
If it's important to get the walnut meat out whole, soak overnight in salt water before cracking gently.

Pecan Poofs

yield 20 cookies

½   cup butter, room temperature
2   T. sugar
1   tsp. vanilla
1   cup finely ground pecans
1   cup sifted cake flour
     powdered sugar

Preheat oven to 300 degrees. Beat the butter until soft, then add sugar and blend until creamy. Add the vanilla, pecans and flour; blend well.

Break off pieces of dough slightly smaller than a walnut and roll with floured hands into a crescent shape.

Place on a well-buttered baking sheet and bake for 15 minutes or until pale brown. Gently roll the crescents in powdered sugar while they are hot. (They will be fragile at this stage but will harden as they cool.) Roll them a second time when they have cooled. They can be kept for a week or so in a cookie tin, and are very nice to serve after dinner with coffee.

Chocolate Macaroons

yield 20 sandwich cookies

Macaroons:
3½   oz. bittersweet chocolate
1   tsp. vanilla
2   large egg whites
1   8 oz. can almond paste
1¼   cups sugar
1   T. unsalted butter (to butter cookie sheet)

Filling:

1¾   oz. bittersweet chocolate
2   T. heavy cream

Preheat oven to 275 degrees. In a saucepan, over very low heat, melt 3½ ounces of chocolate, then add the vanilla to the chocolate.

With an electric mixer at low speed, mix the egg whites, almond paste and sugar until well blended. Add the melted chocolate mixture and continue beating until thoroughly blended.

Butter a cookie sheet. Spoon the batter onto the pan, allowing one teaspoon of batter for each macaroon. You should have 40 cookies.Bake for 18 to 20 minutes, or until macaroons are firm not dry. Transfer the macaroons to a rack to cool.

Meanwhile prepare the filling. In a small saucepan, over very low heat, melt the bittersweet chocolate; add the heavy cream and stir until blended.

When the macaroons and filling have cooled, spread a scant teaspoon of the filling on half the macaroons and cover each with a second macaroon, making a sandwich.These are best when served within a few hours.

Note: Use a fine chocolate, preferably a Belguim chocolate.

Chocolate Pecan Crinkles

yield 2 dozen

¼ cup butter (½ stick)
¾ cup light brown sugar, firmly packed (4 oz.)
½ cup dark sweet chocolate bits
1 cup (4 oz.) chopped pecans (chop fine)
1 egg
1 tsp. vanilla

Preheat oven to 350 degrees. In a heavy metal saucepan, melt butter and sugar; stir until mixture dissolves and begins to boil around the edges. Add the chocolate and continue to cook over low heat until chocolate thoroughly dissolves, stirring constantly. Remove from heat and stir in the pecans. Add the egg and vanilla and beat until this forms a thick paste.

Grease foil-lined cookie sheet with butter. Drop the batter by rounded teaspoons onto the foil leaving 2 inches between cookies; they spread while baking. Bake 10-12 minutes. The cookies will be thin and lacey when cooked. They should be a little chewy in the center and if overcooked, they will be hard and gummy.

Chill in the refrigerator when removed from the oven. When cold, remove from foil and store in tin box lined with wax paper. They will keep fresh up to two weeks.

French Lace Cookie Baskets

yield 3 dozen

½ cup corn syrup
½ cup butter
⅔ cup brown sugar
1 cup flour
1 cup nuts, chopped fine (optional)
1 tsp. vanilla

Preheat oven to 350 degrees. Put corn syrup, butter and sugar in a saucepan and bring to a boil, stirring constantly. The minute the mixture boils remove from heat and add flour and nuts; if using them. Add vanilla. Drop by teaspoons onto a well greased baking sheet placing well apart as they spread. Bake 5-6 minutes until lightly browned. Let them cool on pan placed on a rack for about 2 minutes until you can lift them off with a spatula. At this point you can roll them around a wooden spoon handle or anything else handy. Another pretty idea: mold cookie over the top of an inverted mason jar or egg custard cup.

When cold they make nice baskets for crème caramel, ice cream, custard or Ganache, a slightly thick mousse.

Ganache:
5 oz. chocolate
1 oz. cocoa butter (found in drugstores or health food store)
⅔ cup heavy cream
1 tsp. instant coffee dissolved in 2 tsp. hot water

Melt chocolate and cocoa butter in a double boiler. Bring cream to a boil, add to chocolate and mix well, beating with a wooden spoon until light in color. Add dissolved coffee and mix again.

Tasty Trivia
Coating chocolate may be substituted for the chocolate chips and paraffin.

Individual Cheesecakes

8 cakes

Preheat oven to 350 degrees.

¼ lb. butter
9 oz. cream cheese
1 tsp. vanilla
½ cup sugar
2 beaten eggs
1 cup sour cream
5 T. sugar
  strawberries or cherries for garnish

Cream butter and cheese, then add vanilla. Mix in sugar and eggs. Don't overbeat. Pour into muffin cups. (use double thickness.) Bake for 20 minutes. Remove from oven and let stand 15 minutes.

Mix sour cream and sugar. Spoon on top. Bake 5 to 10 minutes more. Chill. Serve with a strawberry or pretty red cherry on top.

This recipe is a great traveler when you must entertain on vacation. It keeps in the refrigerator for days and is a handy snack for anyone with a sweet tooth. It can, of course, be made well in advance of a dinner party.

Lace Cookies with Chocolate

yield 4 dozen

1 cup flour
1 cup coconut
½ cup light corn syrup
½ cup brown sugar, packed
½ cup margarine
1 tsp. vanilla
1 6 oz. pkg. chocolate chips

Preheat oven to 350 degrees. Mix flour and coconut. In a heavy pan bring to a boil the corn syrup, sugar and margarine, stirring constantly. Remove from heat and gradually stir in flour-coconut mixture, then vanilla.

Drop onto foil-covered cookie sheet by scant teaspoonfuls about 3 inches apart.

Cook 8-10 minutes. Cool 3-4 minutes until they can be taken off the foil and put on a paper towel. Melt chocolate chips (may be done in a microwave on Medium Heat for about 4 minutes) and spread thinly over top of cookies.

These are very tasty and nice to serve for a cocktail buffet dessert.

Minted Brownie Cookies

yield 4 to 5 dozen

14 chocolate minted cookies (Oreo), chilled
3 egg whites, beaten
  dash salt
¾ cup sugar
½ cup chopped nuts
½ tsp. vanilla

Preheat oven to 350 degrees. Roll chilled cookies between wax paper to make crumbs. Beat egg whites and salt together until soft peaks form. Gradually beat in sugar until stiff peaks form. Fold in cookie crumbs, nuts and vanilla. Drop by teaspoonfuls on a greased cookie sheet. Bake for 6-8 minutes.

Track Talk
Of the 40,000 thoroughbreds born every year, only 400 or so
will be good enough to be nominated for the Derby.

Lemon Crispies

yield 3-4 dozen

½   cup sifted flour
½   tsp. salt
⅔   cup sugar
1   cup shortening
2   eggs
1   tsp. lemon extract
1   tsp. lemon rind, grated
1   cup rolled oats

Preheat oven to 350 degrees. Sift the flour, salt and sugar. Blend in shortening, eggs, lemon extract and grated lemon rind; beating until smooth, about 2 minutes. Stir in 1 cup rolled oats.

Drop the batter from a teaspoon onto a greased and foil-lined cookie sheet, allowing 2 inches between each cookie. Flatten to about ¼-inch thick with a wet rubber spatula. Bake for 10-12 minutes, or until golden brown at the edges. Once brown, they will quickly overcook so watch carefully. Cool on wire cooling racks.

Melt Aways

yield 4 dozen

1   cup butter, room temperature
⅓   cup powdered sugar
1   tsp. vanilla
1   cup sifted flour
¾   cup cornstarch

Icing:
1   cup powdered sugar
2   T. melted butter
1   tsp. vanilla
     milk
     lemon juice and rind of one
        lemon, optional

Preheat oven to 350 degrees. Cream butter, powdered sugar and vanilla. Sift flour and corn starch and add to butter mixture. Spread in 9 x 13 pan and bake for 12-14 minutes. Cool and ice with the following:

Mix ingredients for icing, adding milk if needed to have proper consistency for spreading. When icing has hardened, cut into squares.

Mint Julep Kisses

yield 2 dozen

2   egg whites, stiffly beaten
¾   cup sugar
½   tsp. peppermint extract
2   drops green vegetable coloring
6   oz. chocolate bits

Preheat oven to 325 degrees. Beat egg whites until stiff, gradually adding sugar, Add peppermint and green coloring. Stir in chocolate bits. Drop by spoonfuls on cookie sheet. Put in preheated oven and turn off immediately. Leave in oven overnight or for several hours. Store in tin box.

Mrs. Field's Faux Chocolate Chip Cookies

yield 6 dozen

2	cups butter, room temperature
2	cups dark brown sugar
2	cups granulated sugar
4	eggs
2	tsp. vanilla
4	cups flour
5	cups old fashioned oatmeal
1	tsp. salt
2	tsp. baking soda
18	oz. Hershey bars, grated
3	cups chopped nuts
24	oz. chocolate chips

Preheat oven to 375 degrees. Cream butter and both sugars. Add eggs, one at a time, and vanilla. Stir in flour and oatmeal (blended, if desired). Add salt, soda and grated chocolate. Add chopped nuts and chocolate chips last. Mix well. Place golf ball size mounds of dough onto greased cookie sheet. Bake for 10 to 12 minutes.

Rumtoertchen

yield 6-7 dozen

1	cup butter, room temperature
1	cup sugar
2	large eggs
3	cups sifted flour
1	tsp. baking powder
	T. vanilla
1	red raspberry preserves
5	T. water, approximately
2	T. Rum or Brandy

Preheat oven to 350 degrees. Mix butter, sugar and eggs. Add flour and baking powder. Mix together well. Stir in vanilla. The dough is soft and must be chilled for at least an hour. Roll out dough on a floured board until it's very thin. Cut out with a doughnut or round cookie cutter. Place on an ungreased cookie sheet and bake 5-6 minutes. Cool on a rack.

Put about 1 teaspoon red raspberry preserves on each half of the cookies. Use the remaining cookies to make sandwich tops on those spread with preserves. Brush each double cookie with glaze made from confectioners sugar, water and Rum or Brandy.

Swedish Butter Cookies

yields 4 dozen

1	cup butter, room temperature
½	cup powdered sugar
1	tsp. vanilla
1¾	cups flour
1	cup chopped nuts
	granulated sugar

Cream butter and sugar well. Add vanilla, flour and nuts. Divide dough in half and form into 2 rolls. Pat the rolls on all four sides to make square shape. Refrigerate overnight.

Preheat oven to 350 degrees.
Cut ¼-inch thick and bake 10-12 minutes or until edges are lightly browned. Dip in sugar while warm and cool on wire racks.

Sesame Crisps

yield 5 dozen

1	cup sesame seeds
1½	sticks unsalted butter
¾	cup packed light brown sugar
1	egg, room temperature
2	T. dark rum
1¼	cup all-purpose flour
¼	tsp. baking powder
½	tsp. grated nutmeg
⅛	tsp. white pepper
¼	tsp. salt

Preheat oven to 375 degrees. In a large skillet, toss the sesame seeds constantly over moderate heat until light brown and toasted, about 5 minutes. Let cool.

Melt the butter and let cool to room temperature. In a medium bowl, combine the butter, sugar, egg, rum and sesame seeds. Combine and sift the flour, baking powder, nutmeg, salt and pepper. Add the flour mixture to the butter mixture; blend well.

Drop by the rounded ½ teaspoon, about 2-inches apart on buttered baking sheets. Bake in the middle of oven for 7-10 minutes, or until the cookies are golden brown with slightly darker edges. Let cool on wire racks.

Sinful Turtle Squares

yields 3 dozen

2	cups flour
1	cup brown sugar
½	cup butter, room temperature
1½	cups pecan halves
¾	cup butter
⅔	cup brown sugar packed
6	oz. semi-sweet chocolate chips, melted

Preheat oven to 350 degrees. Mix together flour, 1 cup brown sugar and ½ cup butter. Pat into an ungreased 9 x 13 x 2 inch glass baking dish. Sprinkle pecan halves over crust.

In a small saucepan, combine ¾ cup butter with ⅔ cup brown sugar and cook over medium heat, stirring constantly until entire surface begins to boil. Stir and boil for 1 minute. Pour hot mixture evenly over pecan halves and crust. Bake for 20 minutes or until entire surface is bubbly and crust is golden brown. Meanwhile, melt chocolate chips.

Take cookies from oven and immediately pour chocolate over surface of cookie. Cool completely before cutting into squares.

Bran Honey Wafers

yield 5 dozen (2¼ inch in diameter)

½	cup butter
½	cup honey
¼	cup bran cereal
2	cups flour
1	tsp. soda
½	tsp. cloves
¼	tsp. allspice

Preheat oven to 350 degrees. Boil butter and honey together for 1 minute. Cool. Crush bran cereal slightly. Sift flour with soda and spices and add to first mixture with bran cereal. Mix thoroughly. Chill. Roll dough on floured board to about 1/16 thickness; cut out and bake for about 10 minutes, until brown around edges.

Tasty Trivia
When eggs are stuck to the carton, just wet the box and the eggs can be easily removed without cracking the shells.

COOKIES / CANDY

Spice Cakes

yields 3-4 dozen

⅔ cup shortening
1   cup brown sugar
1   egg
3   cups sifted flour
1   tsp. cinnamon
½   tsp. allspice
½   tsp. ginger
1   tsp. baking soda
¾   cup molasses
¼   tsp. vanilla extract
    grape jelly

Cream sugar and shortening and egg. Add dry ingredients which have been sifted together, alternating with molasses. Add vanilla. Dough will be very stiff. Chill dough at least one hour.

Preheat oven to 350 degrees. Shape into small balls and roll in granulated sugar. Place on greased baking sheets. Make an indentation with finger and fill with grape jelly. Bake for 10-12 minutes.

Stretch Brownies

yields 16

2   sq. unsweetened chocolate
1   stick butter
1   cup sugar
2   eggs, beaten
½   tsp. vanilla
¼   cup flour
¼   tsp. salt
1   cup chopped nuts
½   cup raspberry preserves

Preheat oven to 325 degrees. In a saucepan over medium heat, melt chocolate and butter. Remove from heat and add sugar, eggs and vanilla. Beat well. Stir in flour, salt and nuts. Mix well. Pour half of mixture in a greased 8 x 8-inch pan and put in freezer until well frozen. (30 minutes) Remove from freezer and spread on layer of raspberry preserves. Bring back to room temperature, pour remaining chocolate mixture on top of preserves and bake for 40 minutes.

Sugar Squares

yields 2 dozen

¾   cup butter
3   T. sugar
2¼ cup brown sugar
1½ cups flour
3   egg yolks, beaten
1   cup coconut
⅛   tsp. salt
1   cup chopped nuts
3   egg whites
    powdered sugar

Cream butter and sugar. Add flour and mix well. Pour into a 9 x 13-inch pan and bake for 15 minutes at 350 degrees. Cool.

Mix egg yolks, nuts, coconut and salt. Beat egg whites until stiff, and gently fold into coconut mixture. Pour over cooled, baked mixture and bake for 30 minutes at 325 degrees.

Cool and cut into squares. Roll squares in sifted powdered sugar.

240

Swedish Toscas

yields 1-1½ dozen

6	T. butter, room temperature
¼	cup sugar
1	cup flour
½	cup slivered almonds
½	cup sugar
3	T. butter
2	T. cream
2½	tsp. flour

Preheat oven to 350 degrees. Cream 6 tablespoons butter and gradually add ¼ cup sugar. Blend in 1 cup flour and mix well. Divide into 12-18 small 2-inch muffin tins. Press into bottom and up sides. Bake for 10 minutes.

Combine the remaining ingredients in a saucepan and cook until mixture comes to a boil. Remove from heat and pour into each pastry. Cook for 10-15 minutes. Cool at least 5 minutes and pop out of tins. Makes 12-18 pastries.

Mother's Pound Cake Cookies

yield 5 dozen

1	lb. butter, room temperature
2	cups sugar
4	egg yolks
2	tsp. vanilla
5	cups flour

Cream butter and sugar well. Add egg yolks, then vanilla. Stir in flour by hand, cup by cup. Form into cylinders 1½ inches thick. Wrap in waxed paper and chill at least one hour, or perferably overnight.

Preheat oven to 350 degrees. Slice cookies ½-inch thick; place on greased cookie sheets. Bake until light brown, about 20 minutes.

Fudge-topped Granola Bars
(Microwave)

yields 24 bars

⅓	cup butter
½	cup brown sugar
¼	cup light corn syrup
1 ½	tsp. vanilla
¼	tsp. salt
3	T. crunchy peanut butter
1¾	cups oatmeal
1	cup crispy rice cereal
½	cup shredded coconut
2	T. butter
1	T. light corn syrup
1	T. milk
¼	cup brown sugar
1	tsp. cocoa (optional)
¼	tsp. vanilla
1	cup confectioners sugar
1	tsp. hot coffee
3	T. chopped peanuts

Place butter in 8-inch square dish. Microwave at High (100% power) for 1 minute, or until melted. Mix in brown sugar, syrup, vanilla, salt and peanut butter. Microwave at High for 3 minutes, stirring after 1½ minutes. Add oatmeat, cereal and coconut. Microwave at High for 2-3 minutes until mixture is bubbly.

In a small glass bowl, prepare fudge topping: mix butter, syrup, milk, brown sugar and cocoa. Microwave at High 2-2½ minutes, stirring after 1 minute. Mix in vanilla, sugar and coffee. Beat until smooth and creamy. Spread topping on granola bars. Immediately sprinkle with peanuts. Cool before cutting.

Tasty Trivia
The pan to a pressure cooker is the heaviest and best for candy making.

Peanut Butter Cups

yield 12 dozen

1   cup peanut butter
2   cups powdered sugar
½   cup melted butter
2½   pounds chocolate almond bark
     (available at candy stores)
12   dozen (approximately) petit four
     cups, which are 1 inch at base

Mix together the peanut butter, powdered sugar and melted butter. Make small balls of this mixture and flatten slightly. Place on wax paper-covered cookie sheet; chill.

Melt chocolate in a double boiler. Put small amount of chocolate in petit four cups. Add filling and cover with chocolate; chill. These keep well in refrigerator.

Orangerines

Chef Ferré, Maxim's, Paris, France

5   oz. candied orange peel, chopped
     fine (in processor)
2   T. Grand Marnier
1   lb. marzipan
     powdered sugar
1   lb. coating chocolate
3½   oz. candied orange peel for
     decoration

Combine orange peel, Grand Marnier and marzipan in food processor. Sprinkle with powdered sugar and chill for 30 minutes. Roll out ⅜-inch thick. Cut rounds with a very small cutter, (½-¾-inch). Place on waxed paper and leave to dry overnight. Melt covering chocolate carefully and dip each candy. Decorate with a tiny sliver of orange peel.

Kentucky Creams

yield 4 dozen

3   egg whites
1   cup sugar
15   soda crackers, rolled fine
1   cup chopped pecans
1   cup margarine
2   cups powdered sugar
4   squares baking chocolate,
     unsweetened
3   tsp. vanilla-divided
4   eggs
1   tsp. peppermint extract-not oil of
     peppermint
     fresh mint leaves, garnish

Beat egg whites until stiff. Add the sugar, one tablespoon at a time and beat until very stiff. Add 1 teaspoon vanilla. Fold in crackers and pecans until just mixed; do not over mix. Put one tablespoon mixture in bottom of large cup-cake paper cups or 2 scant teaspoons in the bottom of small paper cupcake cups. Bake 20 minutes at 350 degrees until crisp and light brown. Let cool before filling.

Beat margarine and sugar until creamy. Blend in cooled and melted chocolate. Beat in one egg at a time. Add remaining vanilla and peppermint extract. Fill meringue cups and freeze.

Serve on a silver platter and garnish with fresh mint leaves.

Track Talk
Aristides was the first Derby winner in 1875.

Fondant

Fondant is the base for many candies. This basic recipe for fondant is followed by several adaptions.

2	cups granulated sugar
¼	tsp. cream of tartar
½	tsp. salt
2	T. butter
½	cup cream, measured in heat proof measuring cup, then fill to brim with boiling water
¼	tsp. oil of peppermint few drops of green food coloring

Put all ingredients into pan and cook until a soft ball forms. Pour into a large buttered platter. When cool enough to place your hand on it, stir and then knead until creamy. When creamed, add ¼ teaspoon oil of peppermint and a few drops of green food coloring. Using both hands, continue to cream until ready to form into small balls. Refrigerate balls until firm and ready for dipping. After dipping each ball into warm, melted dipping, semi-sweet chocolate, place one pecan on top. (Slightly cook pecans in melted butter in pan in oven for several minutes. Remove and salt.)

Note: Eliminate peppermint and food coloring for variations.

Coconut Candy: Add coconut to basic fondant recipe and cream until it is ready to form into small balls. Refrigerate balls until firm. Dip each ball into warm, melted dipping semi-sweet chocolate.

Bourbon Balls: Make bourbon balls by using Kentucky Bourbon as flavoring, adding 1 cup chopped, toasted nuts and forming balls which are then dipped in warm, melted dipping semi-sweet chocolate.

Tea Mints: Form fondant around an almond and serve without dipping.

Kentucky Bourbon Balls

yield 4 dozen

1	stick butter
1	box powdered sugar
1	cup chopped pecans
4	T. Bourbon
4	oz. semi-sweet chocolate
4	oz. bitter chocolate

One day ahead: Cream the butter and the sugar. Add the chopped pecans, mixing well. Add the Bourbon and quickly shape into balls using about 1 teasoon of the mixture for each ball. Refrigerate overnight.

Next day: Melt both the chocolates in a double boiler until the chocolate has a smooth consistency. Dip the chilled Bourbon balls into the chocolate. Place the candy on waxed paper in the refrigerator to harden.

Spencer County Public Library
210 Walnut
Rockport, IN 47635-1398

243

Tasty Trivia
Helen Mojeska performed at the Macauley Theatre in the 1870's. Mr. Busath's confectionary created a marshmallow-caramel confection in the honor of the actress and called it a Mojeska.

Vanessa's Taffy

½   lb. butter
1¾   cups sugar
¼   cup water
1   cup chopped almonds, warmed
1   large Hershey bar, softened

Combine butter, sugar and water and cook over low heat until mixture reaches hard crack stage (300 degrees). Add ¾ cup almonds which have been warmed slightly in the oven. Pour out onto a greased sheet pan and let candy become firm. While still warm, spread chocolate bar over candy. Sprinkle remaining ¼ cup nuts over chocolate.

Break into pieces when cool and firm.

Microwave Crunchy Toffee   ½ lb. candy

½   cup butter
1⅓   cups sugar
1   T. light corn syrup
2   T. water
1   tsp. vanilla
½   cup semi-sweet chocolate pieces
½   cup sliced almonds

In a 2-quart glass casserole, place butter. Microwave at High for 30 seconds to 1 minute, until melted. Thoroughly stir in sugar, corn syrup and water. Microwave at High for 10 to 14 minutes, stirring every 4 minutes, until syrup dropped in cold water immediately forms hard, brittle balls or strands.

Stir in the vanilla and almonds; pour syrup onto a un-greased cookie sheet. Sprinkle with the chocolate pieces and let stand a few minutes until pieces melt. With knife, spread melted chocolate evenly over toffee. Refrigerate until chocolate is set. When cool, break the candy into pieces.

Note: Remember—syrup gets very hot when boiling candies, so take care in handling.

Modjeskas   yield 3 dozen

1   batch of basic caramel
        (without nuts)
36-40   marshmallows (homemade
        are best)

Pour the caramel, as soon as it has been flavored and stirred, onto an oiled marble slab. Cut the marshmallows in half with wet scissors. When the caramel has cooled slightly, use a spatula to pick up a small sheet of caramel and wrap around each marshmallow half, molding with oiled fingers to cover each. Wrap each candy separately in waxed paper. Store tightly covered in tin boxes. This method gets lots of caramel on each candy.

Diana Hansen's Chocolate Pralines
(Microwave)

20-30 pieces

1   lb. light brown sugar
1   cup whipping cream
1   square (1 oz.) semi-sweet
        chocolate, coarsely chopped
2   T. butter
2   cups whole pecans (½ lb.)

Microwaving is the very best way to make pralines. There's no danger of scorching the sugary mixture, as there is in a saucepan on the range top. You can omit the chocolate to make plain pralines, if you wish.

In a 3 quart microwave casserole, place sugar and whipping cream, Stir well. Microwave uncovered at High for 10 minutes (if your oven is 700 watts) to 14 minutes (if your oven is 625 watts), until a little syrup dropped in a cupful of cold water forms a soft ball. Quickly stir in the chocolate, butter and nuts. Return to microwave at High for 1 to 1½ minutes, just to reliquify. Quickly drop mixture by spoonfuls onto waxed paper. Let stand to cool and firm up. Store in airtight container.

Note: Boiling mixture is very hot. Use glass or high-temperature plastic dish and take care when handling hot mixture.

Peanut Brittle
(Microwave)

2 dozen small pieces

1   cup sugar
½   cup white corn syrup
1   cup dry roasted unsalted peanuts
1   tsp. butter
1   tsp. vanilla extract
1   tsp. baking soda

In 1½ quart casserole, stir together sugar and syrup. Microwave at High level for 4 minutes.

Stir in peanuts. Microwave at High for 3-5 minutes until light brown. Add butter and vanilla to syrup, blending well. Microwave at High for 1-2 minutes more. Peanuts will be lightly browned and syrup very hot. Add soda and stir gently until light and foamy. Pour mixture onto lightly greased cookie sheet. Let cool ½ to 1 hour. When cool, break into small pieces, and store in airtight container.

Tasty Trivia
You can crisp soggy cereal and crackers by putting them on a cookie sheet and heating for a few minutes in the oven.

Helen's Delicate Sweet Treats

yield 3-4 dozen

2	cups flour
1	tsp. baking powder
¾	cup butter, room temperature
1	cup powdered sugar
1	egg, separated
¼	cup milk
¼	tsp. almond extract
¾	tsp. vanilla

Preheat oven to 375 degrees. Sift together the flour and baking powder. In a mixer, cream together the butter and sugar; add egg yolk and mix. Add flour-baking powder mixture and milk, alternately. Add vanilla and almond extract. Whip the egg white and stir in by hand. Drop by teaspoons on a lightly greased cookie sheet and bake for 10 minutes.

Ice if desired with a glaze made by adding sifted powdered sugar to warm milk until proper consistency. Add few drops of almond or vanilla extract. The icing may be lightly tinted.

Praline Cookies

yields 2-2½ dozen

⅓	box Graham crackers
2	sticks butter
½	cup sugar
½	cup chopped nuts

Preheat oven to 325 degrees. Break graham crackers into sections. Place on cookie sheet, letting sides of crackers touch.

Melt butter, add sugar and bring to a boil. Boil for 3 minutes stirring constantly; add nuts and pour over crackers.

Bake for 12 minutes.

Remove from pan at once. Put on foil to cool. May be frozen.

Molasses Crinklers

yield 4 dozen

¾	cup shortening
1	cup dark brown sugar
1	egg, beaten
4	T. molasses
¼	tsp. salt
2	tsp. baking soda
½	tsp. cloves
1	tsp. cinnamon
1	tsp. ginger
2 ¼	cups flour
	granulated sugar
	water

Preheat oven to 375 degrees. Mix well the shortening, brown sugar, beaten egg and molasses. Sift together the salt, baking soda, cloves, cinnamon and ginger with the flour. Mix the flour mixture with the shortening mixture. Chill for 1 hour.

Shape the dough into walnut-size balls. Dip into sugar and "dot" the top with cold water (to make the cookies snappy). Bake for 12-15 minutes.

Caramels

yield 2 ½ dozen

2   cups sugar
1   cup light corn syrup
2   cups heavy cream, warmed and
        divided
½   tsp. salt
½   tsp. vanilla
     Chopped pecans, ½-1 cup,
        depending on taste

In large, heavy saucepan, mix sugar, syrup and 1 cup of the cream. Cook for about 10 minutes, stirring thoroughly to dissolve sugar before it comes to a strong boil. Insert candy thermometer. Thereafter, stir only when necessary, to prevent scorching. Add the other cup of cream slowly so as not to stop cooking. When candy reaches 230 degrees, cook more slowly to 244 degrees. Remove from heat, add salt and vanilla, stirring only enough to blend flavors.

Add chopped pecans according to your taste and pour into oiled 8 x 8 pan. Cool. Refrigerate until hard. Cut into small squares and wrap in waxed paper. Store in tins in refrigerator.

This will be difficult to remove from pan, so lift each corner and remove entire square, then cut into smaller squares on a cutting board.

Turtles

100 candies

1   batch of basic caramel, minus
        chopped nuts
1   lb. whole pecans
1   lb. good chocolate or semi-sweet
        choclate bits

Grease several large baking sheets. Place 3 pecans together, with "feet" pointed out, all over each sheet. Pour caramel over each 3 "feet" to almost cover. When cool, melt chocolate in top of a double boiler and spread on top of caramel. Wrap each candy in waxed paper.

Chocolate Buckeyes

yield 3-4 dozen

1   stick margarine
2   cups crunchy peanut butter
1   lb. powdered sugar
2   cups Rice Krispies (may need
        more)
1   pkg. (12 oz.) chocolate chips
¼   bar paraffin (optional)

Mix margarine, peanut butter and as much powdered sugar as needed. When well-mixed, add the Rice Krispies. Roll into small balls (about the size of a walnut). Put in freezer for about an hour.
Melt chocolate and paraffin (if used) in double boiler over very warm, not boiling, water. Dip balls in chocolate with a toothpick or dipping fork, covering ⅔ of ball, leaving an "eye" for the buckeye. Place on waxed paper. Keep in refrigerator or freezer.

Pistachio Crescents Chef Ferré

110 crescents

1   lb. marzipan (or almond paste)
¾   cup powdered sugar
3½   oz. pistachio nuts, very finely
      chopped
3   T. Kirsch or Amaretto liqueur
      powdered sugar for rolling
1   lb. covering chocolate or ¾ lb.
      semi-sweetchocolate, ¼ lb.
      butter and 3 tablespoons oil
3½   oz. whole pistachio nuts for
      garnish

Knead together the almond paste, powdered sugar, chopped nuts, and liqueur until well blended. Cover and chill until firm, about 30 minutes. Cover two baking sheets with foil. Sprinkle work surface with powdered sugar. Roll out the mixture to ⅜ inch thickness. Cut into scalloped crescent shapes with a 1½ inch fluted cookie cutter. Place them on the prepared baking sheets and leave overnight in a cool dry place. Next day, melt covering chocolate over hot water, stirring until just warm to the touch. Dip each crescent into the chocolate, let excess drip off, carefully flip it onto the baking sheet. Garnish each crescent with a whole pistachio nut, as it is dipped. Candies can be kept in a cool dry place for two months or more.

Truffles

yield 3 dozen

1¾   cups semi-sweet chocolate chips
      (12 oz)
2   T. water
1   cup powdered sugar
5   T. cream
1   tsp. vanilla

Coating: chocolate sprinkles, or toasted chopped nuts, or cocoa, or toasted coconut, or grated orange peel

Melt chocolate and water in double boiler. When melted, remove from heat and add powdered sugar, cream & vanilla. Beat with a wooden spoon until creamy. Chill one hour. Oil hands and make uniform sized balls. Roll in favorite coating. Store in refrigerator. Will keep a week or more.

Index

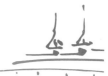

Adeline and Jane's Never-Fail Corn Pudding ... 157
Adlai Stevenson's Dish 139
All Natural Wheat-Bran Muffins 182
Almonds:
  Almond Bavarian Cream with Raspberry
    Coulis and Caramel Sauce 223
  Almond Cream Pie 213
  Amaretto Soufflé 218
  Bisque Ice Cream 210
  Chicken Supreme in
    Toasted Almond Sauce 95
  Chocolate Macaroons 234
  Ice Cream Soufflé 220
  Orangerines 242
  Swedish Toscas 241
  Toasted Almond Sauce 95
Amaretto:
  Amaretto Ice Cream 210
  Amaretto Sauce 176
  Amaretto Soufflé 218
  Chocolate Amaretto Cheesecake 209
Ambrosia from the Sea for Microwave 146
Aniello's Bracciola 110
Anitra Mandarine 105
Appetizers: Cocktail Foods
  Artichoke Dip 22
  Artichoke Nibbles 22
  Asparagus Rounds 22
  Baby Hot Browns, Café Musée 30
  Baked Stuffed Brie 24
  Beer Cheese 23
  Benedictine 84
  Bourbon Glazed Ham Balls 25
  Boursin Cheese Wafers 23
  Café Musée's Caramelized Bacon 23
  Caviar Beggar's Purses 35
  Caviar Mousse 35
  Cheese Puffs 33
  Cheese Timbales with Spinach Sauce 85
  Cheesey Shrimp Mold 39
  Chili Con Queso 24
  Chutney Cheese Canapé 26
  Crêpes 36
  Crusty Havarti 26
  Curried Chicken Paté 30
  Ed's Salsa 24
  Glazed Chicken Wings 31
  Green Chili Hors d'Oeurves 26
  Ham and Green Peppercorn Paté 30
  Ham Balls with Sweet-Sour Pineapple
    Sauce 31
  Herbal Cheesecake 27
  Holly's Mexican Appetizers 27
  Homemade Crackers 194
  Hot Crab Casserole 37
  Hot Mushroom Dip 33
  Indian Feast Popcorn 41
  Julia's Spinach Casserole 164
  Junie's Marinated Shrimp 38
  Mark's Spread 28
  Meatballs in Creamy Dill Sauce 32
  Mock Boursin Cheese 23
  Museum Mushrooms 33
  Mushroom Mousse 34
  Mushrooms 33
  Mushrooms Normandy 34
  Naples Nibbles 40
  Onion Rounds 41
  Ophelia's Derbytime One-Step Tomato
    Sandwiches 41
  Oyster Rockefeller Spread 37
  Oyster Roll 37
  Party Chicken Livers 31
  Peppered Beef 116
  Pimiento Cheese 85
  Pineapple Cheese Ball 28
  Post Time Cheese Mold 28
  "Quick" Beaten Biscuits 186
  Roquefort Walnut Spread 29
  Sausage Balls 32
  Savory Cheese Bites 25
  Seafood Mold 38
  Shantung Torte 29
  Shrimp Cocktail Ball 39
  Shrimp Toast 39
  Shrimp Toast-to-Show 40
  Shrimper's Party Spread 39
  Smearcase 72
  Smokey Salmon Spread 38
  Steak Tartare 32
  Tarragon Dip 29
  Tuna Paté 40
  Watercress Spread 29

Winningham Farm's Baked Clam Dip 36
Zucchini à La Grecque 167
Apples:
  Apple Chutney 175
  Apple Graham Pie 225
  Apple Nut Cake 202
  Bourbon Apple Sauce 134
  Mother's Apple Cheese Crisp 213
Apricots:
  Apricot Bars 232
  Apricot Bread 184
  Apricot Liqueur 44
  Pineapple-Apricot Nut Loaves 191
Artichokes:
  Artichoke Dip 22
  Artichoke Hearts with Gorgonzola 150
  Artichoke Nibbles 22
  Artichokes Au Gratin 150
  Carciofi Imbottiti Alla Siciliana
    (Sicilian Stuffed Artichokes) 151
  Chicken with Artichokes 92
  Cold Pasta Salad with Red Peppers, Chicken
    and Artichoke Hearts 64
  Creamed Shrimp with Artichoke Bottoms 140
Asparagus:
  Asparagus Gratin 151
  Asparagus Rounds 22
  Asparagus Soup with Tarragon 54
  Refreshing Asparagus Salad 74
Aspic, Diamond Beef Filet In Aspic 115
Atlanta Cheesecake 208
Avocado, Warm Scallop and Avocado Salad 66
Baby Hot Browns Café Musée 30
Barbecue Shrimp 139
Barbecue Shrimp Sauce 139
Bacon:
  Capé Musée's Caramelized Bacon 23
  Egg and Bacon Soufflé 87
  Governor's Egg Casserole 87
  Party Chicken Livers 31
Baked Cherries 154
Baked Rice 162
Baked Stuffed Brie 24
Ballotine de Boeuf 111
Bananas:
  Banana Daiquiri 44
  Hummingbird Cake 204
  Processor Bourbon Raisin Banana Bread 192
  Six Threes Ice Cream 211
Barbecued-Grilled:
  Barbecue Sauce 170
  Barbecue Shrimp 139
  Barbecue Shrimp Sauce 139
  Beef Brisket Barbecue 110
  Elizabethtown, Kentucky Trout 134
  Grilled Salmon Stuffed with Rice 137
  Lamb Marinated with Rosemary 118
  Marinated Lamb Chops 122
  Pork Tenderloin in Spiced Bourbon Sauce 128
  Barbecue Sauce 170
  Barbecued Spareribs 124
  Barley Pilaf 151
  Basil Cream Sauce 144
  Bauer's Hot Slaw 69
Beans, green:
  Dilled Green Beans with Walnuts 164
  French Green Bean Salad 72
  Green Beans with Oranges 156
  Green Beans with Persillade 152
  Green Vegetable Medley 166
  Marinated Green Beans 159
Beaten Biscuits 186
Beef Bourguignon 112
Beef with Broccoli and Black Beans 113
Beef, Flank:
  Ballotine de Boeuf 111
  Beef with Broccoli and Black Beans 113
Beef, Ground:
  Celide's Meatballs and Sauce 114
  Meatballs in Creamy Dill Sauce 32
  Steak Tartare 32
Beef, Roast:
  Beef Brisket Barbecue 110
  Diamond Beef Filet in Aspic 115
  Eye of Round Party Platter 116
  Germantown Beef 117
  Marinated Rolled Rib Roast 115
  Peppered Beef 116
  Ribeye Roast 114
  Seldom Seen Brisket, Hot and Cold 117
  Spiced Round of Beef 132
Beef, Steak: Aniello's Bracciola 110
Beef, Stew:
  Beef Bourguignon 112

Dead Heat Kentucky Burgoo 112
Beer Cheese 23
Beets:
  Gingered Red Carrots 153
  Jellied Beet Soup 55
  Mrs. Potter's Borscht 55
Benedictine 84
Berry Sauce 220
Beverages and Punches:
  Apricot Liqueur 44
  Banana Daiquiri 44
  Bimini Planters Punch 45
  Blinker 44
  Bourbon Slush 45
  Café Brûlot Diabolique 45
  Coffee Liqueur 44
  Cranberry Punch 44
  Cricket 45
  Daiquiri 46
  Derby Fizz 46
  Dixie Whiskey 46
  Golden Cadillac 46
  Irvin Cobb's Mint Julep 47
  Kentucky Derby Cranberry Punch 46
  Mint Grape Punch 50
  Mint Juleps 47
  Mock Champagne Punch 48
  Mother's Old Fashioned Custard 50
  Mr. Closson's Mint Julep 47
  Nancy's Mint Julep 48
  Pendennis Champagne Punch 48
  Polar Bear 49
  Rebel Party Sour 50
  Ringer 49
  Shade Seeker Lemonade 51
  Sherry Bolo 49
  Some Stardust Wine Cooler 49
  Spanish Chocolate 51
  The Cookbook Committee's
    Favorite Countertop Tea 51
  White Wine Sangria 50
  Wonderful Hot Chocolate 51
Bill's Chestnuts and Potatoes 156
Bill's Sunday Supper 147
Bill's Thick Pear and Caramel Sauce 176
Bimini Planter's Punch 45
Biscuits for a Party 186
Bisque Ice Cream 210
Bitter Chocolate Biscuits 233
Black Beans, Beef with Broccoli and
  Black Beans 113
Blinker 44
Blueberries:
  Blueberry Muffins 182
  Fresh Blueberry Tart 213
  Pecan Muffins 184
Blue Boar's Lettuce with Cottage Cheese
  Dressing 78
Blue Cheese Dressing 82
Bluegrass Peaches 227
Bonnie and Lucy's Salmon Scallops with Lemon
  Ginger Sauce 136
Bourbon:
  Blinker 44
  Bluegrass Peaches 227
  Bourbon Applesauce 134
  Bourbon Dates 227
  Bourbon Glazed Ham Balls 25
  Bourbon Pork Roast 124
  Bourbon Sauce 177
  Bourbon Slush 45
  Bourbon Waffle Syrup 177
  Bourbon Yams 168
  Derby Fizz 46
  Dixie Whiskey 46
  Fondant 243
  Hot Bourbon Sauce 178
  Hot Brown Sauce 30
  Kentucky Bourbon Balls 243
  Kentucky Bourbon Cake 204
  Kentucky Derby Cranberry Punch 46
  Louisville Bourbon Pie 214
  Mint Juleps 47
  Mr. Closson's Mint Julep 47
  Nancy's Mint Julep 48
  Pork Tenderloin in Spiced Bourbon Sauce 128
  Processor Bourbon Raisin Banana Bread 192
  Ringer 49
  Spiced Bourbon Sauce
    for Pork Tenderloin 128
Boursin Cheese Wafers 23
Boyle County Stuffed Tomatoes 70

Bran:
All Natural Wheat-Bran Muffins 182
Bran Honey Wafers 239
Gem Date Bran Muffins 182
Granola 189
Brandied Chicken 101
Bread, Adaptations:
Chad Mitchell's Bread Pudding 224
Herbed French Bread 190
Bread, Biscuits:
Beaten Biscuits 186
Biscuits for a Party 186
"Quick" Beaten Biscuits 186
Quick Brioches 191
Richard's Delicious Biscuits 187
Bread, Muffins:
All Natural Wheat-Bran Muffins 182
Blueberry Muffins 182
Breakfast Puffs 187
Brown Sugar Muffins 183
Carrot Cake Muffins 183
Gem Date Bran Muffins 182
Pecan Muffins 184
Strawberry Muffins 185
Whole Wheat Ginger Orange Muffins 185
Bread, Quick:
Apricot Bread 184
Broccoli Bread 188
Caraway Cheese Bread 188
Glenis' Egg Cornbread 189
Hot Sausage Bread 190
Hot Water Cornbread 190
Maker's Mark Bourbon Bread 188
Pineapple-Apricot Nut Loaves 191
Plainview Farm Spoon Bread 191
Processor Bourbon Raisin Banana Bread 192
Squash Bread 193
Whole Wheat Biscuits 187
Bread, Rolls and Buns:
Homemade Rolls 195
Mini Cinnamon Wheels 184
Mother's Coffee Cake 199
Mother's Rolls 199
Bread, Yeast:
Cheese Carrot Bread 193
Dee Cunningham's Kuchen 194
French Bread 195
Grace Smith's Honey Wheat Bread 196
Homemade Crackers 194
Horseshoe Derby Bread 200
Kitty's Oatmeal Bread 198
Laurie's Buttermilk Bread 192
Maple Oatmeal Bread 198
Mother's Rolls 199
Raisin Bread 199
Spiral Herb Bread 200
Breakfast Puffs 187
Breakfast Ramekins 86
Brie, Baked Stuffed Brie 24
Broccoli:
Beef with Broccoli and Black Beans 113
Broccoli Bake 150
Broccoli Bread 188
Broccoli Salad 68
Broccoli Sauce 170
Broccoli with Sesame Dressing 152
Broiled Sweetbreads 130
Brown Sugar Muffins 183
Brunch Eggs, Taco Style 88
Brussels Sprouts, Fast Track Soup 60
Bulgar, Tabouli (cold vegetable salad) 75
Butter Bean Salad 69
Butter Crunch Lemon Chiffon Pie 217
Buttermilk:
Gem Date Bran Muffins 182
Laurie's Buttermilk Bread 192
Richard's Delicious Biscuits 187
Butters:
Maple Butter 183
Pistachio Butter 183
Strawberry Butter 185
Butterscotch:
Butterscotch Sauce 177
Hot Butterscotch Sauce 225
Cabbage:
Bauer's Hot Slaw 69
Cadiz Fudge Cake 202
Cadiz Fudge Frosting 202
Café Brûlot Diabolique 45
Café Musée Caramelized Bacon 23
Cajun Blackened Redfish 135
Cakes: see also Breads Quick: Charlotte; Cheesecake; Meringue
Apple Nut Cake 202
Cadiz Fudge Cake 202
Fabulous Spice Cake 214
Fresh Coconut-Carrot Cake 203
German Chocolate Cake with Orange Marmalade 203
Hummingbird Cake 204
Kentucky Bourbon Cake 204
Lutèce Chocolate Cake 206
Mrs. Pollard's Sour Cream Cake 207
Orange Date Cake 208
Pound Cake 206
Snowball 228
13th Century Nun's Cake 207
California Rice 163
Candies:
Caramels 247
Chocolate Buckeyes 247
Diana Hansen's Chocolate Pralines 245
Fondant 243
Kentucky Bourbon Balls 243
Kentucky Creams 242
Microwave Crunchy Toffee 244
Modjeskas 244
Orangerines 242
Peanut Brittle 245
Peanut Butter Cups 242
Pistachio Crescents Chef Ferré 248
Truffles 248
Turtles 247
Vanessa's Taffy 244
Caramel:
Almond Bavarian Cream with Raspberry Coulis and Caramel Sauce 223
Bill's Thick Pear and Caramel Sauce 176
Caramels 247
Caramel Icing 210
Caramel Sauce 177
Crème Caramel 205
Jam Caramel Pie 216
Modjeskas 244
Turtles 247
Caraway Cheese Bread 188
Carciofi Imbottiti Alla Siciliana (Sicilian Stuffed Artichokes) 151
Carrots:
Carrot Cake Muffins 183
Carrots and Celery with Pecans 153
Carrots with Mustard and Dill 168
Clubhouse Carrot Casserole 152
Fresh Coconut-Carrot Cake 203
Gingered Red Carrots 153
Stuffed Carrots 153
Timbales of Carrot Mousse 154
Walnut Carrots 155
Casserole of Shrimp in a Cream Sauce 141
Cauliflower:
Cauliflower Medley 155
Cauliflower with Poppy Seeds 154
Curried Cauliflower Aspargus Soup 60
Caviar:
Caviar Beggar's Purses 35
Caviar Mousse 35
Celery:
Carrots and Celery with Pecans 153
Celery Casserole 155
Celide's Meatballs and Sauce 114
Cereal,Granola 189
Chad Mitchell's Bread Pudding 224
Champagne:
Mock Champagne Punch 48
Pendennis Champagne Punch 48
Charlottes:
White Charlotte Russe and Hot Butterscotch Sauce 225
Cheese: see also individual varieties
Apple Cheese Crisp 213
Artichoke Hearts with Gorgonzola 150
Artichokes au Gratin 150
Baked-Stuffed Brie 24
Beer Cheese 23
Benedictine 84
California Rice 163
Caraway Cheese Bread 188
Cheese Carrot Bread 193
Cheese Pastry for Torta 167
Cheese Puffs 33
Cheese Sandwiches 84
Cheese Soup 57
Cheese Timbales with Spinach Sauce 85
Cheese Waffles 189
Cheesey Shrimp Mold 39
Chili Con Queso 24
Chutney Cheese Canapé 26
Crusty Havarti 26
Dee Cunningham's Kuchen 194
Fettuccine Casserole 89
Green Chilies Hors d'Oeuvre 26
Grits Casserole 86
Herbal Cheese Cake 27
Houseguest Eggs 86
Make-ahead Quiche 89
Mark's Spread 28
Peas Creole 161
Pimiento Cheese 85
Pineapple Cheese Ball 28
Post Time Cheese Mold 28
Roquefort Walnut Spread 29
Savory Cheese Bites 25
Shantung Torte 29
Swiss Potatoes 162
Veal Chops Stuffed with Bel Paese and Sundried Tomatoes 128
Cheesecake:
Atlanta Cheesecake 208
Chocolate Amaretto Cheesecake 209
Herbal Cheese Cake 27
Individual Cheese Cakes 236
Pumpkin Cheese Cake 209
Cherries, Baked Cherries 154
Chestnuts, Bill's Chestnuts and Potatoes 156
Chèvre and Leek Flan 88
Chèvre Sauce 89
Chicken:
Brandied Chicken 101
Chicken á la Roma 107
Chicken and Fruit Salad 64
Chicken and Green Grapes 94
Chicken Breast with Dressing 93
Chicken Dijonnaise 100
Chicken Piccata 95
Chicken Salad with Wild Rice 65
Chicken Supremes in Toasted Almond Sauce 95
Chicken with Artichokes 92
Chicken with Cashews and Pineapple 93
Chicken with Taj Mahal Barbecue Sauce 102
Cold Pasta Salad with Red Peppers, Chicken and Artichoke Hearts 64
Country Chicken Pie 108
Country Ham, Chicken and Mushroom Timbale 119
Country Terrine 125
Crumb Chicken Casserole 108
Curried Chicken Paté 30
Curried Chicken with Rice Salad 65
Dead Heat Kentucky Burgoo 112
Elegant Chicken 96
Glazed Chicken Wings 31
Grandstand Chicken Casserole 96
Hawaiian Chicken 97
Hot Chicken Salad 97
Idie and Herman's Marinade for Grilled Chicken 173
Kelaguen Monnok (Chicken Mannock) 98
Lemon Roasted Chicken 99
Mancho Manteles 99
Party Chicken Livers 31
Poulet in Papillote with Fresh Ginger and Lemon 98
Roxanne's Boursin Chicken 92
Snow on the Mountain 102
Stir-fry Chicken with Snow Peas 94
Stuffed Chicken Breasts 103
Track Time Terrine 101
Chili Peppers:
Chili Con Queso 24
Ed's Salsa 24
Green Chili Hors d'Oeurves 26
Chilled Chocolate Raspberry Soufflé 221
Chinese:
Beef with Broccoli and Black Beans 113
Broccoli with Sesame Dressing 152
Steamed Fish 135
Stir-fry Chicken with Snow Peas 94
Chocolate:
Bitter Chocolate Biscuits 233
Cadiz Fudge Cake 202
Chilled Chocolate Raspberry Soufflé 221
Chocolate Amaretto Cheesecake 209
Chocolate Buckeyes 247
Chocolate Cookies 233
Chocolate Fudge Pie 215
Chocolate Macaroons 234
Chocolate Pecan Crinkles 235
Chocolate Sabayon Pie 219

Chocolate Sauce for Pears ... 226
Diana Hansen's Chocolate Pralines ... 245
Fondant ... 243
Fudge-Topped Granola Bars ... 241
Ganache ... 235
German Chocolate Cake With Orange Marmalade ... 203
German Chocolate "Pig Out" ... 232
Hill's Chocolate Coconut Squares ... 233
Kentucky Bourbon Balls ... 243
Kentucky Creams ... 242
Kentucky Derby Museum Pie ... 216
Lace Cookies with Chocolate ... 236
Lemon or Chocolate Pie ... 219
Lutèce Chocolate Cake ... 206
Minted Brownie Cookies ... 236
Mrs. Field's Faux Chocolate Chip Cookies ... 238
Orangerines ... 242
Peanut Butter Cups ... 242
Pistachio Crescents Chef Ferré ... 248
Sinful Turtle Squares ... 239
Snowball ... 228
Spanish Chocolate ... 51
Stretch Brownies ... 240
Sugar Squares ... 246
Truffles ... 248
Wonderful Hot Chocolate ... 51
Chutney:
Apple Chutney ... 175
Chutney Cheese Canapé ... 26
Mark's Spread ... 28
Peach Chutney ... 180
Post Time Cheese Mold ... 28
Sausage Balls ... 32
Sprinter Turkey Salad ... 65
Clams, Winningham Farm's Baked Clam Dip ... 36
Clubhouse Carrot Casserole ... 152
Club Salad ... 70
Coconut:
Fondant ... 243
Fresh Coconut-Carrot Cake ... 203
Gainesborough Tart ... 216
Granola ... 189
Hill's Chocolate Coconut Squares ... 233
Kelaguen Mannok (Chicken Kelaguen) ... 98
Mamie's Coconut Pie ... 212
Sugar Squares ... 246
White Charlotte Russe and Hot Butterscotch Sauce ... 225
Coffee:
Café Brûlot Diabolique ... 45
Coffee Liqueur ... 44
Cold Pasta Salad with Red Peppers, Chicken and Artichoke Hearts ... 64
Cold Spinach-Cucumber Soup ... 61
Condiments:
Mrs. Rodes Green Tomato Catsup ... 171
Seasoned Salt ... 179
Confetti Rice Salad ... 71
Cookies:
Apricot bars ... 232
Bitter Chocolate Biscuits ... 233
Bran Honey Wafers ... 239
Chocolate Cookies ... 233
Chocolate Macaroons ... 234
Chocolate Pecan Crinkles ... 235
French Lace Cookie Baskets ... 235
Fudge-Topped Granola Bars ... 241
German Chocolate "Pigout" ... 232
Ginger Snaps ... 232
Helen's Delicate Sweet Treats ... 246
Hill's Chocolate Coconut Squares ... 233
Lace Cookies with Chocolate ... 236
Lemon Crispies ... 237
Melt Aways ... 237
Minted Brownie Cookies ... 236
Mint Julep Kisses ... 237
Molasses Crinklers ... 246
Mother's Pound Cake Cookies ... 241
Mrs. Field's Faux Chocolate Chip Cookies ... 238
Pecan Poofs ... 234
Praline Cookies ... 246
Rumtoertchen ... 238
Sesame Crisps ... 239
Sinful Turtle Squares ... 239
Spice Cakes ... 240
Stretch Brownies ... 240
Sugar Squares ... 246
Swedish Butter Cookies ... 238
Swedish Toscas Cookies ... 241
Corn and Cornmeal:
Adeline and Jane's Never Fail Corn Pudding ... 157
Cornbread Salad ... 71
Corn on the Cob with Mint Butter ... 156
Curry Cream of Corn Soup ... 58
Fried Corn ... 157
Glenis Egg Cornbread ... 189
Hot Water Cornbread ... 190
Kentucky Corn Fritters ... 157
Mother Dunlop's Corn Pudding ... 157
Plainview Farm Spoon Bread ... 191
Cornish Game Hens:
Duckling or Cornish Hens Far East Style ... 100
Grape-Stuffed Cornish Game Hens with Orange Butter ... 106
Cottage Cheese:
Blue Boar Lettuce with Cottage Cheese Dressing ... 78
Boyle County Stuffed Tomatoes ... 70
Country Chicken Pie ... 108
Country Crust Bread ... 197
Country Ham, Chicken and Mushroom Timbale ... 119
Country Ham, Cooked Mike Best's Way ... 118, 132
Country Terrine ... 125
Crab:
Adlai Stevenson's Dish ... 139
Crabmeat Blanche ... 143
Elizabethtown, Kentucky Trout ... 134
Hot Crab Casserole ... 37
Maryland Crab Cakes ... 143
Seafood Mold ... 38
Crackers:
Boursin Cheese Wafers ... 23
Cheese Puffs ... 33
Homemade Crackers ... 194
Naples Nibbles ... 40
Cranberries:
Cranberry Punch ... 44
Kentucky Derby Cranberry Punch ... 46
Cream:
Crème Fraiche No. 1 ... 178
Crème Fraiche No. 2 ... 178
Cream of Cucumber Soup ... 55
Cream of Leek Soup ... 56
Creamed Potatoes ... 160
Creamed Shrimp with Artichoke Bottoms ... 140
Creamy Dill Sauce ... 32
Crème Anglaise ... 230
Creme Caramel ... 205
Cream Cheese:
Boursin Cheese Wafers ... 23
Chicken Breasts with Dressing ... 93
Cream Cheese Frosting ... 204
Cream Cheese Pastry ... 211
Holly's Mexican Appetizers ... 27
Mock Boursin Cheese ... 23
Oyster Roll ... 37
Roulades de Jambon ... 120
Roxanne's Boursin Chicken ... 92
Creole Squash ... 164
Crèpes:
Caviar Beggar's Purses ... 35
Ham and Mushroom Crepes ... 120
Crested Butte Teriyaki ... 170
Cricket ... 45
Crumb Chicken Casserole ... 108
Crusty Havarti ... 26
Cucumbers:
Cold Spinach-Cucumber Soup ... 61
Cream of Cucumber Soup ... 55
Cucumbers with Snow Peas ... 156
Dilled Cucumbers ... 71
Curried Cauliflower-Asparagus Soup ... 60
Curried Chicken Paté ... 30
Curried Chicken and Rice Salad ... 65
Curry Cream of Corn Soup ... 58
Custards:
Crème Anglaise ... 226
Creme Caramel ... 205
Derby Sabayon ... 178
Lil's Irish Trifle ... 226
Daily Double Shrimp and Scallops ... 138
Daiquiri ... 46
Dates:
Bourbon Dates ... 227
Gem Date Bran Muffins ... 182
Orange Date Cake ... 208
Dead Heat Kentucky Burgoo ... 112
Dee Cunningham's Kuchen ... 194
Derby Fizz ... 46
Derby Sabayon ... 178
Derby Salad ... 79
Desserts: see Index; cakes, candy, pie, etc.
Diamond Beef Filet in Aspic ... 115
Diana Hansen's Chocolate Pralines ... 245
Dijon Dressing ... 79
Dill:
Creamy Dill Sauce ... 32
Dill Sauce ... 137
Dilled Cucumber Slices ... 71
Dilled Green Beans with Walnuts ... 164
Meatballs in Creamy Dill Sauce ... 32
Tomato and Dill Salad ... 76
Dips:
Artichoke Dip ... 22
Cheese Sandwiches ... 84
Chili Con Queso ... 24
Ed's Salsa ... 24
Hot Mushroom Dip ... 33
Tarragon Dip ... 29
Winningham Farm's Baked Clam Dip ... 36
Dishwasher Salmon ... 134
Dixie Whiskey ... 46
Doves In Tomato Sauce ... 105
Dressings: see Salad Dressings
Duck:
Anitra Mandarine ... 105
Duckling or Cornish Hens Far East Style ... 100
Duck Soup ... 59
Wild Duck Gumbo ... 61
Ed's Salsa ... 24
Eggs: see also Quiche; Souffle's
Breakfast Ramekins ... 86
Brunch Eggs, Taco Style ... 88
Egg and Bacon Soufflé ... 87
Egg and Watercress Sandwiches ... 87
Five Color Fritatta for Microwave ... 84
Governor's Egg Casserole ... 87
House Guest Eggs ... 86
Jennie Benedict's Eggs Baked in Tomatoes ... 88
Make-Ahead Quiche ... 89
Eggplant:
Eggplant Pie ... 158
Moussaka ... 121
Ratatouille Supreme ... 168
Elegant Chicken ... 96
Elizabethtown, Kentucky Trout ... 134
Elkridge Tomatoes ... 165
Eye of Round Party Platter ... 116
Fabulous Spice Cake ... 214
Fast Track Soup ... 60
Feathered Rice ... 162
Fettuccine Casserole ... 89
Fettuccine Fredo al Pronto ... 72
Figs, Pork Medallions in Fig Coulis ... 126
Fillings, Dessert
Lutèce Chocolate Cake ... 206
Orange Date Cake ... 208
Fish: see also individual varieties
Ambrosia From the Sea for Microwave ... 146
Bill's Sunday Supper ... 147
Bonnie and Lucy's Salmon Scallops with Lemon Ginger Sauce ... 136
Cajun Blackened Redfish ... 135
Creamed Shrimp with Artichoke Bottoms ... 140
Dishwasher Salmon ... 134
Elizabethtown, Kentucky Trout ... 134
Fish Creole ... 143
Flounder Dijon ... 135
Grilled Salmon Stuffed with Rice ... 137
Maryland Crab Cakes ... 143
New Orleans Seafood Gumbo ... 145
Paupiettes en Papillotes ... 136
Poached Fish with Vegetables for Microwave ... 147
Salmon Mousse with Green Peppercorn Sauce ... 148
Scallop Kabobs ... 146
Shad Roe ... 141
Sole Dugleré ... 148
Sole Stuffed with Shrimp and Ginger ... 138
Steamed Fish ... 135
Five Color Fritatta for Microwave ... 84
Flank Steak Marinade ... 171
Flounder:
Flounder Dijon ... 135
Paupiettes en Papillotes ... 136
Fondant:
Bourbon Balls ... 243
Coconut Candy ... 243
Fondant ... 243
Tea Mints ... 243

French Bread, Processor 195
French Green Bean Salad 72
French Lace Cookie Baskets 235
French Pheasant 107
Fresh Blueberry Tart 213
Fresh Coconut-Carrot Cake 203
Fresh Strawberries in Port 229
Fresh Tomato Sauce 172
Fried Corn 157
Fried Green Tomatoes 165
Fried Oysters Country Style 144
Frostings:
Cadiz Fudge Frosting 202
Caramel Icing 210
Cream Cheese Frosting 204
Lutèce Frosting 206
Frozen Lemon Soufflé 222
Frozen Tomato Salad 72
Fruit: See also specific varieties
Ginger Honey Fruit Salad 67
Hot Fruit Compote 158
Idie's Schaum Torte 229
Fudge-Topped Granola Bars 241
Fusilli with Chévre Sauce 89
Gainesborough Tart 216
Galatoire's Remoulade Sauce 172
Game:
Anitra Mandarine 105
Doves in Tomato Sauce 105
French Pheasant 107
Quail, Kentucky Style 106
Sauce for Game or Pork 175
Ganache 235
Gem Date Bran Muffins 182
German Chocolate Cake with Orange Marmalade 203
German Chocolate "Pig-Out" 232
Germantown Beef 117
Ginger:
Ginger Honey Fruit Salad 67
Ginger Snaps 232
Gingered Red Carrots 153
Peach Chutney 180
Poulet en Papillote with Fresh Ginger and Butter 98
Sole Stuffed with Shrimp and Ginger 138
Whole Wheat Ginger Orange Muffins 185
Glaze, Mike Best's Favorite Ham Glaze 118
Glazed Chicken Wings 31
Glenis' Egg Cornbread 189
Goat Cheese:
Chèvre and Leek Flan 88
Chèvre Sauce 89
Fusilli with Chèvre Sauce 89
Kentucky Goat Cheese Salad 80
Golden Cadillac 46
Governor's Egg Casserole 87
Grace Smith's Honey Wheat Bread 196
Grandstand Chicken Casserole 96
Granola 189
Grapes:
Chicken and Green Grapes 94
Grape Stuffed Cornish Game Hens with Orange Butter 106
Grecian Shrimp 140
Green Beans with Oranges 156
Green Beans with Persillade 152
Green Chilies Hors d'Oeurve 26
Green Peppercorn Sauce 172
Green Tomato Casserole 166
Green Vegetable Medley 166
Grilled Salmon Stuffed with Rice 137
Grits Casserole 86
Guadeloupe Vinaigrette 81
Ham:
Bourbon Glazed Ham Balls 25
Country Ham, Chicken and Mushroom Timbale 119
Country Ham Cooked Mike Best's Way 118, 132
Elizabethtown, Kentucky Trout 134
Ham and Green Peppercorn Paté 30
Ham and Mushroom Crepes 120
Ham Balls with Sweet Sour Pineapple Sauce 31
Roulades de Jambon 120
Hasenour's Raspberry Soufflé 220
Hawaiian Chicken 97
Hazelnuts, Veal with Hazelnut Butter Sauce 129
Helen's Delicate Sweet Treats 246
Henry Bain Sauce I 173
Henry Bain Sauce II 173
Herbed Vinaigrette Dressing 80
Herbs:
Herbal Cheesecake 27
Herbed French Bread 190
Horseshoe Derby Bread 200
Spiral Herb Bread 200
Hill's Chocolate-Coconut Squares 233
Historic Recipes:
Beaten Biscuits 186
Benedictine 84
Country Ham Cooked Mike Best's Way 118, 132
Dead Heat Kentucky Burgoo 112
Henry Bain Sauce I 173
Henry Bain Sauce II 173
Idie's Schaum Torte 229
Jennie Benedict's Eggs Baked in Tomatoes 88
Kentucky Derby Museum Pie 216
Liberty Hall Pudding Sauce 179
Mildred's Chess Pie 215
Modjeskas 244
Normandy Inn Salad 81
13th Century Nun's Cake 207
Wilted Lettuce Salad 77
Holly's Mexican Appetizers 27
Homemade Crackers 194
Homemade Rolls 195
Honey Nut Glaze 197
Hors d'Oevres: see Appetizers
Horseshoe Derby Bread 200
Hot Bourbon Sauce 178
Hot Butterscotch Sauce 225
Hot Chicken Salad 97
Hot Crab Casserole 37
Hot Fruit Compote 158
Hot German Potato Salad 80
Hot Mushroom Dip 33
Hot Orange Soufflé 222
Hot Sausage Bread 190
Hot Water Cornbread 190
Houseguest Eggs 86
Hubbard Squash 159
Hummingbird Cake 204
Ice Cream:
Amaretto Ice Cream 210
Bisque Ice Cream 210
Ice Cream Soufflé 220
Peach Ice Cream 210
Six Threes Ice Cream 211
Vanilla Ice Cream 211
Iced Honey Raisin Bread 197
Idie and Herman's Marinade for Grilled Chicken 173
Idie's Schaum Torte 229
Indian Feast Popcorn 41
Individual Cheese Cakes 236
Inverness Sauce 174
Irvin Cobb's Mint Julep 47
Jam Caramel Pie 216
Jellied Beet Soup 55
Jennie Benedict's Eggs Baked in Tomatoes 88
Jezebel Sauce 174
Julia's Spinach Casserole 164
Junie's Marinated Shrimp 38
Kelaguen Mannok (Chicken Kelaguen) 98
Kentucky Bourbon Balls 243
Kentucky Bourbon Cake 204
Kentucky Corn Fritters 157
Kentucky Creams 242
Kentucky Derby Cranberry Punch 46
Kentucky Goat Cheese Salad 80
Kentucky Spring Salad 82
Kentucky Style Quail 106
Kitty's Oatmeal Bread 198
Lace Cookies with Chocolate 236
Lamb:
Dead Heat Kentucky Burgoo 112
Lamb Marinated with Rosemary 118
Marinated Lamb Chops 122
Moussaka 121
Roast Lamb Vino 122
Spring Veal or Lamb Ragout 123
LaPeche Shrimp 142
Laurie's Buttermilk Bread 192
Leeks, Cream of Leek Soup 56
Lemon:
Butter Crunch Lemon Chiffon Pie 217
Frozen Lemon Soufflé 222
Lemon Chess Pie 215
Lemon or Chocolate Pie 219
Lemon Crispies 237
Lemon Roasted Chicken 99
Lemon Sauce 179
Lemon Sherbet with Mint Sauce 211
Shade Seeker Lemonade 51
Liberty Hall Pudding Sauce 179
Lil's Irish Trifle 226
Lime:
Derby Salad Dressing 79
Sherry Bolo 49
Lobster, Maisonette Lobster Bisque 59
Louisiana Shrimp 142
Louisville Bourbon Pie 214
Lutèce Chocolate Cake 206
Lutèce Frosting 206
Macerated Oranges 205
Maisonette-Lobster Bisque 59
Make-Ahead Quiche 89
Maker's Mark Bourbon Bread 188
Mamie's Coconut Pie 212
Mancho Manteles 99
Maple:
Maple Butter 183
Maple Oatmeal Bread 198
Marinades:
Crested Butte Teriyaki 170
Idie and Herman's Marinade for Grilled Chicken 173
Inverness Sauce 174
Junie's Marinated Shrimp 38
Marinade for Flank Steak 171
Marinade for Rolled Rib Roast 115
Spiced Bourbon Sauce for Pork Tenderloin 128
Marinated Green Beans 159
Marinated Lamb Chops 122
Marinated Pork Roast 125
Marinated Rolled Rib Roast 115
Marinated Vegetable Salad 73
Mark's Spread 28
Marmalade, Peach 176
Maryland Crab Cakes 143
Meatballs in Creamy Dill Sauce 32
Melt Aways 237
Meringue:
Apricot Bars 232
Chad Mitchell's Bread Pudding 224
Fabulous Spice Cake 214
Idie's Schaum Torte 229
Mamie's Coconut Pie 212
Meringue Dessert Shells 229
Mint Julep Kisses 237
Minted Brownie Cookies 236
Microwave:
Ambrosia from the Sea for Microwave 146
Apple Graham Pie 225
Bourbon Glazed Ham Balls 25
Brunch Eggs, Taco Style 88
Butterscotch Sauce for Microwave 177
Carrots with Mustard and Dill 168
Chicken à la Roma 107
Diana Hansen's Chocolate Pralines 245
Dilled Cucumber Slices 71
Duckling or Cornish Hens Far East Style 100
Fish Creole 143
Five Color Fritatta for Microwave 84
Fudge-Topped Granola Bars 241
Hot German Potato Salad 80
Microwave Cruchy Toffee 244
Peanut Brittle 245
Pears, Poached in Microwave 217
Poached Fish with Vegetables for Microwave 147
Savory Cheese Bites 25
Vegetable Lasagna for Microwave 159
Mighty Mustard 174
Mike Best's Favorite Ham Glaze 118
Mildred's Chess Pie 215
Milk:
Spanish Chocolate 51
Wonderful Hot Chocolate 51
Mini Cinnamon Wheels 184
Mint:
Corn on the Cob with Mint Butter 156
Irvin Cobb's Mint Julep 47
Mint Grape Punch 50
Mint Juleps 47
Mr. Closson's Mint Juleps 47
Nancy's Mint Julep 48
Mint Juleps—See Beverages
Mint Julep Kisses 237
Minted Brownie Cookies 236

Mock Boursin Cheese....23
Mock Champagne Punch....48
Modjeskas....244
Molasses Crinklers....246
Molded Gazpacho....74
Mother Dunlop's Corn Pudding....157
Mother's Apple Cheese Crisp....213
Mother's Coffee Cake....199
Mother's Old Fashioned Custard....50
Mother's Pound Cake Cookies....241
Mother's Rolls....199
Mother's Stuffed Pork Chops....124
Mountain Top Bread....196
Moussaka....121
Mousse:
Caviar Mousse....35
Mushroom Mousse....34
Timbales of Carrot Mousse....154
Mr. Closson's Mint Julep....47
Mrs. Field's Faux Chocolate Chip Cookies....238
Mrs. Pollard's Sour Cream Cake....207
Mrs. Potter's Borscht....55
Mrs. Rodes' Green Tomato Catsup....171
Muffins, see Bread, Muffins
Museum Winner's Pie....216
Mushrooms:
Country Ham, Chicken and Mushroom Timbale....119
Ham and Mushroom Crèpes....120
Hot Mushroom Dip....33
Museum Mushrooms....33
Mushroom Mousse....34
Mushroom Soup....61
Mushroom-Spinach Salad with Parmesan Dressing....81
Mushrooms....33
Mushrooms Normandy....34
Sherried Cream of Mushroom Soup....61
Veal Filets in Mushroom and Cream Sauce....129
Winner's Circle Mushrooms....158
Mustard:
Dijon Dressing....79
Guadeloupe Vinaigrette....81
Mighty Mustard....174
Mustard Pickle....180
Nancy's Mint Julep....48
Naples Nibbles....40
New Orleans Seafood Gumbo....145
Normandy Inn Salad....81
Nuts, see specific varieites
Oatmeal:
Blueberry Muffins....182
Granola....189
Kitty's Oatmeal Bread....198
Lemon Crispies....237
Maple Oatmeal Bread....198
Mrs. Field's Faux Chocolate Chip Cookies....238
Onion Rounds....41
Ophelia's Derbytime One-Step Tomato Sandwiches....41
Oranges:
Anitra Mandarine....105
German Chocolate Cake with Orange Marmalade....203
Grape-Stuffed Cornish Game Hens with Orange Butter....106
Green Beans with Oranges....156
Hot Orange Soufflé....222
Macerated Oranges....205
Orange Date Cake....208
Pickled Oranges....176
Watercress-Orange Salad....82
Whole Wheat Ginger Orange Muffins....185
Orangerines....242
Oysters:
Fried Oysters Country Style....144
New Orleans Seafood Gumbo....145
Oyster Rockefeller Spread....37
Oyster Roll....37
Pancakes and Waffles:
Cheese Waffles....189
Potato Pancakes....161
Potato Zucchini Pancakes....161
Park Cottage Tomato Soup....56
Party Bundt Bread....197
Party Chicken Livers....31
Pasta:
Cold Pasta Salad with Red Peppers, Chicken and Artichokes Hearts....64
Fettuccine Casserole....89
Fettuccine Freddo Al Pronto....72
Fusilli with Chèvre Sauce....89
Pasta Primavera with Seafood in Basil Cream....144
Pasta Seafood Salad....66
Ravioli Dominic....148
Summer Orzo Salad....75
Veal Pesto with Orzo....131
Vegetable Lasagna for Microwave....159
Pastry, see also Piecrusts
Butter Crunch Lemon Chiffon Pie....217
Cheese Pastry for Zucchini Torta....167
Cream Cheese Pastry....211
Fresh Blueberry Tart....213
Rich Shortcut Pastry (Processor Method)....212
Rich Shortcut Pastry (Conventional Method)....212
Patés and Terrines:
Country Terrine....125
Ham and Green Peppercorn Paté....30
Track Time Terrine....101
Triple Crown Paté....130
Tuna Paté....40
Paupiettes en Papillotes....136
Pavé à Lite....224
Peaches:
Bluegrass Peaches....227
Louisville Bourbon Pie....214
Peach Chutney....180
Peach Ice Cream....210
Peach Marmalade....176
Peach Praline Pie....216
Peanut Brittle....245
Peanut Butter:
Chocolate Buckeyes....247
Peanut Butter Cups....242
Peanut Butter Pie....218
Pears:
Bill's Thick Caramel-Pear Sauce....176
Pears à La Bomhard....228
Pears Poached in Microwave....217
Peas:
Green Vegetable Medley....166
Peas Creole....161
Peas Italian....164
Pretty Party Peas....160
Stuffed Squash....165
Pecans:
Carrots and Celery with Pecans....153
Chocolate Pecan Crinkles....235
Kentucky Derby Museum Pie....216
Pecan Muffins....184
Pecan Poofs....234
Sinful Turtle Squares....239
Turtles....247
Pendennis Champagne Punch....48
Peppers: see also Chili Peppers
Pretend Pimientos....160
Red Pepper Sauce....174
Peppered Beef....116
Pesto, Veal with Orzo....131
Pheasant, French Pheasant....107
Phyllo, Pork in Phyllo Dough....127
Pickles, Pickled
Mustard Pickle....180
Pickled Oranges....176
Pie Crust: see also Pastry
Chocolate Sabayon Pie....219
Meringue Dessert Shells....229
Peanut Butter Pie....218
Pie crust with Lard, Southern Style....212
Pies and Tarts: see also Pie crusts; Pastry
Almond Cream Pie....213
Apple Graham Pie....225
Butter Crunch Lemon Chifffon Pie....217
Chocolate Fudge Pie....215
Chocolate Sabayon Pie....219
Fresh Blueberry Tart....213
Gainsborough Tart....216
Idie's Schaum Torte....229
Jam Caramel Pie....216
Lemon Chess Pie....215
Lemon or Chocolate Pie....219
Louisville Bourbon Pie....214
Mamie's Coconut Pie....212
Mildred's Chess Pie....215
Mother's Apple Cheese Crisp....213
Museum Winner's Pie....216
Peach Praline Pie....216
Peanut Butter Pie....218
Strawberry Chess Pie....215
Sugar Cream Pie....218
Pimiento Cheese....85
Pineapple:
Chicken with Cashews and Pineapple....93
Chutney Cheese Canape....26
Ham Balls with Sweet-Sour Pineapple Sauce....31
Hummingbird Cake....204
Pineapple-Apricot Nut Loaves....191
Pineapple Cheese Ball Spread....28
Pistachio Butter....183
Pistachio Crescents Chef Ferré....248
Plainview Farm Spoon Bread....191
Poached Fish with Vegetables for Microwave....147
Poached Pears with Crème Anglaise....230
Polar Bear....49
Pork:
Barbecued Spareribs....124
Bourbon Pork Roast....124
Celide's Meatballs & Sauce....114
Country Terrine....125
Mancho Manteles....99
Marinated Pork Roast....125
Mother's Stuffed Pork Chops....124
Pork Chops in Sauce....126
Pork in Phyllo Dough....127
Pork Medallions in Fig Coulis....126
Pork Tenderloin in Spiced Bourbon Sauce....128
Sauce for Game or Pork....175
Triple Crown Paté....130
Post Time Cheese Mold....28
Pot of Gold Soup....57
Potatoes:
Bill's Chestnuts and Potatoes....156
Cream of Leek Soup....66
Creamed Potatoes....160
Hot German Potato Salad....80
Potato Pancakes....161
Potato-Zucchini Pancakes....161
Swiss Potatoes....162
Poulet en Papillote with Fresh Ginger, Lemon and Butter....98
Poultry: see Index Capon, Chicken, Cornish Game Hens, etc.
Pound Cake....206
Praline Cookies....246
Preserves: see Chutneys; Condiments; Marmalades
Pretend Pimientos....160
Pretty Party Peas....160
Processor Bourbon Raisin Banana Bread....192
Puddings:
Chad Mitchell's Bread Pudding....224
Pavé à Lite....224
Puff Pastry:
Baked Stuffed Brie....24
Crusty Havarti....26
Pumpkin:
Pumpkin Cheese Cake....209
Pumpkin Salad....73
The Clark Handicap....58
Punch: see Beverages and Punches
Quail, Kentucky Style....106
Quiche:
Chèvre and Leek Flan....88
Make-Ahead Quiche....89
Quick Brioche....191
"Quick" Beaten Biscuits....186
Raisins:
Grace Smith's Honey Wheat Bread....196
Processor Bourbon Raisin Banana Bread....192
Raisin Bread....199
Raspberries:
Almond Bavarian Cream with Raspberry Coulis and Caramel Sauce....223
Berry Sauce....220
Chilled Chocolate Raspberry Soufflé....221
Hasenour's Raspberry Soufflé....220
Raspberry Coulis....221, 223
Ratatouille Supreme....168
Ravioli Dominic....148
Rebel Party Sour....50
Red Fish Cajun Blackened Redfish....135
Red Peppers:
Cold Pasta Salad with Red Peppers, Chicken and Artichoke Hearts....64
Pretend Pimientos....160
Red Pepper Sauce....174
Red Snapper, New Orleans Seafood Gumbo....145
Refreshing Asparagus Salad....74
Ribeye Roast....114
Rice:
Baked Rice....162
California Rice....163
Casserole of Shrimp in a Cream Sauce....141

Chicken Salad and Wild Rice ... 65
Club Salad ... 70
Confetti Rice Salad ... 71
Curried Chicken and Rice Salad ... 65
Elegant Chicken ... 96
Feathered Rice ... 162
Grilled Salmon Stuffed with Rice ... 137
Snow on the Mountain ... 102
Tasty Wild Rice ... 162
Uptown Rice ... 163
Wild Rice Salad ... 77
Rich Shortcrust Pastry (conventional) ... 212
Rich Shortcrust Pastry (processor method) ... 212
Richard's Delicious Biscuits ... 187
Ringer ... 49
Roast Lamb Vino ... 122
Rolls: see Breads, Rolls and Buns
Roquefort Walnut Spread ... 29
Roulades de Jambon ... 120
Roxanne's Boursin Chicken ... 92
Rum: see also Beverage and Punches
Banana Daiquiris ... 44
Bimini Planter's Punch ... 45
Daiquiri ... 46
Rum Sauce ... 179
Rumtoertchen ... 238
Run For the Roses Soup ... 54
Salad Dressings:
Blue Cheese Dressing ... 82
Confetti Rice Dressing ... 71
Cottage Cheese Dressing ... 78
Derby Salad Dressing ... 79
Dijon Dressing ... 79
Guadeloupe Vinaigrette ... 81
Herbed Vinaigrette Dressing ... 80
Hot Slaw Dressing ... 69
Island Salad Dressing ... 68
Kentucky Boiled Dressing ... 82
Molded Salad Dressing ... 74
Parmesan Dressing ... 81
Smearcase ... 72
Summer Orzo Salad Dressing ... 75
Walnut-Cheese Salad Vinaigrette ... 79
Wild Rice Salad Dressing ... 77
Salads: see also Gelatin Salads
Salads: Fruit
Chicken and Fruit Salad ... 64
Ginger Honey Fruit Salad ... 67
Island Salad ... 68
Sour Cream Cranberry Salad ... 66
Springtime Fruit Salad ... 68
Strawberry Salad ... 69
Watercress-Orange Salad ... 82
Salads: Gelatin
Molded Gazpacho ... 74
Refreshing Asparagus Salad ... 74
Sour Cream Cranberry Salad ... 66
Salads: Main Dish
Chicken and Fruit Salad ... 64
Chicken Salad with Wild Rice ... 65
Cold Pasta Salad with Red Peppers, Chicken and Artichoke Hearts ... 64
Curried Chicken and Rice Salad ... 65
Fettuccine Freddo Al Pronto ... 72
Pasta Seafood Salad ... 66
Sprinter Turkey Salad ... 65
Warm Scallop and Avocado Salad ... 66
Salads: Pasta and Rice
Chicken Salad with Wild Rice ... 65
Club Salad ... 70
Confetti Rice Salad ... 71
Curried Chicken and Rice Salad ... 65
Fettuccine Freddo Al Pronto ... 72
Pasta Primavera with Seafood with Basil Cream ... 144
Pasta Seafood Salad ... 66
Summer Orzo Salad ... 75
Tortellini Vegetable Salad ... 76
Wild Rice Salad ... 77
Salads: Tossed Greens or Lettuce
Derby Salad ... 79
Kentucky Goat Cheese Salad ... 80
Kentucky Spring Salad ... 82
Mushroom-Spinach Salad with Parmesan Dressing ... 81
Normandy Inn Salad ... 81
Peas Italian ... 164
Walnut-Cheese Salad ... 79
Wilted Lettuce Salad ... 77
Salads: Vegetable
Bauer's Hot Slaw ... 69
Boyle County Stuffed Tomatoes ... 70
Broccoli Salad ... 68
Butter Bean Salad ... 69
Chinese Slaw ... 70
Cornbread Salad ... 71
Dilled Cucumbers ... 71
French Green Bean Salad ... 72
Frozen Tomato Salad ... 72
Hot German Potato Salad ... 80
Marinated Vegetable Salad ... 73
Molded Gazpacho Salad ... 74
Pumpkin Salad ... 73
Refreshing Asparagus Salad ... 74
Summer Orzo Salad ... 75
Tabouli-Cold Vegetable Salad ... 75
Tomato and Dill Salad ... 76
Tortellini Vegetable Salad ... 76
Zucchini à la Grecque ... 167
Salmon:
Bonnie and Lucy's Salmon Scallops ... 136
Dishwasher Salmon ... 134
Grilled Salmon Stuffed with Rice ... 137
Smokey Salmon Spread ... 38
Sandwiches:
Baby Hot Browns Café Musée ... 30
Benedictine ... 84
Cheese Sandwiches ... 84
Egg and Watercress Sandwiches ... 87
Eye of Round Party Platter ... 116
Germantown Beef ... 117
Onion Rounds ... 41
Ophelia's Derbytime One-step Tomato Sandwiches ... 41
Peppered Beef ... 116
Pimiento Cheese Spread ... 85
Pork Tenderloin in Spiced Bourbon Sauce ... 128
Spiced Round of Beef ... 132
Tuna Paté ... 40
Sauces: Dessert
Amaretto Sauce ... 176
Berry Sauce ... 220
Bill's Thick Pear and Caramel Sauce ... 176
Bourbon Apple Sauce ... 134
Boubon Sauce ... 177
Bourbon Waffle Syrup ... 177
Butterscotch Sauce ... 177
Caramel Sauce ... 177
Chilled Chocolate Raspberry Soufflé ... 221
Chocolate Sauce ... 230
Crème Anglaise ... 230
Derby Sabayon ... 178
Hot Bourbon Sauce ... 178
Hot Butterscotch Sauce ... 225
Lemon Sauce ... 179
Liberty Hall Pudding Sauce ... 179
Raspberry Coulis ... 221, 223
Rum Sauce ... 179
Vanilla Sauce ... 220
Sauces: Main Course
Barbecue Sauce ... 170
Barbecue Shrimp Sauce ... 139
Basil Cream Sauce ... 144
Beef Brisket Barbecue Sauce ... 110
Broccoli Sauce ... 170
Cheese Timbales with Spinach Sauce ... 85
Chèvre Sauce ... 89
Creamy Dill Sauce ... 32
Dill Sauce ... 137
Fig Coulis ... 126
Fresh Tomato Sauce ... 172
Galatoire's Remoulade Sauce ... 172
Green Peppercorn Sauce ... 172
Henry Bain Sauce I ... 173
Henry Bain Sauce II ... 173
Inverness Sauce ... 174
Jezebel Sauce ... 174
Lemon Sauce ... 179
Mighty Mustard ... 174
Pesto ... 131
Red Pepper Sauce ... 174
Rum Sauce ... 179
Sauce for Celide's Meatballs ... 114
Sauce for Game or Pork ... 175
Spinach Sauce ... 85
Sweet-Sour Pineapple Sauce ... 31
Tarragon Cream ... 103
Toasted Almond Sauce ... 95
Tomato Cream Sauce ... 175
Sausage:
Celide's Meatballs and Sauce ... 114
Hot Sausage Bread ... 190
Make-Ahead Quiche ... 89
Sausage Balls ... 32
Savory Cheese Bites ... 25
Scallops:
Daily Double Shrimp and Scallops ... 138
Galatoire's Remoulade Sauce ... 172
Pasta Primavera with Seafood in Basil Cream ... 144
Warm Scallop and Avocado Salad ... 66
Scallop Kebabs ... 146
Seafood: see index; Crab, Shrimp, etc.
Seasoned Salt ... 179
Seldom Seen Brisket, Hot or Cold ... 117
Sesame Crisps ... 239
Shad Roe ... 141
Shade Seeker Lemonade ... 51
Shantung Torte ... 29
Sherbet, Lemon with Mint Sauce ... 221
Sherried Cream of Mushroom Soup ... 61
Shrimp:
Adlai Stevenson's Dish ... 139
Barbecue Shrimp ... 139
Bill's Sunday Supper ... 147
Casserole of Shrimp in a Cream Sauce ... 141
Cheesey Shrimp Mold ... 39
Creamed Shrimp with Artichoke Bottoms ... 140
Daily Double Shrimp and Scallops ... 138
Galatoire's Remoulade Sauce ... 172
Grecian Shrimp ... 140
Junie's Marinated Shrimp ... 38
LaPeche Shrimp ... 142
Louisiana Shrimp ... 142
New Orleans Seafood Gumbo ... 145
Pasta Primavera with Seafood in Basil Cream ... 144
Pasta Seafood Salad ... 66
Seafood Mold ... 38
Shrimp Cocktail Ball ... 39
Shrimper's Party Spread ... 39
Shrimp Toast ... 39
Shrimp Toast-to-Show ... 39
Sole Stuffed with Shrimp and Ginger ... 138
Side Dishes:
Baked Cherries ... 154
Hot Fruit Compote ... 158
Sinful Turtle Squares ... 239
Six Threes Ice Cream ... 211
Smearcase ... 72
Smokey Salmon Spread ... 38
Snow Peas:
Cucumber with Snow Peas ... 156
Pretty Party Peas ... 160
Stir-fry Chicken with Snow Peas ... 94
Snowball ... 228
Snow on the Mountain ... 102
Sole:
Sole Stuffed with Shrimp and Ginger ... 138
Some Stardust Wine Cooler ... 149
Soufflés:
Amaretto Soufflé ... 218
Chilled Chocolate Raspberry Soufflé ... 221
Egg and Bacon Soufflé ... 87
Frozen Lemon Soufflé ... 222
Hasenour's Raspberry Soufflé ... 220
Hot Orange Soufflé ... 222
Ice Cream Soufflé ... 220
Soups: Chilled
Asparagus Soup with Tarragon ... 54
Cold Spinach-Cucumber Soup ... 61
Cream of Cucumber Soup ... 55
Cream of Leek Soup ... 56
Curry Cream of Corn Soup ... 58
Jellied Beet Soup ... 55
Mrs.Potter's Borscht ... 55
Pot of Gold Soup ... 57
Run for the Roses ... 54
Spinach Soup ... 57
The Clark Handicap ... 58
Soups: Hot
Asparagus Soup with Tarragon ... 54
Bill's Sunday Supper ... 147
Cheese Soup ... 57
Curried Cauliflower Asparagus Soup ... 60
Curry Cream of Corn Soup ... 58
Cream of Cucumber Soup ... 55
Cream of Leek Soup ... 56
Dead Heat Kentucky Burgoo ... 112
Duck Soup ... 59
Fast Track ... 60
Maisonette Lobster Bisque ... 59

Mushroom Soup...61
New Orleans Seafood Gumbo.........................145
Park Cottage Tomato Soup...............................56
Pot of Gold Soup...57
Sherried Cream of Mushroom Soup.................61
Spinach Soup..57
The Clark Handicap Soup.................................58
Wild Duck Gumbo..61
Sour Créam Cranberry Salad............................66
Spanish Chocolate...51
Spice Cakes..240
Spiced Round of Beef....................................132
Spinach:
Cheese Timbales with Spinach Sauce..............85
Cold Spinach-Cucumber Soup..........................61
Julia's Spinach Casserole..............................164
Mushroom Spinach Salad with Parmesan
Dressing...81
Special Spinach Casserole.............................163
Spinach Sauce..85
Spinach Soup..57
Track Time Terrine...101
Spiced Bourbon Sauce for Pork.....................128
Spiced Round of Beef....................................132
Spiral Herb Bread..200
Spreads:
Beer Cheese...23
Benedictine..84
Caviar Mousse..35
Cheese Sandwiches..84
Cheesey Shrimp Mold......................................39
Chutney Cheese Canapé..................................26
Curried Chicken Paté.......................................30
Green Chilies Hors d'Oeuvres..........................26
Julia's Spinach Casserole..............................164
Mark's Spread..28
Mock Boursin Cheese......................................23
Mushroom Mousse...34
Oyster Rockefeller Spread................................37
Oyster Roll...37
Pimiento Cheese Spread..................................85
Pineapple Cheese Ball Spread.........................28
Post Time Cheese Mold...................................28
Roquefort Walnut Spread..................................29
Seafood Mold..38
Shantung Torte..29
Shrimp Cocktail Ball..30
Shrimper's Party Spread...................................39
Smokey Salmon Spread....................................38
Tuna Paté..40
Watercress Spread..29
Winningham Farm's Baked Clam Dip.................36
Sprinter Turkey Salad.......................................65
Springtime Fruit Salad......................................68
Spring Veal or Lamb Ragout............................123
Squash: see also Zucchini
Creole Squash...164
Hubbard Squash..159
Pot of Gold Soup...57
Squash Bread..193
Stuffed Squash..165
Steak Tartare..32
Steamed Fish..135
Stews: see specific main ingredients
Stir-fry Chicken with Snow Peas........................94
Strawberries:
Berry Sauce..220
Derby Sabayon..178
Fresh Strawberries in Port..............................229
Pavé à Lite...224

Strawberry Butter..185
Strawberry Chess Pie.....................................215
Strawberry Muffins...185
Strawberry Salad...69
Stretch Brownies...240
Stuffing:
Ballotine de Boeuf..111
Carciofi Imbottiti Alla Siciliana (Sicilian
Stuffed Artichoke).......................................151
Grilled Salmon Stuffed with Rice.....................137
Stuffed Chicken Breasts..................................103
Stuffing for Cornish Game Hens......................106
Stuffed Carrots..153
Stuffed Chicken Breasts..................................103
Stuffed Squash..165
Sugar Cream Pie..218
Sugar Squares..240
Summer Orzo Salad...75
Swedish Butter Cookies..................................238
Swedish Toscas...241
Sweetbreads, Broiled......................................130
Swiss Potatoes..162
Tabouli (cold vegetable salad)...........................76
Tarragon:
Asparagus Soup with Tarragon..........................54
Tarragon Cream...103
Tarragon Dip...29
Tasty Wild Rice..162
Tea, The Cookbook Committee's Favorite Coun-
tertop Tea...51
Terrine: see Pate's and Terrines
Timbales of Carrot Mousse.............................154
The Clark Handicap Soup.................................58
13th Century Nun's Cake.................................207
Toasted Almond Sauce.....................................95
Tomatoes:
Boyle County Stuffed Tomatoes.........................77
Creole Squash...173
Ed's Salsa..24
Elkridge Tomatoes...165
Fresh Tomato Sauce.......................................172
Fried Green Tomatoes.....................................165
Frozen Tomato Salad.......................................72
Grecian Shrimp...140
Green Tomato Casserole.................................166
Jennie Benedict's Eggs Baked in
Tomatoes..88
Molded Gazpacho..74
Mrs. Rodes' Green Tomato Catsup...................171
Ophelia's Derbytime One-Step Tomato
Sandwiches...41
Park Cottage Tomato Soup...............................56
Ratatouille Supreme.......................................168
Run for the Roses..54
Sauce for Celide's Meatballs...........................114
Tomato Casserole..165
Tomato Cream Sauce......................................175
Tomato and Dill Salad......................................76
Zucchini Casserole..166
Torta, Zucchini..167
Tortellini Vegetable Salad.................................76
Track Time Terrine...101
Trifle, Lil's Irish Trifle....................................226
Triple Crown Paté..130
Trout, Elizabethtown Kentucky Trout...............134
Truffles..248
Tuna, Tuna Paté..40
Turkey:
Baby Hot Brown Café Musée.............................30

Sprinter Turkey Salad.......................................65
Turkey Hash..100
Turtles...247
Uptown Rice..163
Vanilla Ice Cream...211
Vanilla Sauce..220
Veal:
Country Terrine..125
Dead Heat Kentucky Burgoo............................112
Meatballs in Creamy Dill Sauce.........................32
Spring Veal or Lamb Ragout............................123
Sweetbreads, broiled......................................130
Triple Crown Paté..130
Veal Chops Stuffed with Bel Paese and Sun
Dried Tomatoes..128
Veal Filets in Mushroom and Cream Sauce.....129
Veal with Hazelnut Butter Sauce......................129
Veal Pesto with Orzo......................................131
Vegetables: see also specific varieties and
salads
Dead Heat Kentucky Burgoo............................112
Green Vegetable Medley..................................166
Marinated Vegetable Salad...............................73
Molded Gazpacho Salad...................................74
Pasta Primavera with Seafood in Basil
Cream...144
Ratatouille Supreme.......................................168
Tabouli (cold vegetable salad)...........................75
Tortellini Vegetable Salad.................................76
Vegetable Lasagna for Microwave....................159
Vinaigrette, Vinaigrette Dressing, Herbed........80
Walnut:
Apple Nut Cake..202
Dilled Green Beans with Walnuts.....................164
Roquefort Walnut Spread..................................29
Walnut Carrots..155
Walnut-Cheese Salad......................................79
Warm Scallop and Avocado Salad......................66
Watercress:
Egg and Watercress Sandwiches......................87
Watercress-Orange Salad.................................82
Watercress Spread..40
White Charlotte Russe and Hot Butterscotch
Sauce..225
Whole Wheat:
All Natural Wheat-Bran Muffins........................182
Carrot Cake Muffins.......................................183
Fresh Coconut Carrot Cake.............................203
Whole Wheat Biscuits.....................................187
Whole Wheat Ginger Orange Muffins................185
Wild Duck Gumbo..61
Wild Rice Salad...77
Wilted Lettuce Salad..77
Wine:
Sherry Bolo..49
Some Stardust Wine Cooler..............................49
White Wine Sangria..50
Winner's Circle Mushrooms.............................158
Winningham Farm's Baked Clam Dip.................36
Wonderful Hot Chocolate..................................51
Yams, Bourbon Yams....................................168
Yeast Breads, see Breads, Yeast
Zucchini:
Ratatouille Supreme.......................................168
Zucchini à la Grecque....................................167
Zucchini Casserole..166
Zucchini Torta...167

Contributors

The Kentucky Derby Museum Cookbook Committee would like to thank the many people who so graciously contributed their recipes for this cookbook. These recipes were tested for quality and edited for clarity. Similarity of content and limitation of space prevented us from including all of the recipes.

A — Abell, Julie
Altsheler, Mrs. Edward
Aniello's Ristorante Italino
Anderson, Anne
Anderson, Trude
Arnell, Julie
Arthur, Mrs. Stanley
Asbury, Connie
B — Badame, Marilyn
Bailey, Nancy
Barnett, Gil
Bart, Robert
Bauer's Restaurant
Beale, Sandy
Bell, Eugenia
Bender, Betty J.
Besten, Betty
Best, Mike
Biggs, Franklin
Blackmon, Ann
Blue Boar Cafeteria (Wesley Johnson)
Boden, Lila
Bond, Kathy
Borries, Bets
Bortner, Judy
Bowers, Chef
Bramley, Margaret
Bratcher, Teri Lynn
Brennwald, Marion
Briscoe, Jean
Brittain, Tippy
Broecker, Bradley
Brohos, Chef
Brooks, Peggy
Brown, Mrs. Owsley III
Bucayne, Linda
Bugai, Henry Chef Bowes Harbor Inn, Traverse City Michigan
Bucayne, Linda
Buice, Nell
Busath's Confectionary
C — Café Musée
Callahan, Ed
Callahan, Jill
Campbell, Anne
Campbell, Sally
Carpenter, Mrs. John R., Jr.
Casa Grisanti
Chapman, Gary
Childress, Shirley
Clark, Mary
Cleesattle, Bland
Colombo, Alice

Conway's Cake Decorating & Candy Supply
Corn, Elaine
Courier Journal and Louisville Times
Courteney, Mary Anderson
Cox, Mrs. Millard III
Crain, Mary
Cromer, Mary
Crawford, Mrs. H.D. Sr.
Crawford, Carroll Watson
Cuneo, Barbara
Cunningham, Dee
D — Dabney, Pat
DeBeer, Vanessa
Donohue, Gage
Dunlap, Mrs. George
Durham, Billie
Dymond, Celide
E — Eberhardt, Ms. Daniel L.
Edelen, Emily
Edwards, Kitty
Egerton, George Anne
Ellis, Ophelia
Ensenat, Taylor
Evans, Mrs. Wilson
F — Fawcett, Betty
Ferre, Chef
Fink, Estelle
Fischer, Roberta
Fitzgerald, Elinor
Frigon, Anne Marie
Flexner, Marion
Folsom, Connie
Fox, Marilyn
Friebert, Babs
Fulcher, Carol
Fulton, Kaye
G — Galatoire's
Gallrein, Glyna Meredith
Garrett, Mrs. Charles E., Jr.
General Electric Corp.
Giesel, Norma
Gillim, Mary Jo
Glass, Mrs. Frank M.
Glenn, Camille
Gray, Norma
Gregory, Carmelia
Griffin, Bunch
Griffin, Annaliese
H — Hackett, Mary
Hansen, Diana
Harcourt, Hill
Harcourt, Nancye

Hasenour's Restaurant
Hay, Tonia
Hayunga, Ainez
Hayunga, Jean
Hazelip, Mary
Heaven Hill Distilleries
Hendrix, Mrs. Pete
Hertels Parkway Confectionary
Heumann, Joanne
Heun, Martha
Hilliard, Mary
Hoagland, Adeline
Hollingsworth, Mark
Horine, Louise
Houghton, Valerie
Howard, Libby
Huber, Betty J.
Huber, Jeanne L.
Hughes, Sarah Ann
Hungerford, Emily, M.D.
J — Jackson, Barbara
Jelsma, Mrs. Franklin
Jenkins, Chef Richard
Johnson, Mrs. Harold S.
Johnston, Anise
Johnstone, Sara
Jones, Betty
Jones, Janet
Jones, Mrs. Warner
Joseph, Anne
Juckett, Martha
K — Kathy's Kitchens Inc.
Keene, Mrs. Catherine
Kernen, Mary Dunlap
Kessinger, Debbie
Knoefel, Franca
Kohler, Peachy
Kute, Mary
L — Laffoon, Henrietta
Lander, Thelma C.
La Peche
La Plante, Col. Jack
Larimore, Sharon
Larson, Karen
Lavin, Betsy
Lawrence, Marjorie
Leatherman, Portia
Leister, Sandy
Lensing, Richard
Ligon, Betty
Ligon, Eleanor

Lisby, Betty
Lombardo, Jean Ming
Lorson, Mrs. Karen Garrett
Lowry, Paula
Lussky, Bill
Lussky, June
Lussky, Laurie
Lynch, Emily
M — Maddux, Judy, Winingham Farm
Maisonette
Major, Betty
Maker's Mark Distillery
Marion, Alice
Marshall, Lillian
Mayfield, Patty
McAllister, Amy.
McAllister, M. B.
McAllister, Nancy
McNeil, Martine
Miles, Berry
Milham, Suzanne
Miller, Norma
Minton, Dorothy
Mitchell, Chad
Mitchell, Josephine M.
Mitchell, Helen
Moore, Laura
Murray, Jossie
N — Nader, Dottie V.
Nancy's Cuisine
Nash, Jan
New, Mr. Dwight D.
Newcom, Mrs. Forrest T.
Newman, Eleanor
Nichols, Amelia
Nichols, Macie
Normandy Inn (Paul O'Brien)
O — Oates, Margaret Ann
Old Fitzgerald Distillery, Inc.
Osborne, Glenis
Otte, Marylene
P — Page, Josie
Parrent, Mrs. Homer, Jr.
Pasquale, Connie
Patrick, Tandy
The Phantom Cook
Pollard, Kathlene
Portis, Hattie
Potter, Genie
Potter, Lib
Prittie, Helen
Prospect Store (Shane Best)

Q — Quilted Giraffe
R — Radford, Nina
Ragan, Nancy
Rankin, Ann
Rhawn, Helen
Rigsby, Mrs. Robert T.
River Valley Club
Roberts, Maugee
Robertson, Beverly
Robertson, Laverne
Rodes, Barbara
Rodway, Leta
Rosen, Sue
Rounsavall, Jef
Rudd, Eleanor
Rudd, Judy
Rue, Lee
S — Sackleh, Rosemary
Sampson, Lillian
Sams, Betsy
Sams, Ruth
Sanford, Joan
Schmied, Tari
Schneider, Sally
Scott, Marion
Segell, Inez
Serratore, Dominic
Shallcross, Marjorie Ann
Shaw, Shirley M.
Shaw, Holly
Shelton, Elizabeth
Sheridan, Virginia
Siegel, Alyce
Sims, Karen
Sixth Avenue
Sloan, Donald E.
Slucher, Hazel
Smiley, Mrs. Roger
Smith, Annette J.
Smith, Bonnie
Smith, Grace
Smith, Martha
Smith, Nancy
Smith, Pauline
Smythe, Sue
Sotsky, Shirley
Southworth, Doris Beck
Spaulding, Pam
Speed, James
Spizzirri, Mary
Spears, Amy
Stallion Stakes
Stokes, DeeDee

Stokes, Jessie C.
Stough, Jane
Strickler, Cathy
Syers, Sue
T — Tate, Jane O.
Terry, Louise C.
Tharp, Ann
Thomas, Barbie Tafel
Thomas, Phyllis
Thompson, William A.
Thorp, Ann
Tichenor, Kitty
Tway, Carol
Twenty-Four Carrot
U - University of Kentucky Club
Cookbook
V — Vance, Evelyn
Vatter, Jonnie
Veatch, Priscilla
Vitucci, Joan
W — Weaver, Rochelle
West, Anne R.
West, Beth
West, Pat
White. Mrs. M. A.
Whitsett, Nancy & Gavin
Whittenberg, Jo D.
Whittenberg, Joan
Wicks, Mrs. D.
Wilhelm, Mr. Jack
Will, Marlene
Willett Family
Willis, Nancy W.
Wine, Berry, Chef and Owner of
"Quilted Giraffe Restaurant"
Wirth, Julia
Wiser, Helen
Y — Yates, Ann Marie

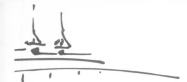

Heart Healthy Substitutions

Instead of...	Use...
1 whole egg	¼ cup egg substitute (or) 2 egg whites
1 cup butter, lard, margarine shortening	1 cup non-fat yogurt* (plain or flavored) (or) ¾ cup vegetable oil
½ cup shortening	½ cup non-fat yogurt (or) ⅓ cup vegetable oil
1 cup whole milk	1 cup skim milk
1 cup light cream	1 cup evaporated skim milk
1 cup heavy cream	1 cup evaporated skim milk
1 cup sour cream	1 cup fat free sour cream alternative (or) 1 cup fat-free yogurt
1 oz. regular cheese	1 oz. fat-free or low-fat cheese (less than 5 grams fat per ounce)
Ricotta cheese	non-fat cottage cheese
butter or oil for sauteeing	spray pan with cooking spray (or) use defatted beef, chicken or vegetable broth, or wine
butter for flavoring	butter substitute (Butter Buds or Molly McButter)
mayonnaise (in salad dressings)	fat-free or low fat mayonnaise
marinades, vinaigrettes	fat-free Italian salad dressing
sandwich spreads or mayonnaise-based salad dressings	non-fat mayonnaise blended with pickle relish, garlic, Ranch seasoning mix or other spices to taste
baking chocolate	replace each oz. with 3 T. cocoa powder and up to 1T. vegetable oil

General Guidelines to De-Fat Recipe

Use non-stick cook-ware and bake-ware or spray with vegetable cooking spray instead of adding oils.

For recipes calling for high-fat cheese, use half the amount of cheese indicated or substitute a fat-free or low-fat cheese. When a recipe calls for Cheddar use ¼ the amount sharp Cheddar and the other ¾ fat-free mozzarella. The sharp Cheddar will give the flavor, the fat-free mozzarella will give the texture.

Nuts are almost pure fat; use them sparingly-no more than ¼ to ½ cup per recipe of 8 servings.

Up to one half of the shortening in muffins, quick breads, coffee cakes, bar cookies or soft cookies can be replaced with unsweetened applesauce or any other pureed fruit. Use on-fat yogurt for the other half and your recipe is now fat-free.

If a recipe calls for mayonnaise, whole milk, sour cream, vinaigrette or bottled salad dressing, use the non-fat version of these products.

KENTUCKY DERBY MUSEUM
PO Box 3513
Louisville, Kentucky 40201

Please send me _____ copies of The Kentucky Derby Museum Cookbook at $22.00 per copy plus $3.00 postage. Kentucky Residents add $1.32 tax per book. Mail the book to:

_____
Name

_____
Address

_____
City   State   Zip   Phone

_____ Check or Money Order Enclosed

_____ VISA/Mastercard # _____ Exp. Date _____

Signature _____

Proceeds from this book go directly to support The Kentucky Derby Museum.

THE KENTUCKY DERBY MUSEUM
P.O. Box 3513 — Louisville, KY 40201

To: _____
Address: _____
City: _____
State _____
Zip _____

Mailing Label — Please Print

KENTUCKY DERBY MUSEUM
PO Box 3513
Louisville, Kentucky 40201

Please send me _____ copies of The Kentucky Derby Museum Cookbook at $22.00 per copy plus $3.00 postage. Kentucky Residents add $1.32 tax per book. Mail the book to:

_____
Name

_____
Address

_____
City   State   Zip   Phone

_____ Check or Money Order Enclosed

_____ VISA/Mastercard # _____ Exp. Date _____

Signature _____

Proceeds from this book go directly to support The Kentucky Derby Museum.

THE KENTUCKY DERBY MUSEUM
P.O. Box 3513 — Louisville, KY 40201

To: _____
Address: _____
City: _____
State _____
Zip _____

Mailing Label — Please Print

KENTUCKY DERBY MUSEUM
PO Box 3513
Louisville, Kentucky 40201

Please send me _____ copies of The Kentucky Derby Museum Cookbook at $22.00 per copy plus $3.00 postage. Kentucky Residents add $1.32 tax per book. Mail the book to:

_____
Name

_____
Address

_____
City   State   Zip   Phone

_____ Check or Money Order Enclosed

_____ VISA/Mastercard # _____ Exp. Date _____

Signature _____

Proceeds from this book go directly to support The Kentucky Derby Museum.

THE KENTUCKY DERBY MUSEUM
P.O. Box 3513 — Louisville, KY 40201

To: _____
Address: _____
City: _____
State _____
Zip _____

Mailing Label — Please Print